English Unlimited

C1 Advanced
Teacher's Pack

Adrian Doff, Johanna Stirling & Sarah Ackroyd

CAMBRIDGE UNIVERSITY PRESS
Cambridge, New York, Melbourne, Madrid, Cape Town, Singapore,
São Paulo, Delhi, Dubai, Tokyo, Mexico City

Cambridge University Press
The Edinburgh Building, Cambridge CB2 8RU, UK

www.cambridge.org
Information on this title: www.cambridge.org/9780521175593

© Cambridge University Press 2011

This publication is in copyright. Subject to statutory exception
and to the provisions of relevant collective licensing agreements,
no reproduction of any part may take place without the written
permission of Cambridge University Press.

First published 2011

Printed in the United Kingdom at the University Press, Cambridge

A catalogue record for this publication is available from the British Library

ISBN 978-0-521-17559-3 Advanced Teacher's Pack
ISBN 978-0-521-14445-2 Advanced Coursebook with e-Portfolio
ISBN 978-0-521-16973-8 Advanced Self-study Pack (Workbook with DVD-ROM)
ISBN 978-0-521-14446-9 Advanced Class Audio CDs

Cambridge University Press has no responsibility for the persistence or
accuracy of URLs for external or third-party internet websites referred to in
this publication, and does not guarantee that any content on such websites is,
or will remain, accurate or appropriate. Information regarding prices, travel
timetables and other factual information given in this work is correct at
the time of first printing but Cambridge University Press does not guarantee
the accuracy of such information thereafter.

Contents

Introduction

The thinking behind *English Unlimited*	4
How a unit is organised	6
A more detailed look at the features of *English Unlimited*	11
The Self-study Pack	16
The e-Portfolio	18
The Teacher's Pack	19
Assessing your learners with *English Unlimited*	20
The Common European Framework of Reference for Languages (CEF)	22

Teaching notes

Unit 1	23
Unit 2	31
Unit 3	40
Unit 4	48
Unit 5	58
Unit 6	67
Unit 7	75
Unit 8	84
Unit 9	92
Unit 10	101
Unit 11	109
Unit 12	118

The thinking behind *English Unlimited*

The aim of *English Unlimited* is to enable adult learners to communicate effectively in English in real-life situations. To achieve this, *English Unlimited* is:

1 a **practical** course
2 an **authentic** course
3 an **international** course
4 a **flexible** course

1 A practical course

Each unit of *English Unlimited* is designed to help learners achieve specific **communicative goals**. These goals are listed at relevant points throughout the Coursebook. For example, you and your learners will see these goals at the top of the first lesson in Unit 5:

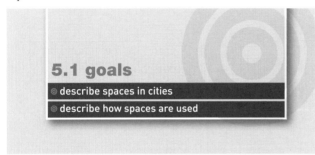

All the goals are of a practical 'can do' nature, chosen to enable Advanced learners to deal with a wide range of concepts, styles and topics in English. Of course, a substantial amount of each unit is dedicated to learning lexical phrases, collocations and grammar – but the goals come first. We've identified goals which we think will be useful for Advanced learners to work on, and then selected topics and areas of grammar and vocabulary to help them do this.

Where exactly do the goals come from?

The goals for the course have been taken from the **Common European Framework of Reference for Languages (CEF)**, and adapted and supplemented according to our research into the needs of Advanced learners.

The goals in the Coursebook are based on the CEF goals but they have been reworded to make them less 'technical' and more motivating and accessible for learners and teachers.

What is the CEF?

The CEF uses 'Can Do' statements to describe the abilities of learners of English (or any other language) at different levels. The focus is on **how to do things in the language**, rather than on abstract knowledge of the language itself. For example, here are some CEF goals which describe learners' speaking abilities at the end of Advanced:

- Can give clear, detailed descriptions of complex subjects.
- Can give elaborate descriptions and narratives, integrating sub-themes, developing particular points and rounding off with an appropriate conclusion.
- Can give a clear, well-structured presentation of a complex subject, expanding and supporting points of view at some length with subsidiary points, reasons and relevant examples.
- Can handle interjections well, responding spontaneously.

The CEF originated in Europe but is used increasingly widely around the world as a guide for curriculum design and assessment. It can be used with learners of any nationality or first language.

What's the level of the course?

The CEF is divided into 6 main **levels**, sometimes with 'plus' levels in between. This table shows the CEF levels and how they relate to the Cambridge ESOL exams:

CEF levels		Cambridge exams
C2	'Mastery'	CPE
C1	'Operational proficiency'	CAE
B2+		
B2	'Vantage'	FCE
B1+		
B1	'Threshold'	PET
A2+		
A2	'Waystage'	KET
A1	'Breakthrough'	

English Unlimited Advanced is based on 'Can Do' statements at the C1 level of the Common European Framework.

2 An authentic course

Because it is based on practical goals, *English Unlimited* teaches authentic language – that is, the kind of language which is really used by native speakers and proficient non-native speakers of English in everyday situations and when talking about abstract topics. An important tool for identifying useful language to include in the course has been the **Cambridge International Corpus (CIC)**.

What is the CIC?

The CIC is an electronic collection of more than a billion words of real text, both spoken and written, which can be searched by computer to discover the most common words, expressions and structures of the language, and the kinds of situation in which they are used.

How has it been used in the course?

The CIC has been used throughout *English Unlimited* to ensure that learners are taught **the most useful and appropriate words and expressions** for meeting their communicative goals. For example, Unit 1 introduces a range of expressions (*fit in, be accepted, make an effort, be an outsider*) which the CIC shows are often used for talking about adapting to a new culture.

The CIC has also been used in checking **collocations**, which form an important part of the language taught at Advanced level. For example, Unit 5 introduces common collocations used when describing cities and urban spaces (*urban planning, living space, public spaces, city dwellers*) – these have been carefully matched with examples in the CIC.

The CIC has also been used in the preparation of **grammar** sections, both to select structures to be taught and to identify realistic contexts for presentation. For example, subject–object inversion (Unit 10) is introduced through common expressions where we want to give emphasis (*No way would I want to live there*), while the present progressive active and passive (Unit 11) are reviewed in the context of describing gradual changes (*Climate change is being felt all over the world*).

A further use of the CIC is in the **Keywords pages** which appear in every unit. At Advanced level, each Keywords page focuses on a 'family' of important words used to express a particular meaning, as well as on useful expressions based around those words (for example, Unit 6 Keywords teaches ways of expressing aim and purpose: *aim to, aim for, with the aim of, for the purpose of*).

How else is English Unlimited *an authentic course?*

In addition to being informed by the CIC, *English Unlimited* contains a large amount of **unscripted audio and video material**, recorded using non-actors, both native and non-native speakers. Listening texts are also taken from authentic sources such as radio news items and web-based interviews.

What are the benefits for learners of using 'authentic' listening material?

Listening to spontaneous, unscripted speech is the best way for learners to experience English as it is spoken in the real world and become accustomed to the natural rhythm and intonation of English speech. We also find that authentic recordings are more motivating and engaging for learners in general.

3 An international course

In what ways is English Unlimited *'international'?*

Firstly, *English Unlimited* is an **inclusive** course, catering to learners of different backgrounds from all around the world. We have taken care to select topics, texts and tasks which will appeal to a broad range of learners. We've tried to avoid topics which learners may find uncomfortable or simply uninteresting, and we don't assume a knowledge of a celebrity culture, but focus instead on more universal themes, accessible to all. In particular, we include topics which relate to learners' own lives and which touch on learners' own attitudes and feelings.

English is most often used nowadays between non-native speakers from different places. How does the course take this into account?

A second strand to the 'internationalism' of the course is that it includes features which will help learners become more effective communicators in international contexts.

In every unit there is an **Across cultures** page which focuses on a particular topic of cultural interest or an issue which is of international importance. The aim of these pages is to increase learners' awareness of how the values and assumptions of people they communicate with in English might differ from – or be similar to – their own. Learners who have this awareness are likely to be more sensitive and effective communicators in international environments.

Listening sections use recordings of **speakers with a range of accents** in order to familiarise learners with the experience of hearing both native and non-native speakers from a wide variety of places. These include international varieties of English, such as Canadian English, West African English and Indian English, as well as non-native speakers from a range of different language backgrounds. Regardless of accents, care has been taken to ensure that recordings are of appropriate speed and clarity and that they are error-free. All non-native speakers are competent users of English and should provide learners with strong and motivating role models to help them progress and achieve greater confidence in English.

For the purposes of language production, taught grammar, vocabulary and pronunciation follow a British English model, but by exposing learners to a wide range of accents and models, we are helping to enhance their ability to use English in real international contexts.

4 A flexible course

The next five pages show how a typical unit of *English Unlimited Advanced* is organised.

As you'll see, the first four pages are connected to each other and make up the 'core' of the unit, leading up to a Target activity which reflects the main goals of the unit. After that, there is the **Explore** section, three pages of activities which have a topical or linguistic link to the unit, but which can be used separately. These include an **Across cultures** section, which deals with a topic of international or intercultural interest related to the theme of the unit. On the last two pages of each unit is the **Look again** section, which focuses more closely on particular areas of grammar and vocabulary which arise from the unit.

This means that *English Unlimited* can be adapted not only for lessons of different lengths, but also for shorter and longer courses. For example, just using the 'core' of each unit would be suitable for a course of about 50 hours, while using all the material, including the **Explore** and **Look again** pages, would give a course length of 80 or 90 hours.

The flexibility of *English Unlimited* is further enhanced by an extensive range of supplementary materials. These include **Grammar reference pages** at the back of the Coursebook, the **Teacher's DVD-ROM** containing three extra activities for each unit of the Coursebook, **Achievement and Progress tests**, and the **Self-study Pack**, which offers more than 50 hours of additional language and skills practice material in the Workbook and on the Self-study DVD-ROM.

In the rest of this introduction you'll find:
- a plan showing how a unit is organised *pages 6 to 10*
- more detailed notes on the different sections of the units *pages 11 to 15*
- information about the other components of the course *pages 16 to 21*
- more detailed information about the CEF *page 22*

We hope that you and your learners will enjoy using *English Unlimited*.

Adrian Doff
Ben Goldstein

How a unit is organised

The course consists of 12 units, each of which has 10 pages.

Each unit covers a general **unifying topic** or **theme**. **The first two pages** are a single lesson with goals based on the CEF. You can of course spread the material over more than one lesson if you want. ⏱ *about 90 minutes*

Lessons include a **language focus**, which deals with important words, expressions and collocations, as well as **reading**, **listening**, **speaking** and **writing** activities. Lessons always finish with a communicative speaking task, often involving role play or discussion. *See pp11–12 for details of language and skills sections.*

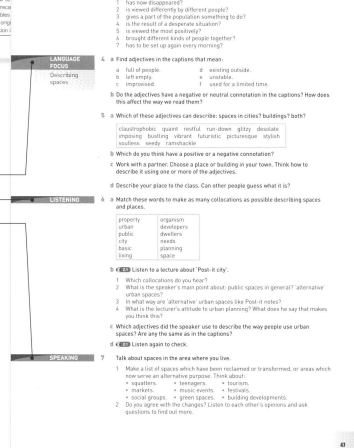

6   Introduction

> **The next two pages** are another lesson related to the topic of the unit, with goals based on the CEF.
> ⏱ *about 90 minutes*

5.2 Surveillance

5.2 goals
- talk about crime and surveillance
- comment on experiences

READING

1. a What do the images show?
   b Talk together.
   1. Where can you find surveillance cameras in your town? What do you think is their main purpose?
   2. Do you think they have helped to reduce crime? If so, how?

2. a Read the article.
   1. Where is the writer and why is he there?
   2. Does he think CCTV cameras are useful, useless or sinister? What evidence can you find in the article to support this?
   3. How does his attitude change in the second paragraph?
   4. Who runs the operation? Why does that seem to be a good idea?

IN Manchester, I watch the man as he fumbles in his pocket, rolls a cigarette and lights it. He is young, thin, and seems nervous. He also seems oblivious to the camera through which I am watching him. He is outside, in the city centre; I am in front of a bank of screens, at the NCP car park. This is the control centre for Manchester's CCTV camera surveillance operation: five operators controlling over 250 cameras, covering public spaces throughout the greater Manchester area 24 hours a day. One of the operators had noticed something unusual about our man, but his suspicions, honed by hours of watching street activity, were soon allayed, and his attention turned elsewhere. At one end of the screens, an operator is observing the car park. A police officer is on shift for referrals for action. The operation has had its successes: nearly 50 football hooligans rampaging in the city centre before last year's UEFA cup final between Rangers and Zenit St Petersburg have been identified; mobile wireless cameras have assisted in a successful police operation against gangs in Moss Side.

It is not always so exciting. The operator showed me his computerised log of recent incidents: a man on a garage forecourt looking at the camera, a group of youths on bicycles, someone acting suspiciously here, a shoplifter being brought out of a shop there. The centre's manager is keen to stress that CCTV is there "to improve the quality of life, not just to catch criminals". The cameras are alert to fly tipping, traffic congestion, illegal street traders. "We want to be the fourth emergency service, watching out for the people of Manchester," the manager says. She also thinks this collection of functions and separation of powers between council and police is the proper model for CCTV, allowing checks and balances. Certainly, to the observer, the operation smacks more of the familiar British piecemeal pragmatism than any sinister desire for control.

b What do you think the highlighted words mean? How else can you express the same idea?
1. as he fumbles in his pocket
2. seems oblivious to the camera
3. his suspicions were allayed
4. honed by hours of watching
5. rampaging in the city
6. smacks more of ... pragmatism

3. Read two more paragraphs from the article on p129. Then answer the questions.

LANGUAGE FOCUS
Legal and illegal activities

4. a These words are used to describe things people do in streets or in buildings. Explain what they mean.

mugging	burglary	vandalism	riots	pick-pocketing	squatting	writing graffiti
busking	robbery	protest marches	shoplifting	street trading
hooliganism	begging	demonstrations	sleeping rough	gang warfare

b Which words have a different verb form? Is there a noun for the people who do these activities?

mugging → mug → mugger
writing graffiti → graffiti artist

c Choose *five* of the activities you find interesting.
1. In your country, which are legal, which are illegal, and which can be either?
2. Which do you think should be legal / illegal? Why?
3. Do you think any could (or should) be controlled by surveillance cameras?
4. Are any a particular problem where you live?

Security

LISTENING

1. Look at the photos. What forms of security do they show? What is their purpose?

2. 🔊 Listen to Jane, Uri, Patrick and Tina talking about security measures.
   1. What security measure do they talk about?
   2. Are they in favour of them, against them, or do they have mixed feelings?

LANGUAGE FOCUS
Commenting on experiences

3. a The speakers comment on things that happened to them. Try to complete the gaps.
   1. JANE I did think it was _____, as, you know, I wasn't really doing anything that dangerous.
   2. JANE _____ any schoolchildren were actually crossing the road.
   3. URI I think they serve _____.
   4. URI Then they speed up again – it's _____.
   5. PATRICK I think _____, but sometimes I think it's just a bit _____.
   6. PATRICK But at no point did they actually ask to see my passport – it was _____. _____ getting priorities wrong!
   7. TINA I do think they're _____, I mean, if you think about it, it does make it safer to buy things.
   8. TINA There was a huge queue of people standing behind me – it was _____.

b 🔊 Listen again to check.

SPEAKING

4. a What do you think are the pros and cons of the four security measures?
   b Comment on an experience you have had.
   1. Think about an experience you have had with security measures.
      - What happened?
      - How do you feel about the experience?
      - What comments would you like to make about it?
   2. Talk about your experiences and how you feel about them. Listen to each other and ask questions to find out more.

> Language focus sections expand **vocabulary** and focus on **functional expressions** used in reading or listening.

Introduction 7

The fifth page is the heart of the unit, the **Target activity**. Learners prepare for and carry out an **extended task** which draws on language taught in earlier lessons in the unit. *See p13 for details.*

The Target Activity and the next five pages will take about 45 minutes each.

Target activities **recycle goals** from the earlier lessons of the unit.

Task language sections provide learners with **useful language** for the task.

Target activities include a **preparation stage** and have a **clear outcome**.

Each unit has an **Across cultures** page which gives learners the chance to explore topics which touch on learners' own lives but also reflect differences – and similarities – between cultures. *See p13 for details.*

The Explore section is made up of activities which extend and broaden the language and skills taught in the core part of each unit. On the first page is the **Across cultures** section. This is followed by the **Keywords** section. On the third page is either **Explore writing** or **Explore speaking**.

Across cultures sections usually contain a strong **visual** element to stimulate discussion.

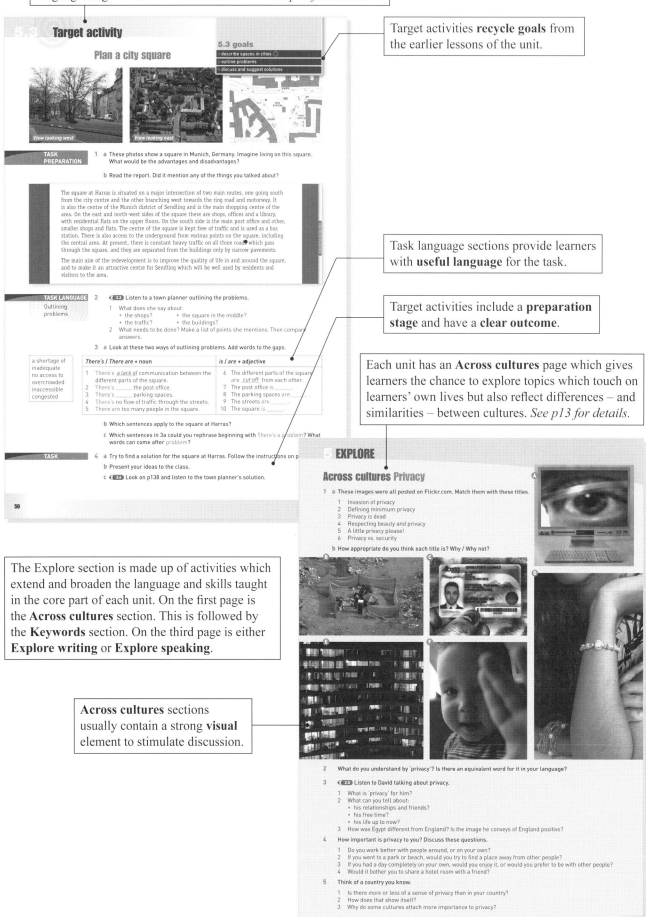

8 Introduction

All units have a **Keywords** page. Each one focuses on a commonly used English word, or a collection of words used to express a similar meaning. *See p14 for details.*

Exercises focus not only on individual words but on **phrases and collocations**.

Odd-numbered units have **Explore speaking** pages dedicated to developing learners' speaking skills and strategies. *See p14 for details.*

Even-numbered units have **Explore writing** pages which enable learners to write a range of different text types. *See p14 for details.*

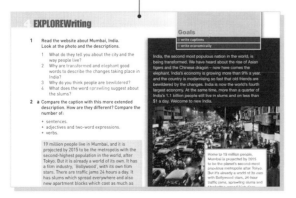

Introduction 9

The last two pages of each unit, **Look again**, are a series of short classroom activities which focus on key grammar and vocabulary points which arise from the unit. *See p15 for details.*

Grammar activities review and expand important areas of grammar. *See p15 for details.*

There is a **Grammar reference section** for each unit at the end of the book.

Vocabulary activities pick up on important vocabulary areas from the unit and focus on words, expressions and collocations in more detail. *See p15 for details.*

At the end of each unit is a **Self-assessment** for learners to complete.

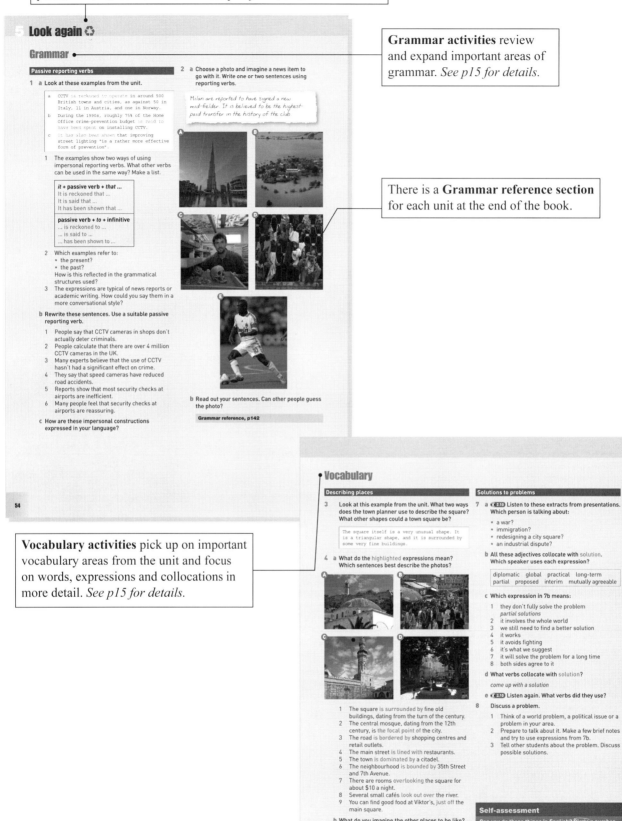

10 Introduction

A more detailed look at the features of *English Unlimited*

Lexical areas

Each unit of *English Unlimited Advanced* focuses on important **lexical areas** which correspond to the topics and communicative goals of the unit. In most units, at least one lexical area is introduced in each of the main lessons and in the Target activity, and further lexical areas are introduced in the **Keywords**, **Across cultures**, **Explore writing** and **Explore speaking** sections, as well as on the Vocabulary page of the **Look again** section.

These lexical areas include:
- important **vocabulary** such as words and expressions for describing Internet crime (*piracy, hacking, copyright*) or for talking about nutrition (*processed food, wholemeal, cereals*)
- **expressions and phrases** such as ways of talking about membership (*sign up for, become a member of, team up with*)
- **collocations** such as adverb/adjective combinations (*hideously ugly, blissfully happy*), words that go together in describing an experiment (*conduct an experiment, devise a test, assess performance*) or words that collocate with 'effect' (*a calming effect, a detrimental effect, a far-reaching effect*)
- **word families** such as ways of using *suppose* (*suppose, supposedly, supposing*) or adjectives and nouns that begin with *self-* (*self-sufficient, self-contained, self-esteem, self-confidence*)
- **frames** which can be used to express language functions at an advanced level, such as ways of talking about aims and priorities (*My main aim is …, I need to concentrate on …*) or ways of softening criticism (*It seems to me that …, Perhaps it would have been better to …*)

The focus on collocations and longer items as well as single words will enable learners to express themselves more fluently, naturally and effectively.

The Advanced level of *English Unlimited* also goes beneath the surface of words and explores **connotations** and **implied meaning**, such as the way *just* and *only* affect the meaning of a sentence, how adjectives which describe a town (*soulless, quaint, bustling*) have a positive or a negative connotation, and what effect is achieved by descriptive words such as *snooze, pristine* and *grimy*.

Attention is also given to common **language strategies** that are important for speaking and writing, for example how to backtrack and reformulate successfully, how to capture the listener's attention, how to make a brief written description concise and vivid.

The lexical areas focused on are generally drawn from texts which learners have already read or listened to as part of a skills section of a lesson. In other words, lexis is placed in **clear contexts** which help learners work out what it means and how it's used.

Grammar

At the Advanced level of *English Unlimited*, we assume that learners will have already covered the main grammar of English, so the course does not set out to teach grammar as if for the first time. Grammar is dealt with in two main ways through the course.

- Grammar points are focused on as they arise **as part of the main lessons**, often through **noticing activities**. For example, in Unit 2, learners read the story of how someone met her partner; they complete a text with correct verb forms and discuss what tenses are used. In Unit 10, learners read texts about football and notice how inversion is used as a way of being emphatic.

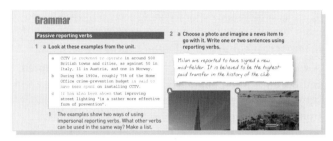

- **Key areas** of grammar that arise in each unit are focused on in the Grammar part of the **Look again pages**. These provide a chance for **review** of grammar: for example, Unit 2 covers tenses used in narration, and Unit 11 deals with the present progressive active and passive. They also focus on grammar that may be **new** to learners or which they haven't covered in depth before: for example, Unit 4 focuses on comparisons involving different verbs and tenses, and Unit 5 deals with passive reporting verbs. Both in the main lessons and in the Look again sections, the grammar is based on what is naturally used in the unit (in reading and listening texts and in speaking and writing activities), so it is closely linked to the unit goals.

Grammar reference

In each Look Again section, you'll see a label like this …

… which directs learners to a **Grammar reference section** at the end of the book.

Each Grammar reference section gives a summary of the grammar area in question, using simple language and a range of examples.

Introduction 11

Pronunciation

Pronunciation is focused on wherever this is an important part of **expressing meaning** or **communicating effectively**, and special attention is paid to **rhythm, stress and intonation patterns** of remarks. For example, in Unit 10 Look again, learners mark the stressed words used in sentence inversion; in Unit 12 Target activity, they decide where to place the stress in a remark in order to sound positive and self-confident.

Listening

There is at least one major listening section in each of the main lessons, and other listening activities occur frequently in the **Across cultures** and **Explore speaking** sections.

A wide range of recordings, both **authentic** and **scripted**, is used, including monologues, topical conversations between friends and colleagues, interviews and excerpts from web-based programmes.

Authentic recordings are unscripted and feature both native and non-native speakers from a variety of backgrounds, usually talking at natural speed. These provide exposure to a range of accents and to the rhythm of natural spoken English, as well as to features of the spoken language such as vague language, rephrasing and hesitation devices.

Scripted recordings are based on real-world recordings and corpus data to guarantee the inclusion of natural expressions and features of English. They are often used in contexts which would naturally be scripted, for example a radio feature or interview, and also to exemplify specific language points.

Texts are exploited using **a range of tasks** designed to develop specific listening skills and help learners to focus on the main points of what they hear, and also to use what they hear as a source of language they can use themselves. Listening activities are usually preceded by a **pre-listening task** to raise interest and help learners predict what they will hear, often using **visual images**.

For example, this listening task from Unit 5 includes:
- pre-listening activity (1).
- listening for gist (2).
- interpreting speaker's attitude (2).
- focus on language used (3a, b).

Reading

Each main lesson of the unit has at least one major reading section. Smaller reading texts are used in **Target activities** and can be found in **Across cultures** and **Explore writing** pages.

A wide range of text types is used, both **printed and electronic**: newspaper, magazine and online articles, web postings, brochures, adverts, interviews and personal correspondence.

Reading texts:
- are drawn from sources around the world in order to appeal to as many learners as possible.
- are authentic, or based on authentic texts, ensuring that learners are exposed to natural language and preparing them for the experience of reading outside the classroom.
- are slightly above learners' productive language level, so that learners have opportunities to notice new language.
- provide a context for the main lexical areas to be focused on.

Our response to the reading needs of advanced learners has not simply been to make texts longer. We have:
- included **more demanding texts** and text types, often featuring specialist or colloquial language and dealing with abstract topics.
- included tasks which encourage learners to read the text in more **depth** and explore implied meaning and stylistic features.
- used the texts as a rich source of **authentic language** for learners to notice and make use of themselves.

For example, a text about childhood memories in Unit 1 has the following tasks:
- prediction task (3a).
- reading for gist (3b).
- focus on style and the writer's intention (3c).
- in-depth reading of the text (3d).
- language focus (4a).

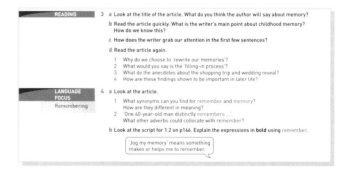

For further reading practice, the Self-study Pack contains six **Explore reading** pages, each of which focuses on a different real-life reading scenario, sometimes with longer texts to practise extended reading skills.

Target activity

The target activity is **an extended speaking task**, which **draws on goals, vocabulary and grammar from the previous two lessons**. It is the conclusion of the first five, topically linked pages of the unit.

As part of the task preparation, the Target activity also provides further listening or reading skills development, and further language input. Target activity pages have **three sections**.

Task listening or **Task reading** sections have three objectives: they introduce the topic of the Target activity, they provide a context for the language which will be focused on and needed for the Task, and they provide further receptive skills development.

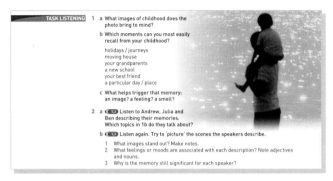

The **Task language** is drawn from the listening or reading above, and focuses on useful language for the task to follow:

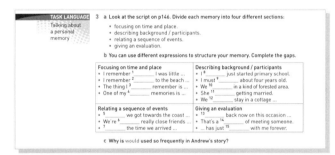

In the **Task** section, learners are given the chance to think about the ideas and the language they want to use before they begin, meaning that they will be able to focus on accuracy as well as fluency when they do the task itself:

Intercultural awareness

More and more people around the world are learning English in order to live, work, study and travel in other countries. The increasingly global nature of business, travel, education and personal relations in today's world means that **intercultural awareness** is an area of growing interest and need for learners everywhere. The Common European Framework of Reference for Languages (CEF) identifies intercultural awareness as a key sociolinguistic competence (chapter 5.1.1–3). Learners who are interculturally competent are more sensitive and effective communicators in international situations.

Intercultural awareness is developed at the Advanced level of *English Unlimited* in three main ways:

- through the choice of topics throughout the course which have **an international perspective** and explore **intercultural issues**. For example, Unit 1 looks at the experience of children growing up in a different culture; Unit 3 contains extracts from novels which describe contact with different cultures; Unit 4 deals with nutrition in different countries of the world and how this is changing; Unit 10 discusses football as a uniting factor between different parts of the world.
- through the choice of topics which are **global in their significance** rather than being limited to any particular culture or country. For example, Unit 8 discusses the marketing of international brands; Unit 9 looks at 'icons' of global significance which are representative of our age; Unit 12 deals with the international impact of technology on learning styles.
- through the **Across cultures** sections which appear in each unit.

Across cultures

The **Across cultures** pages are intended to help learners to:

- be able to view topics and issues from an international perspective.
- be more aware of the kinds of differences and similarities that can exist both between and within cultures.
- reflect on aspects of their own and other cultures in an objective, non-judgmental way.
- contribute to an exchange of ideas about cultures by drawing on their own observations and experiences.

Each Across cultures section looks at a particular topic which is of intercultural interest or which involves cross-cultural issues. They are structured like an ordinary lesson, and are concerned with developing fluency rather than specific language input. They typically include a brief lead-in, a listening or reading text for further skills development, and a speaking stage where learners talk about their own and other cultures.

Keywords

The Keywords sections in each unit focus on a group of **high-frequency words** which are used to express a particular **area of meaning** in English. Examples are ways to describe skill and ability (Unit 2), using the word *need* (Unit 5), using the words *effect* and *affect* (Unit 8), and describing similarities and differences (Unit 11). As in other sections in the course, attention is paid not just to the words themselves but how they are used in **expressions and collocations**.

In each unit, the Keywords section revisits words that have occurred and been significant in the unit, and are often illustrated using examples from the current or previous units:

This is followed by a practice stage which focuses on contexts and collocations.

Explore speaking

Explore speaking pages occur in **odd-numbered units** (alternating with Explore writing), and link to and develop the topic of the unit.

Explore speaking is a complete, free-standing page which aims to equip learners with **skills and strategies for improving their spoken interaction** at an advanced level. It addresses real-life, immediate needs of Advanced learners, such as:
- telling an anecdote effectively.
- using repetition, paraphrasing and fillers to get points across.
- giving an effective presentation using images.
- taking turns in a discussion and interrupting politely.
- 'softening' criticism and responding appropriately.
- reporting and reacting to an opinion.

Each Explore speaking page includes:
- **listening** to an example of the interaction (for example, a discussion, a presentation, a conversation) containing the language and strategies that will be focused on. This enables learners to hear the target language in an authentic context.
- **the listening script** on the same page. This enables learners to see and study the target language straight away without having to flick to the back of the book.

- activities in which learners **notice the target language** in different ways, such as categorising expressions according to their function.
- **controlled practice exercises** which build familiarity and confidence with the target language.
- **a freer practice task**, such as a role play, which gives learners the chance to use the target language in a real-life situation.

Explore writing

Explore writing pages occur in **even-numbered units** (alternating with Explore speaking).

This page is dedicated to improving learners' writing skills through a sequence of activities which build towards a practical, purposeful writing task. As with Explore speaking, the page is linked to and develops the topic of the unit.

Specifically, Explore writing pages will help learners to:
- **write a range of text types** appropriate to the level, e.g. a cover letter to apply for a job, a caption accompanying a webpage image, a description of an organisation.
- **understand genre-specific conventions and strategies**, e.g. presenting yourself in a positive light, writing economically, using persuasive language.
- **extend their abilities** in writing by planning and discussing ideas with peers, talking about and improving texts together, and building from shorter to longer texts.

Each Explore writing page contains one or more models of the text type learners will produce at the end of the lesson. The sequence of exercises will usually require learners to:
- **read the model texts** for meaning.
- **notice** specific language features in the texts and strategies employed by the writer.
- **practise** applying the new language and strategies.
- **plan** a piece of writing (e.g. learners may be asked to generate ideas in pairs or groups, then organise their ideas into paragraphs).
- **write** their own texts.
- **read** each other's texts and **respond**, or **use** the text as a basis for a speaking activity.

You can, of course, set some of the later stages of the writing process as homework if you prefer.

Look again

The Look again pages are divided into two main sections, **Grammar** and **Vocabulary**. Both sections pick up and focus more closely on key language areas that have arisen in the main part of the unit.

The Grammar section picks up on key grammar areas, and gives a chance to review and practise them. So, for example, the first lesson of Unit 4 includes a text predicting the world's population in 2050. In Look again, this is focused on and used as the basis to review and explore ways of expressing future time.

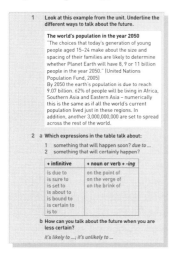

The Vocabulary section picks up on key areas of vocabulary that have appeared in the unit, and gives a chance to expand on them and explore collocations, synonyms and word families. So, for example, the first lesson of Unit 10 is about groups and group membership. Look again reviews this and introduces a range of words used to describe groups (e.g. *horde*, *mob*, *clique*), and explores meaning differences and common collocations.

Self-assessment

Each unit concludes with a Self-assessment box for learners to complete either in class or at home. Many learners find it useful and motivating to reflect on their progress at regular intervals during a course of study.

For teachers, the Self-assessment will be a valuable means of gauging learners' perceptions of how much progress they've made, and of areas they need to work on further. Self-assessments can also be useful preparation for one-to-one tutorials in which the learner's and teacher's perceptions of progress are compared and discussed.

The Self-study Pack

About the Self-study Pack

English Unlimited Advanced Self-study Pack offers a wealth of activities for learners to **reinforce what they have learned in class**. It has been designed to offer **flexibility and depth** to your English teaching, whatever the specific needs of your learners. The Workbook and Self-study DVD-ROM provide a wide range of language and skills practice activities to accompany each unit of the Coursebook, so you can:

- set homework tasks based on the Coursebook lessons.
- supplement your lessons with further language and skills practice.
- use authentic video activities in class, or get learners to watch in their own time.

Your learners can:

- consolidate their knowledge of language and skills taught in class.
- practise and check their pronunciation.
- learn and practise essential speaking skills.
- create tests on specific language areas quickly and easily, which allows learners to focus on either grammar-based or vocabulary-based questions or both from any unit or combination of units.
- check their progress and get feedback on their level of English and any specific areas of difficulty.
- record and listen to themselves speaking in everyday conversations, using the audio materials.

In the Workbook

English Unlimited Advanced Workbook contains:

- activities which practise and extend the vocabulary and grammar taught in the Coursebook units.
- further reading and writing skills practice.
- numerous opportunities in each unit for learners to personalise what they are learning to their own interests and situations.

The first three pages of each unit consist of **vocabulary and grammar practice activities** to consolidate and reinforce what has been taught in the Coursebook which can either be used in class or set for homework. **Over to you** activities suggest ways for learners to practise and personalise the language and skills they have learned in a more open way.

Explore reading, in even-numbered units, offers practice in reading, understanding and responding to a range of everyday texts, such as news stories, personal texts, blogs and emails. As Advanced learners are expected to be able to deal with longer and in-depth reading tasks, each Explore reading section is two pages long. This allows for an extended reading task, with detailed comprehension, language and exploitation work.

Explore writing, in odd-numbered units, gives learners key pointers on structure and language, to enable them to produce a wide range of written texts, focusing on such areas as reports, summaries and tributes. Taken alongside the Explore writing pages in even-numbered units of the Coursebook, this means that there is a dedicated writing lesson for every unit of the course.

The last page of each odd-numbered unit has a set of activities that link up directly with the **authentic video** on the Self-study DVD-ROM. Learners have the chance to watch authentic documentaries on topics connected to the unit.

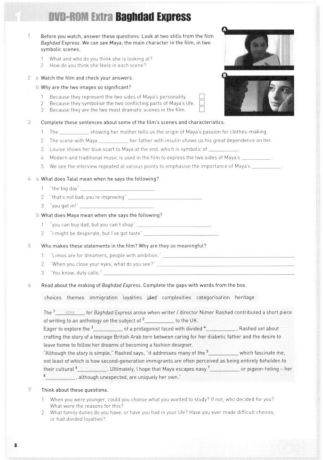

On the Self-study DVD-ROM

The *English Unlimited Advanced Self-study DVD-ROM* offers your learners over 300 interactive activities which they can use to practise and consolidate what they have learned in class, while providing a number of easy ways to check their progress at every step of the course.

Just click on the icon for each unit and the learners will find a wide range of engaging and easy-to-use activities, from picture matching and drag-and-drop categorisation to cloze exercises. Learners are also able to record themselves, practising pronunciation or taking part in conversations, and compare their recordings with the original audio. If learners have used their e-Portfolio from the Coursebook, they are able to save their conversation recordings direct to their e-Portfolio.

Each unit's activities practise and extend the vocabulary, grammar and Keyword areas focused on in the Coursebook, as well as providing further pronunciation practice. Learners can also generate tests quickly and easily, using the Quick check test question bank. They can choose which units they want to test and how many questions they want the test to consist of, and Quick check will randomly select from the 700 questions in the bank.

Learners can also keep track of their progress as they work through the course with the Progress page, which shows which exercises they have attempted and their scores. Learners can therefore quickly see the language areas where they need to do more work and can retry the relevant exercises.

In addition to language practice, each unit of the Self-study DVD-ROM also contains Explore Speaking and Explore Listening activities. Explore speaking trains learners to notice key speaking skills, such as involving the listener, or reformulating what you say, and then incorporate these techniques into their own spoken English. Listening activities expose learners to useful everyday listening texts, often extended, such as lectures, a radio phone-in show and personal conversations.

In most language courses, it is rare for learners to get the chance to listen to themselves in conversation, but if there is a microphone available, this can be done easily using the recorded dialogues on the DVD-ROM. Learners listen to the dialogues, take a closer look at the language used, and then have the opportunity to record themselves and play back to hear how they sound in the conversations. If they have installed the e-Portfolio from their Coursebook, they can save this conversation directly to the My work section. Learners can also record and listen to themselves during any exercise, for example, to practise pronunciation.

In every odd-numbered unit of the Self-study DVD-ROM, you will also find video, which can be used by the teacher with the whole class or by the learners outside class, using the last page (or two) of each unit of the Workbook, or just watching them to get extra exposure to real language. At Advanced level, there are six authentic videos on interesting contemporary topics from leading documentary and short-film makers and animators:

- short documentaries: *Iconic buildings*; *Health Food Junkies*; *Dead Icons* and *Garbage Warrior*.

- a short film and an animation: *Baghdad Express*; *Forgetfulness*.

These videos on the Self-study DVD-ROM are available in full-screen version with optional subtitles, or inset alongside an onscreen transcription. In the full-screen version, subtitles can be easily toggled on and off, so learners can find extra support for any part of the video if they need it.

The e-Portfolio

The *English Unlimited Advanced e-Portfolio* is an interactive DVD-ROM which learners can use as a progress check, a reference tool and a store of written and spoken texts. It contains useful features to help reinforce learning and record and encourage progress. Learners click on one of the four icons on the start-up menu to start using these features.

Self-assessment

The **Self-assessment** feature allows learners to reflect on their own progress through the course. They do this by choosing a number between one and five to assess how well they feel they can complete each communicative goal from the Coursebook units. This encourages learners to take responsibility for their own progress and also motivates them by giving a visual record of the goals which they feel they are able to achieve. These rankings are recorded and can be revised when learners feel they have made improvements.

Word list

The **Word list** feature gives learners a comprehensive reference tool for checking the spelling, meaning and pronunciation of the words and expressions presented in the Coursebook. Learners can search by Coursebook unit or by topic group. Clear definitions show how each word or expression is used in the Coursebook, and both British and North American pronunciation guides allow learners to listen and compare with their own pronunciation.

The Word list also allows learners to enter and save new information about each word or expression. They can make notes on a word or expression, or add an example sentence which they have heard or read. New words that learners discover for themselves can also easily be added to the list, giving learners the chance to extend and personalise the Word list.

My work

The **My work** feature gives learners a convenient repository in which they can build a portfolio of their work as they progress through the course. Divided into **Reading and writing** and **Speaking and listening** folders, My work allows learners to import recorded examples of speaking and written work directly from the Self-study Pack or to import documents and files directly from their computer.

Developing a bank of their own written and spoken work provides another opportunity for review over a longer term and can be exceptionally motivating for learners. **My work** also offers a simple solution for English courses in which the production of coursework counts towards a learner's end-of-course grade.

Word cards

The **Word cards** feature encourages the review of words and expressions from the Coursebook. A series of words and expressions can be generated randomly by unit or topic, with the number of 'cards' set by the learner. Cards are then dragged and dropped into categories based on how well the learner can recall the word. A learner can check the meaning of the word by turning over the card. There is also the option for learners to include new words which they have added in the Word list. This is a fun and easy-to-use way of reinforcing vocabulary acquisition.

The Teacher's Pack

We understand that no two teachers or classes are alike, and that the role of a Teacher's Pack accompanying a language course is to cater for as diverse a range of pedagogical needs as possible. The materials in this Teacher's Pack serve to enhance the flexibility of *English Unlimited* to meet the needs of teachers who:

- are teaching courses of different lengths;
- want to supplement the Coursebook materials;
- have different class sizes and types;
- are teaching in different parts of the world;
- are addressing different assessment needs;
- want to use video materials in the classroom.

English Unlimited Advanced Teacher's Pack offers a **step-by-step guide to teaching** from the Coursebook, **three sets of photocopiable activity worksheets per unit** to extend and enrich your lessons and a **complete testing suite**. The Teacher's Pack consists of the **Teacher's Book** and the **Teacher's DVD-ROM**.

In the Teacher's Book

Teacher's notes

In the Teacher's Book, there are more than 100 pages of teacher's notes (pp23–125) to accompany the Coursebook material. These notes are a comprehensive and easy-to-follow guide to using the *English Unlimited Advanced Coursebook*, and have been written with a broad range of class types and teaching styles in mind.

Each unit's notes take you smoothly through the different stages of the Coursebook lessons. Answers are clearly highlighted, and the Individual, Pair and Group work symbols show at a glance what interaction is suggested for each stage.

On most pages, there are instructions for alternative activities, clearly boxed, to offer greater variety and interest. There are also suggestions throughout for adapting activities to stronger and weaker classes, multilingual and monolingual classes, and to different class sizes and environments.

On the Teacher's DVD-ROM

A teacher-friendly resource

English Unlimited Advanced Teacher's DVD-ROM offers a large suite of language and skills practice, assessment and video materials in an easy-to-use package. It also contains unit-by-unit PDF files of the Teacher's Book.

It is designed to offer flexibility to teachers who may want to use materials in digital and paper format. So you can:

- display activity worksheets and tests on a screen or whiteboard as well as distributing paper copies to learners. This is useful if you want to: demonstrate an activity; go through answers with the whole class; zoom in on an area of a worksheet; display Progress or Achievement tests as learners attempt them, or when you go through the answers;
- display answers to Progress tests, so that learners can mark their own papers;
- print out just the unit of the Teacher's Book that you are using, rather than carrying the book around;
- display answer keys to Coursebook exercises from the Teacher's Book;
- watch videos with your learners.

Photocopiable activities

There are 36 photocopiable activity worksheets on the Teacher's DVD-ROM (three for each unit), ready to print out and use straight away. These offer extra vocabulary and grammar practice, extra reading and writing work, role plays and games which further activate the language that learners have been introduced to in the Coursebook, and build their fluency, confidence and communication skills.

Each activity is accompanied by a page of clear, step-by-step instructions, with answer keys and extra teaching ideas. At the end of each unit of the Teacher's notes, there is a page to help you find the activities you need, and there are also boxes in the unit notes which suggest when particular activities might be used.

Progress and Achievement tests

The *English Unlimited* testing suite consists of 12 unit-by-unit Progress tests and three skills-based Achievement tests to motivate your learners and give you and them a clear idea of the progress that they are making. These and other methods of assessment are discussed in detail on pp20–21.

Videos

The videos from each odd-numbered unit of the Self-study Pack are also included on the Teacher's DVD-ROM, as this is easily adaptable for use in class, either using the video exercises from the Workbook, or just for extra listening practice and class discussion. The six documentaries and short films are each linked topically to their corresponding unit, and so they offer extension and consolidation of the work done in the Coursebook, as well as giving learners the chance to listen to authentic and engaging speech from a range of native and non-native English speakers. The subtitles toggle on and off, so you can easily show any sections of text which learners find difficult to understand.

The book on the disk

English Unlimited Advanced Teacher's DVD-ROM also contains the whole Teacher's Book in PDF format, so that you can print out the unit or section that you want, instead of carrying the book around with you.

There are also CEF tables, which show how *English Unlimited Advanced* completes CEF level C1 by mapping the relevant 'can do' statements from the CEF to specific pages and tasks in the Coursebook.

Assessing your learners with English Unlimited

There are many ways of assessing learner progress through a language course. For this reason *English Unlimited* offers a range of testing and assessment options, including progress tests, skill-based achievement tests, assessment using the e-Portfolio, self-assessment and continuous assessment.

Tests on the Teacher's DVD-ROM

There are two types of test available as PDFs on the Teacher's DVD-ROM: Progress and Achievement tests.

Progress tests

There is one Progress test for each of the 12 units of the course. These assess the learners' acquisition of language items taught in the main Coursebook material. Each test carries 40 marks and includes questions assessing language items taught in the unit. These are not intended to be 'high stakes' tests but rather quick checks that will help the teacher and learner judge which language points have been successfully acquired and understood, and which areas individual learners or the whole class may need to study again.

We suggest that each test should take no more than 30 minutes in the classroom. Tests can be copied and distributed to each learner and taken in class time. The tests are designed for quick marking with the provided Answer Key. Teachers may choose to mark tests, or, alternatively, learners can mark each other's work. A mark can be given out of 40. If particular problem areas are identified, learners can be directed to do extra work from the Self-study Pack.

Achievement tests

There are three Achievement tests, designed to form the basis of formal learner assessment.
- **Achievement test 1** can be taken after Unit 4.
- **Achievement test 2** can be taken after Unit 8.
- **Achievement test 3** can be taken after Unit 12.

These tests are based on the four skills: Reading, Listening, Writing and Speaking.

Reading tests

Each test is based on a short text and we advise allowing no more than 15 minutes for each test. As with the Coursebook and Listening tests, there may be a few unfamiliar items in the text, but the tasks are graded so unknown items should not hinder the learners' ability to answer the questions. The teacher may mark the tests or it may be acceptable for learners to mark each other's work.

Listening tests

The audio tracks for these are found at the end of the three Class Audio CDs. Achievement test 1 is track 31 on CD1; Achievement test 2 is track 34 on CD2; Achievement test 3 is track 36 on CD3.

We suggest carrying out tests under controlled conditions, with the recording played twice. Each test should take no longer than ten minutes. As with the Coursebook audio, there may be a few unfamiliar language items in the listening text, but tasks are graded to the level of the learner, so unknown items should not hinder the learners' ability to answer the eight questions. The tests are simple and quick to mark. They can be marked by the teacher or it may be acceptable for learners to mark each other's work.

Writing tests

Learners are set a writing task based on themes from the Coursebook and the teacher assesses work using the Writing assessment scales provided. Tasks are designed to simulate purposeful, real-life, communicative pieces of writing. The teacher should endeavour to identify the band the work falls in for each category. This marking scheme can give learners a profile of the strong and weak points of their written work, creating a virtuous circle of improvement through the course.

If the tests are to be used under timed conditions in class, 40 minutes should be allowed for the learners to produce their texts – planning and redrafting may be encouraged by the teacher at the outset.

Another way is to set the tasks as assessed writing assignments to be done as homework. In these cases, the teacher should interpret the band scales according to the time available and the availability of dictionaries and other reference materials.

The option chosen will depend on your learning environment. A timed test may help you assess learners under equal conditions, but can be a rather artificial, pressured environment. Written homework assignments are less controlled, but could be a better way of encouraging learners to work at their writing and feel satisfied with a polished piece of written work. The Explore writing tasks in the Coursebook and Self-study Pack may also be used as assessed assignments and marked using the assessment scales.

Speaking tests

These are designed to be carried out by an assessor, who may be the learners' regular teacher, or another teacher in the institution. Learners do the tests in pairs. The ideal environment is for the test to take place in a separate room from the rest of the class, who can be engaged in self-study work while the testing is taking place. It is best if seating is set up as a 'round table' if possible, rather than the assessor facing both learners across a desk, so as not to suggest an interrogation! Each test takes 14 minutes.

The assessor should be familiar with the Speaking assessment scales for the Speaking tests before the test and have a copy of the Mark Sheet for each learner with their names already filled in. Screen the Mark Sheets from the learners.

The assessor will need the Teacher's Notes, which provide a script of prompts for the test. Each test is in two parts. In

Part 1 (three minutes), the assessor asks the learners in turn a selection of questions from the Notes, based on themes from the Coursebook. The assessor may depart from the script to elicit further responses, maintaining a friendly, encouraging manner. The assessor may begin to note down some marks based on the scales for each learner.

In Part 2 (six minutes), learners are provided with prompts for a communicative task, which they carry out between themselves. Learners may need some encouragement, or to have the instructions explained more than once.

During this section, the assessor should withdraw eye contact, making it clear that the learners should talk to each other, listen closely and revise the marks from Part 1, gradually completing the grid.

In Part 3 (five minutes) the assessor asks learners questions related to the task in Part 2. The assessor may now make any final necessary adjustments to the learners' marks.

The assessor should not correct learners at any point during the test.

Filling in the Mark Sheets

Once all four papers of the Achievement tests have been carried out, the teacher can provide marks for each learner. This includes analytical marks for the Speaking and Writing tests, and an average mark out of five for each one; and marks out of eight for the Reading and Listening tests. This gives the learners a snapshot of their performance in the four skills. The learners should be encouraged to reflect on what they found easy or difficult, and given strategies to improve performance in different skills. The marks can be used as the basis for course reports or formal assessment.

Self-assessment

Assessment is not just about tests. Self-assessment encourages more reflective and focused learning. *English Unlimited* offers a number of tools for learner self-assessment.
- Each unit of the Coursebook ends with a Self-assessment grid in which learners are encouraged to measure their own progress against the unit goals, which in turn are based on the can-do statements of the *Common European Framework of Reference for Languages*.
- Progress with the activities on the Self-study DVD-ROM can be analysed in detail on the Progress screen.
- The Self-study DVD-ROM also contains Quick check tests, using a bank of 700 multiple-choice questions. Learners select which units they want to be tested on and how long they want the test to be – new tests will be randomly generated each time.

Using the e-Portfolio

Portfolio-based assessment is a useful tool for both self-assessment and formal assessment, particularly for teachers seeking an alternative to traditional timed writing tests. The e-Portfolio allows learners to:
- assess their progress against can-do statements and revise their assessments later in the course depending on progress made.
- build up a personal e-Portfolio of written work associated with the course. The learner may then select their best work, as an alternative to tests, or at the end of the course to be provided as a Portfolio. This may include word-processed documents, project work and even audio files. Some of the Explore writing tasks may lend themselves well to portfolio work, and in some classrooms, learners may be asked to record personal audio files based around speaking tasks in the Coursebook. The satisfaction of producing a polished *spoken* text is a rare one in a language course, but if the learner or the centre has access to a microphone, it is relatively easy to do.

Written texts and audio in a learner's e-Portfolio may be assessed using the same analytical scales as the Writing and Speaking Achievement tests. You can find more information about the e-Portfolio on p18.

Continuous assessment

Finally, some teachers and institutions may prefer to dispense with tests and adopt a form of continuous assessment. This can be demanding on teacher's time but perhaps no more so than the marking load created by frequent formal tests. The important thing is to explain the system to learners early in the course, and regularly show them their Mark Sheets to indicate how they are getting on. How actual assessment is carried out may differ between institutions, but here are some guidelines and ideas.
- It is possible to assess learners using the Speaking assessment scales regularly through the course. The Target activities, where learners are involved in more extended discourse, offer an opportunity for this.
- Tell learners when their speaking is being assessed and the teacher can monitor particular groups.
- Learners should be assessed several times during the course or they may rightly feel they were let down by a single bad performance, even if the assessment is not 'high stakes'.
- An atmosphere of gentle encouragement and striving for improvement should always accompany this kind of assessment. Some learners can get competitive about this, which can have a negative effect on class atmosphere and demotivate less confident learners.
- The Explore writing tasks can be used for continuous written assessment, using the Writing assessment scales.

A final word

Testing and assessment can be a vital tool for teachers and learners in assessing strengths and weaknesses, building awareness and encouraging improvement. But it can be frustrating for a learner to feel that they are being assessed too often, at the expense of actually learning, and while there are certainly learners who like being tested, there are many others who certainly don't!

English Unlimited aims to help learners communicate in real-life situations, and the testing and assessment tools provided should be used with that purpose in mind. Testing and assessment should never take precedence over learning, but serve as useful checks on the way to increasing confidence, competence and fluency.

The Common European Framework of Reference for Languages (CEF)

A goals-based course

English Unlimited is a practical, goals-based course for adult learners of English. The course goals are taken and adapted from the language-learning goals stated in the Common European Framework of Reference for Languages (CEF).

The goals of the CEF are divided into a number of **scales** which describe abilities in different kinds of communication. We've chosen the scales which we felt to be the most useful for adult general English learners at Advanced level. These are:

Speaking
Describing experience
Putting a case
Addressing audiences
Conversation
Informal discussion
Formal discussion and meetings
Information exchange
Interviewing and being interviewed
Compensating
Monitoring and repair
Turntaking

Writing
Creative writing
Reports and essays
Correspondence

Listening
Overall listening comprehension
Understanding conversation
Listening to audio media and recordings

Reading
Overall reading comprehension
Reading correspondence
Reading for orientation
Reading for information and argument

Where the goals are met

As you'll see in the example unit on pp6–10, goals are given for the two lessons at the start of each unit, for the Target activity, and on the Explore speaking and Explore writing pages. They are also listed in the Self-assessment, which learners do at the end of the Look again page.

Listening and reading goals are not usually given on the page, as they are addressed repeatedly throughout the course. The CEF tables on the Teacher's Pack DVD-ROM show which parts of the course deal with the listening and reading goals.

Find out more about the CEF

You can read about the CEF in detail in *Common European Framework of Reference for Languages: Learning, teaching, assessment* (2001), Council of Europe Modern Languages Division, Strasbourg, Cambridge University Press, ISBN 9780521005319.

1 Childhood

1.1

Goal: talk about adapting to different cultures
Core language:
LANGUAGE FOCUS Adapting to another culture

Born everywhere, raised in Britain

READING

1 a To introduce the topic, learners cover p6 and look at photos A–G. Discuss what the children have in common. (*Answer:* They all come from other countries, but grew up in Britain.)

Ask learners what countries or parts of the world the children might be from and what makes them think this.

   b *Reading for gist.* Learners read the quotes and identify the children in the photos. Check that they know where these countries are.

> A Uganda
> B St Lucia
> C Brazil
> D Bahrain
> E Peru
> F Macedonia
> G Ivory Coast

> **Alternative**
> During the pre-reading phase, write the countries on the board and learners match them with the photos. Then ask learners how they imagine each country might be different from Britain for children. Learners read the quotes to check what the children say.

2 a *Reading for detail.* Learners read the quotes again and answer the questions. Then they discuss the answers. Possible answers:

> 1 Mauricio, Indi, Collins
> 2 Sara
> 3 Amna, Inza, Luis, Indi
> 4 Inza, Indi
> 5 Mauricio, Indi, Collins

   b Make sure learners understand *ambivalent*. Look in turn at what each child says and discuss what their attitude seems to be. Focus on particular expressions that reveal their attitude. Possible answers:

> Mauricio: probably negative ("the problem is")
> Amna: positive ("People are accepting within this city")
> Inza: ambivalent ("There's no big deal")
> Sara: negative ("need to", "get tired of", "a bit grown up")
> Indi: negative ("It's just respect", "take education seriously")
> Luis: negative ("they're just nasty")
> Collins: ambivalent ("quite gruesome", "looks good", "just stay at home")

   c Learners note down any non-standard or colloquial expressions they notice. Then discuss these together. For each one, ask what the more 'standard' equivalent would be. Possible answers:

> my dad, he decided (= my father decided)
> at the house (= in or around the house)
> I guess because (= I think it's because)
> they wasn't answering (= they weren't answering)
> there's no big deal (= it isn't important)
> more kid-like (= like children, childlike)
> stuff like that (= things of that kind)
> is a big thing (= is important)
> take the mick out of (= laugh at, imitate)

> **Option**
> After **1b**, each pair / group focuses on two or three of the children and answer questions **2a**, **b** and **c** just about those children. Then learners report back to the class and compare answers.

LANGUAGE FOCUS Adapting to another culture

3 a *Listening.* Play recording **1.1** and learners decide who finds it more difficult (*answer:* Daniel).

   b Focus learners on the highlighted expressions. Note that *expats* is short for *expatriates* (= people living abroad). Play recording **1.1** again. Learners discuss which expressions were used by the speakers.

> fit in: "it was pretty easy to fit in" (Sarah)
> welcoming: "everyone was really welcoming" (Daniel)
> accepted: "I felt accepted"; "I'll never be accepted really until I can speak the language fluently" (Daniel)
> adapt: "I feel that I've adapted to the country" (Sarah)
> outsider: "I feel like an outsider"; "I'll always feel like an outsider" (Daniel)
> expats: "I was lucky to meet a lot of expats here"; "most of the expats that I've met speak English" (Sarah)
> make an effort: "I've also made a real effort to learn the language" (Sarah)
> get used to: "I found that hard to get used to" (Daniel)
> miss: "I really miss my friends at home" (Sarah); "there were lots of things I missed" (Daniel)

 You could use photocopiable activity 1A on the Teacher's DVD-ROM at this point.

SPEAKING

4 a Discuss each question in turn with the class.

> **Alternative**
> 1 Learners choose either question 1 or 2, depending on their experience. They make notes on it.
> 2 They compare their answers with other learners.

b To introduce the discussion, talk about a country yourself. If it is a country you have lived in, ask the class to imagine what might be easy or difficult about living there. Then tell them your experience. If it is a country you can imagine living in, discuss together what might be easy, interesting or difficult about living there.

👥 Learners choose a country and discuss it. If learners have lived in the country, they can tell the others their experiences of it.

Round-up. One learner from each group reports back to the class on what they discussed.

1.2

Goal: talk about memory
Core language:
LANGUAGE FOCUS   Remembering

Memory

SPEAKING

1 a To introduce the topic, tell the class they are going to test their memory. They look at pictures A and B for one minute (time them).

👥 Learners turn to p126 and answer the questions. Go through the questions together. Then learners check on p8.

b Discuss the questions and refer back to what happened when learners did the test. As you do this, present these expressions:
– *short-term / long-term memory*
– *have a* (good) *memory for* (names)
– *visual memory*

LISTENING

2 a 👥 / 👥 Look at photos A–E and learners suggest any associations with memory or with forgetting things.

b *Listening for main idea.* Play recording **1.2**. Pause after each speaker and answer the questions.

> Liam: E (good)
> Jane: A (bad)
> Olga: D (bad)
> Uri: C (good)
> Tina: B (bad)

Alternative
Tell the class they will hear five people saying how good their memory is. Look at the photos and learners predict what the people might say. Then play recording **1.2** and check.

c Learners correct the statements. Then play recording **1.2** again to check.

> 1 He needs to see something he recognises, then he remembers where he is.
> 2 She forgets to check her pockets.
> 3 She writes them in an address book.
> 4 His memory is fading, but he can still remember numbers.
> 5 She can remember most things, but she can't remember names.

Optional extra
Ask further questions, e.g. – *What kind of memory does the first speaker have?* – *What happens when he's in a place he has been to before?*

Optional presentation
Key expressions for talking about memory are introduced in **4b**. Focus on some of these as you go through answers to **2c**.

d Ask round the class who identifies with each of the speakers and why.

READING

3 a *Pre-reading.* Learners cover the article and look at the title. Discuss what the author might say.

b *Skim reading.* Learners read the article quickly (give a time limit). Discuss the question. Possible answer:

> We don't remember accurately what happened to us in childhood.

c Discuss the question. Possible answer:

> The writer makes a statement that most readers will believe is true, then contradicts it.

d 👥 *Reading for detail.* Learners read the article again and answer the questions. Discuss the answers together. Possible answers:

> 1 Perhaps because we only remember fragments and so invent the rest; or perhaps because our 'rewritten' memories are more pleasant.
> 2 The process of taking other elements from our life or things we have read or heard about, to fill the gaps between the fragments that we really remember.
> 3 That we may be sure we remember something even if it is false; that our childhood memories are unreliable and may come from something we read or were told about.
> 4 They affect our behaviour and attitudes.

LANGUAGE FOCUS Remembering

4 a Learners find synonyms for *remember* and *memory* in the article. Elicit the following verb and noun forms and ask how they differ in meaning:

Verb	Noun
remember	memory
reminisce	reminiscence
recollect	recollection

> *reminisce* = *talk or think about your memories*
> *recollect* = *remember something from a long time ago, or that you had nearly forgotten*

On the board, write *One man <u>distinctly</u> remembers ...* and learners suggest other adverbs that could collocate with *remember*. Possible answers:

> clearly   vividly   fondly   vaguely   dimly   still

b 👤/👥 Learners look at the script on p146 and discuss what the highlighted expressions mean. Then discuss these together and give further examples of any difficult items.

> it all comes back to me = I remember it all again
> I've got a mental block = I can't remember something
> to remind me = to help me remember
> I don't have a very good memory = I have problems remembering things
> as reminders = to help me remember
> my memory started to fade = my ability to remember things got worse
> (faces) look familiar = I think I remember (their faces)
> my mind goes blank = I can't remember anything
> on the tip of my tongue = I can almost remember

SPEAKING

5 👥/👥👥 Learners discuss the questions.

Round-up. Learners report back on what they found out from their partner and whether it was similar to their own experience.

> **Alternative**
>
> 👥👥 One learner in each group interviews the others and makes notes.
> *Round-up.* The 'interviewer' from each group summarises what he / she found out.

1.3 Target activity: Describe a childhood memory

Goals: talk about a personal memory
evoke the feelings and moods of a past event
Core language:
TASK LANGUAGE   Talking about a personal memory
1.2 LANGUAGE FOCUS   Remembering

TASK LISTENING

1 a Discuss what images of childhood are suggested by the photo. To focus this more, learners brainstorm words and expressions that the photo brings to mind (e.g. *security, wonder, seaside, safe, the future*).

b, c 👥/👥👥 Learners consider each topic in turn and discuss:
– how easily they can remember it.
– what triggers the memory of it.

Round-up. Each pair or group tells you one or two things they talked about.

> **Note**
>
> In **4**, learners will prepare a longer description of a childhood memory, so avoid going into very detailed memories at this stage.

2 a *Listening for general idea.* Play recording **1.3**. After each speaker, pause and establish which topic the person talked about.

> Andrew: a holiday by the sea
> Julia: a particular day (washing wool)
> Ben: a new school and his best friend

b 👤/👥 *Intensive listening.* Play recording **1.3** again, pausing after each speaker. Learners make notes of images, feelings and moods that they catch from the recording.

Discuss each speaker's story together. Build up a list of images and feelings on the board.

TASK LANGUAGE Talking about a personal memory

3 a Check that learners understand the section descriptions (e.g. participants = the people in the story; giving an evaluation = commenting on the story; relating a sequence = saying what happened in order).

👤/👥 Learners mark the sections for each speaker in the script on p146. Then discuss this together.

b, c 👤/👥 Learners complete the expressions.

Check the answers together or learners check in the script.

> 1 when   2 going   3 really   4 earliest   5 As   6 still
> 7 By   8 had   9 have been   10 were staying   11 was
> 12 'd (would)   13 Looking   14 happy memory
> 15 stayed

> **Language note**
>
> After *I remember* we can use *-ing* or a clause:
> – *I remember going to the seaside.*
> – *I remember (that) we often went to the seaside.*
> To give the background, you can use:
> – the past perfect to talk about previous events (*I had just started ...*).
> – the past progressive to talk about things going on at the time (*We were staying ...*).
> You *look back on* or *think back on* something that happened in the past:
> – *Looking / Thinking back on it now, ...*
> – *When I look / think back on it now, ...*
> You use *would* to talk about repeated or habitual actions in the past:
> – *We'd often go to the seaside.*
> – *... and we'd all open the windows ...*

TASK

4 👤 *Preparation.* Learners think about a childhood event and make an outline of how they will tell the story, using the four categories from **3a**.

👥/👥👥 *Telling the story.* In turn, learners tell their story to the others and ask further questions.

Round-up. A learner from each group says how their stories were similar or different.

 You could use photocopiable activity 1B on the Teacher's DVD-ROM at this point.

1 Explore

Across cultures: Attitudes to children

Goal: to make learners aware of different social attitudes towards children

1   Learners cover the text and look at the photos. Discuss what they seem to show.

> A babies having a massage
> B a baby learning to swim
> C a 'baby 'n' book' session (someone reads to mothers and their babies)

Ask what the feature might say about Norway's attitude to babies (e.g. that good facilities are provided for mothers and babies; that women are encouraged to have babies; that children's development is encouraged from an early age).

2   *Reading to check.* Learners read the feature and make a note of anything they find surprising, or different from their own country.

Ask questions to check the main points of the feature, e.g.
– What do you think the UN Human Development Index shows?
– What's unusual about Norway?
– How does the government support mothers of young babies?
Ask learners what points they noted down.

3   *Discussion.* Learners discuss the questions together.

Round-up. Discuss the questions together, asking different learners what conclusions they came to. Ask further questions to extend the discussion of each point, e.g.
 1 Is there as much support for fathers as for mothers? Should there be?
 2 Are facilities provided for by the government (as in Norway)? Or are they private? What facilities are there for poorer people?
 3 What are the risks for smaller children? (traffic? injury? hygiene?) How 'safety-conscious' is society?
 4 Have attitudes changed? If so, how? Is it better or worse? Do younger adults see children differently from older people?
 5 If attitudes have changed, why do you think this is? Is it for the better or the worse?

Mixed-nationality classes

1 Learners from the same country work together in groups. Then get feedback from each group about their own country.
2 Learners work in groups with learners from different countries. Then in the feedback stage, ask learners what differences and similarities they discovered between their countries.

Keywords: describing habits and tendencies

Goal: to describe habits, repeated actions and tendencies
Core language:
will, would, used to, have a tendency to, tend to, always + -ing, liable to, prone to

1 a   *Focus on 'will' and 'would'.* Look at the examples together and establish the meaning of *will* or *would* in each one. Discuss other ways to express the same meaning. Point out that in these examples:
– *will* and *would* are used to express the idea of habitual or repeated action.
– *will* does not have a future meaning.
– *would* does not have a conditional meaning.
Possible answers:

> 1 Habitual action in the present (= they don't usually say ...; they never say ...)
> 2 Habitual action in the present (= I normally just stay at home ...)
> 3 Habitual action in the past (= as we drove (which happened every year), the trees started ...)
> 4 Habitual action in the past (= we always packed ...)

   b   Learners complete the sentences. Possible answers:

> 2 will play
> 3 will play / will go out
> 4 will babble
> 5 would spend
> 6 would never say

   c   Discuss which sentences could also use *used to*. Make the following points:
– sentences 1 and 5 could use *used to*.
– sentence 6 could use *used not to* or *didn't use to*.
– there is no difference in meaning in these examples, but *used to* can also be used to talk about past states: *When I was a child, we used to live in London.*

   d   Learners correct the mistakes. As you go through the answers, focus on why the sentences are not correct.

> 1 I used to ride my bike with friends. ('used to' = past form)
> 2 I had / I used to have lots of friends when I was little. (the sentence is describing a state, not a habitual action)
> 3 I still remember my fifth birthday. ('remember' is a state verb – it has no progressive form)

2 a   *Focus on other expressions.* Learners underline the expressions. Then go through the answers by building up expressions on the board:
– *have a tendency to*
– *tend to*
– *(be) always (-ing)*
– *(be) liable to*
– *(be) prone to*

Language note

1 *tend to*, *have a tendency to* and *be liable to* are all followed by infinitive.
2 *be prone to* can be followed by infinitive, or by a noun or verb + -ing:
– *I'm prone to put on weight.*
– *I'm prone to putting on weight.*

---

26   Unit 1 Childhood

b Look at the examples again, and establish that:
- *tend to* and *have a tendency to* are neutral (= it often happens).
- *be liable to* and *be prone to* are especially used for negative tendencies (e.g. falling ill, forgetting things).
- *be always* + *-ing* suggests 'it's annoying' or 'it happens too much'.

3 a *Pre-listening discussion.* Tell learners they will hear four conversations about the people / things in photos A–D. Ask what they think they might say, using the expressions in **2a**.

> **Option**
>
> 👥 / 👥👥 Learners look at the photos and brainstorm ideas. Then discuss them together and build up ideas on the board.

b *Listening.* Play recording **1.4**, pausing after each conversation. Match the conversations with photos A–D and discuss answers to questions 1 and 2.

> 1 C (A dog owner and visitor, in the dog owner's home. He's warning her about the dog, which might attack while he's out.)
> 2 D (In a car. The passenger is warning the driver about a slippery bend.)
> 3 A (In an office. Someone is warning a colleague about a computer program that is liable to crash.)
> 4 B (In a school staffroom or classroom. The class teacher is warning a colleague about a bright pupil who annoys the others.)

Ask learners what expressions from **2a** the speakers used. Play recording **1.4** again if necessary.

> 1 He does <u>have a tendency</u> to get a bit excited.
> 2 It<u>'s liable to</u> get really slippery when it's raining.
> 3 It <u>tends to</u> crash suddenly.
> 4 She <u>tends to</u> know all the answers. / She<u>'s always</u> putting her hand up.

4 *Speaking.* Give time for learners to think of someone and make a few notes.

👥 Learners describe the person to their partner.

Round-up. Ask a few learners what their partner told them.

> **Alternative: Mingling activity**
>
> 👥👥 Learners move freely round the class, telling other learners about their person.
> *Round-up.* A few learners tell the most interesting description they heard.

Explore speaking

Goals: tell an anecdote effectively
keep people interested in a story

Core language:
Strategies for keeping the listener's interest
Colourful, descriptive language

1 Look at the photo and discuss the questions. Possible answers:

> 1 They're listening to a story (or watching a film).
> 2 They're interested / fascinated / captivated; they're paying attention, listening carefully.
> 3 The subject, but also the way it's told.

> **Alternative**
>
> Discuss in more detail how to make a story interesting to listen to. Build up ideas on the board.

2 a *Listening.* Learners cover the page. Play recording **1.5** and discuss the questions. Point out that:
- the speaker had a monotonous, flat tone of voice.
- he sounded a bit bored and distant, not really involved in what he was saying.
- he sounded as if he was reading it or reciting it by heart.
- he didn't vary the pace.
- he didn't involve the audience or address them directly.

b *Listening.* Learners keep the page covered. Play recording **1.6**, then ask how it was different from the first version. Point out that:
- the speaker varied his pace and tone of voice more
- he sounded involved in the story himself, and seemed to be enjoying telling it.
- he sounded more spontaneous.
- he involved the audience by addressing them directly and asking questions
- he used more vivid, descriptive language.

3 *Listening and reading. Focus on story-telling strategies.* Play recording **1.6** again. Learners follow by reading the script. They highlight examples of the strategies mentioned. Discuss the strategies together. Possible answers:

> 1 They say the youngest are the spoilt ones, don't they? / Can you believe how cheeky you have to be ...?
> 2 ... with cameras and everything; vanished into thin air: you should have seen everyone's faces; beaming like mad
> 3 'Where's he gone now? Where's the troublemaker?'
> 4 ... as I'm sure you can imagine; you should have seen everyone's faces; Can you believe ...?
> 5 You know, the usual, just terrible. Well, I'd better get back to my anecdote! Nothing's changed really.
> 6 suddenly

4 *Focus on descriptive language.* Learners find the synonyms. Then discuss the answers.

> 2 beaming like mad
> 3 vanished into thin air
> 4 horrified
> 5 saw the funny side
> 6 let me get away with it
> 7 messing about

5 a 👥👥 *Speaking.* Learners look at the story. Together, they discuss how they could make it interesting to listen to. They then develop an outline.

They practise telling the story in their group.

b Each group chooses one 'storyteller'. In turn, they tell the story to the rest of the class. After each story, discuss what techniques the storyteller used to make it interesting.

 You could use photocopiable activity 1C on the Teacher's DVD-ROM at this point.

Unit 1 Childhood 27

1 Look again

GRAMMAR would

Optional lead-in

Books closed. Write *would* on the board and learners suggest examples showing different uses of *would*. For each new use, write the example on the board, until you have built up a range of different uses. Learners explain how *would* is used each time. Then do **1a** as a check and summary.

1 a Learners match the examples with the uses of *would*.

> 1B 2E 3A 4C 5D 6F

Elicit the following information.

1. We use *would* to talk about a habitual action in the past (*we would often walk home*).
2. Using *would* makes requests and offers less direct and so more polite. Compare *Would you prefer?* and *Do you want?*.
3. In reported speech, the verb often changes 'one tense back', so *will* becomes *would* (the person actually said *There will be hundreds out of work.*).
4. This use is similar to reported speech. Because it is set in the past, the verb changes 'one tense back'. (People said at the time *They won't win the match.*).
5. When we imagine an unreal, hypothetical, situation, we use *would* to refer to the present or future. We use *would have* + past participle to refer to the past.
6. Using *would* makes advice less direct – it 'softens' it. Compare *Don't worry about it* and *I wouldn't worry about it*.

b Discuss the question together, and point out that:
– In A and C we could use *was / were going to* instead of *would*.
– In B, we could use *used to* instead of *would*.

2 a Learners re-write the sentences using *would*.

b Learners discuss how their re-writes have changed the meaning of the sentences.

c *Listening.* Discuss the answers together, and play recording **1.7**. Possible answers (stressed examples of *would* are underlined):

> 1 Would you open the door? (Makes the request more polite.)
> 2 I asked him but he <u>wouldn't</u> say a word. (Adds a sense of 'he wasn't willing to'.)
> 3 Would you prefer to go by bus? (Makes the offer more polite.)
> 4 She would never forget that favour. ('Future in the past' – we see it from her point of view at that time.)
> 5 I would go there every August. (Indicates that it was a habitual action.)
> 6 He said he would leave early today. (Makes the message more certain.)
> 7 She <u>would</u> say that. (Emphasises that this is a habit and therefore predictable.)

Language note

Would is normally unstressed. It is only stressed for special emphasis and in the negative form.

3 a Learners complete the sentences.

b Learners tell each other their sentences and ask further questions.

Round-up. Learners tell you something interesting they found out about their partner.

Alternative: Mingling activity

After **3a**, learners choose two sentences they think are most interesting. They move freely round the class, telling each other their sentences and answering further questions.

GRAMMAR Using the -ing form

4 Look at the examples and discuss the questions.

> a 1   b 3 (after 'without')   c 2

5 Learners write the verbs in two lists: verbs followed by *-ing*; other verbs. Go through the answers by building up lists of verbs on the board:

verb + *-ing*		verb + *to* + infinitive
remember	mind	remember
enjoy	risk	manage
finish	suggest	regret
postpone	avoid	offer
regret	imagine	decide
give up		agree
		prepare

Language note

Remember has two meanings:
– remember doing (= recall)
  I remember taking the bus to school.
– remember to do (= don't forget)
  Remember to take some money with you.

6 a Learners add prepositions.

> 1 I get kind of tired of shopping.
> 2 I've no problem with remembering pin numbers.
> 3 That's a happy memory of meeting someone.
> 4 That's how they start talking, by mimicking us adults.

b Discuss which sentences are possible without a preposition (*answers:* 1, 2 and 4).

Language note

I get tired of shopping means I get bored of shopping.
I get tired shopping means that shopping makes me tired.

7 a Learners complete the sentences.

b In turn, learners choose a sentence to read out to the class. The others ask further questions.

VOCABULARY memory

8 a 👥 / 👥👥 *Books closed*. Learners brainstorm collocations with *memory* and write them down. Get suggestions from the class and build up a list on the board. Possible answers:

> short-term memory
> jog someone's memory
> long-term memory
> have a good memory
> a visual memory
> my earliest memory
> a memory for (names)
> a childhood memory
> a vivid memory (of)

b Discuss possible contexts for the expressions, and what they mean.

c Play recording **1.8** to check.

> 1 A news item about rain and floods (= since people can remember).
> 2 A doctor talking about someone with a head injury (= he can't remember things that happened recently).
> 3 A wife talking to a husband who forgot to pay the mortgage (= he has a very bad memory).
> 4 A salesman selling a computer (= computer memory).
> 5 Law students revising for an exam (= she can remember it).
> 6 Police questioning a witness to a crime (= he's not sure what he remembers).

VOCABULARY just

9 👤 / 👥 Learners decide what *just* means in each example. Then discuss the answers together.

> 2 simply   3 only   4 simply   5 simply / really

Language note
Before a noun or a verb, *just* often 'softens' what you are saying (e.g. *it's just respect* = it's nothing more than …). Before an adjective, *just* can either soften what you are saying (e.g. *it's just easier to go by train*) or it can intensify it (e.g. *That play was just awful*).

10 a Discuss the sentences with the class. Possible answers:

> 1 = it's too much to cope with, I haven't got time
>   (e.g. to look after children)
> 2 = there are too many jobs to do at once
>   (e.g. someone doing a very demanding job)
> 3 = it's too risky (e.g. about investing money)
> 4 = there's too much to do
>   (e.g. about running a household)
> 5 = she can't manage it all
>   (e.g. about a very demanding job)

Language note
Sentences 1, 2, 4 and 5 can all be used in similar situations.

b Discuss what syllables to stress in the sentences in **10a**.

c Play recording **1.9** to check. Point out that:
– if *too much* is followed by a noun or verb, *too* and the noun or verb are stressed (*It's too much pressure*).
– if *too much* is on its own, *much* is stressed (*It's just too much*).

d 👥 Learners choose a situation. Together they prepare what they might say about it. Then, learners form new pairs. They take it in turn to tell their new partner about their situation, and ask for advice.

11 a 👥 Learners discuss what the people in cartoons 1–4 are saying. Look at each cartoon in turn and get suggestions from the class.

b Play recording **1.10** to compare. Point out that: *It's just so you* = it really suits you.

c Play recording **1.10** again, pausing after each item. Get learners to repeat, using the correct stress.

Self-assessment

To help focus learners on the self-assessment, read it through, giving a few examples of the language they have learned in each section (or learners tell you). Then learners circle a number on each line.

Unit 1 Childhood 29

Unit 1 Extra activities on the Teacher's DVD-ROM

Printable worksheets, activity instructions and answer keys are on your Teacher's DVD-ROM.

1A Both sides of the argument

Activity type: Speaking – Discussion – Pairs / Groups

Aim: To develop extended discussions on the subject of childhood

Language: Adapting to another culture – Coursebook p7 – Vocabulary

Preparation: Make one copy of the worksheet for each pair.

Time: 25–30 minutes

1B It reminds me …

Activity type: Speaking – Discussion – Pairs / Whole group

Aim: To speculate about and to talk about childhood memories

Language: Talk about a personal memory – Coursebook p10 – Target activity

Preparation: Make one copy of the worksheet for each learner.

Time: 15–20 minutes

1C Embellish a story

Activity type: Speaking and writing – Storytelling – Pairs / Small groups

Aim: To improve skills in telling an anecdote

Language: Telling an anecdote effectively – Coursebook p13 – Explore speaking

Preparation: Make one copy of the worksheet for each pair.

Time: 20–30 minutes

Unit 1 Self-study Pack

In the Workbook

Unit 1 of the *English Unlimited Advanced Self-study Pack Workbook* offers additional ways to practise the vocabulary and grammar taught in the Coursebook. There are also activities which build reading and writing skills, and a whole page of tasks to use with the DVD-ROM video, giving your learners the opportunity to hear and react to spoken English.

- **Vocabulary:** Adapting to another culture; Remembering; *just*
- **Grammar:** *will* to express tendency; *would*; using the *-ing* form
- **Explore writing:** An important event
- **DVD-ROM Extra:** Drama – *Baghdad Express*

On the DVD-ROM

Unit 1 of the *English Unlimited Advanced Self-study Pack DVD-ROM* contains interactive games and activities for your learners to practise and improve their vocabulary, grammar and pronunciation, and also their speaking and listening. It also contains video material (with the possibility for learners to record themselves) to use with the *Workbook*.

- **Vocabulary and grammar:** Extra practice of the Coursebook language and Keywords
- **Explore listening:** Describing change
- **Explore speaking:** Making a story interesting
- **Video:** Drama – *Baghdad Express*

Self

2.1

Goals: talk about personality traits
talk about identity

Core language:
LANGUAGE FOCUS Presenting a self-image
LANGUAGE FOCUS Talking about identity

Your online self

SPEAKING

1 Quickly find out how many learners use Facebook or a similar social networking site and how many have their own page (avoid getting involved in too much discussion at this point). Use this to teach *social networking site*, *personal profile*.

👥 / 👥👥 *Discussion.* Learners look at the image and discuss the four questions. They discuss how they use social networking sites and what they use them for (if you haven't already covered this). Discuss whether social networking sites give an accurate picture of people's character, or whether people portray themselves in an idealised way. Encourage learners to give examples of themselves or people they know.

Round-up. As a class, discuss what the image says about the person. Then discuss images that learners have chosen for themselves. Ask questions to focus the discussion, e.g.
– *Do you think your image says something special about you? If so, what?*
– *How carefully did you think about what image to show of yourself?*
– *Do you think the image you choose is important?*

READING

2 *Reading for main idea.* Learners read the article. Then discuss what it says in answer to the points raised in **1** (*answer:* people present a fairly accurate picture of their personality).

3 a *Intensive reading.* Learners identify the points in the article. Possible answers:

> 1 Far from presenting themselves in a flattering way ...;
> 2 ... reveal both psychological weaknesses and natural physical flaws.
> 3 Far from being idealised versions of themselves ...
> 4 It could be that users ... but in fact fail to do so.
> 5 Social networking sites can in no way be considered ... they are simply another way in which people choose to interact with each other.

b Discuss the question together (*answer:* the writer says what the reader probably thinks, but then says this is not the case; this makes you want to read on).

LANGUAGE FOCUS Presenting a self-image

4 a Learners identify the adjectives.

> **personality traits:** *sophisticated, discerning, intelligent, agreeable, extroverted, conscientious, neurotic, sociable*

b 👥 Learners cover the article. They work together to remember the collocations. Build up the answers on the board.

> create a profile
> portray themselves
> put up a profile
> present an image
> choose interests
> reflect their true personalities
> express their thoughts
> reveal weaknesses / physical flaws

5 👥 / 👥👥 Discuss the questions together. Discuss what type of person might choose each photo as a profile image. You could also ask learners if they would choose images like these and why / why not.

Learners brainstorm other types of profile photo. Build up ideas on the board, e.g.:
– *at work.*
– *doing something typical (e.g. playing the guitar, drinking coffee).*
– *an unusual shot (e.g. very close up, at an angle).*

> **Optional homework**
>
> Ask learners to find out what they can about:
> – *avatars.*
> – *alter-egos.*
> – *virtual worlds (e.g.* Second Life*).*
> Then they report back in the next lesson.

What defines you?

LISTENING

> **Optional lead-in**
>
> Write on the board: *What defines you as a person?*
> Build up on the board a list of things that might define who you are, e.g. your home, your country, your friends, your job, your family, your religion.

1 a *Listening for gist.* Play recording **1.11**. After each speaker, establish what it is that defines them. If you wrote a list on the board, check whether the speaker mentioned one of those factors or something different.

> 1 where he grew up, his language, people around him, living in other countries (the USA, Britain)
> 2 her family, children
> 3 friends, people he spends time with, travelling, being able to live in other cultures
> 4 job, friends

Unit 2 Self 31

b *Intensive listening.* Play the recording again, pausing after each speaker so learners can make notes. Discuss the answers together.

> 1 Norman: *USA and Britain – he adopted some of their values*
> Liam: *Vietnam and France – he learned to adapt to other cultures*
> 2 Olga: *She thought about her own prospects*
> Jane: *She didn't know who she was*
> 3 Norman: *people from his past*
> Olga: *her children*
> Liam: *people he currently spends time with*
> Jane: *a close circle of friends*

> **Alternative**
> Before listening again, learners make notes in answer to the questions. Then discuss the answers together and play recording **1.11** again to check.

LANGUAGE FOCUS Talking about identity

2 a Learners match the sentence halves.

b Go through the answers and ask who made each remark. Learners could check in the script on p147.

> 1 a (Jane)
> 2 h (Jane)
> 3 f (Olga)
> 4 b (Norman)
> 5 g (Liam)
> 6 c (Jane)
> 7 e (Liam)
> 8 d (Norman)

> **Optional presentation**
> *Books closed.* To check key expressions and collocations, write expressions on the board and learners say how they continue, e.g.
> – *I feel part ...*
> – *I see myself ...*
> – *I'm a product ...*
> – *I'm reflected ...*
> – *I identify ...*

3 *Preparation.* Learners look at the categories and think what to say, and think how they could use the expressions in **2a**.

Learners say what defines them and answer questions from other learners.

Feedback. Go through the list of categories. For each one, ask if anyone feels that this defines their identity. Then ask learners which they think are the most and least important categories.

 You could use photocopiable activity 2A on the Teacher's DVD-ROM at this point.

2.2

Goals: understand promotional language
say how you met someone
Core language:
LANGUAGE FOCUS Promotional language
LANGUAGE FOCUS Say how you met someone

Dating agencies

READING

> **Optional lead-in**
> Write *dating agencies* on the board and ask learners who they are for and how they usually work.

1 Discuss the questions together. Bring out these points:
– computerised databases can search for similar people more successfully.
– they are easier to use anonymously.
– as they become more popular, they can offer a wider choice.
– they are becoming more socially acceptable, so more people are encouraged to use them.
– the fact that you have something in common doesn't always mean you will have a good relationship.

2 Learners read the website extracts, then discuss the questions and make notes of their answers.

> A *You make contact using cell phones (= mobile phones) by sending text messages.*
> B *Holidays for single people are available.*
> C *You meet people online, or at a specially arranged party.*

3 Learners decide which agency the sentences describe. As you go through the answers, learners say more about each item, e.g.

1 They have staff at the party who encourage people to mingle and meet each other.

> 1 C (staff help you to mingle)
> 2 B (established in 1969)
> 3 A (you don't have to fill in forms)
>   B (different from other holiday companies)
> 4 A (for cell-phone users) / B (for people who like travelling) / C (for professional people)
> 5 C (a million members online)
> 6 A (you can send text messages immediately)
> 7 B (they share a passion for life)
> 8 C (you get three extra months free if you don't find someone)

LANGUAGE FOCUS Promotional language

4 a To establish the idea of promotional language, ask the class what the aim of the adverts is (to promote their product, to persuade people to join). Point out that the adverts use various language devices which help to sell their product.

Look at the devices and check that learners understand *boast* (= saying something good about yourself) and *pun* (= a play on words).

32 Unit 2 Self

👤/👥 Learners find examples of each device. Possible answers:

> 1 A You'll receive the profiles ... /
>   You may find your perfect ... cell mate!
>   B you will doubtless be holidaying ...
>   C You're sure to love what you see.
> 2 A It's 100% fun and 100% safe!
>   B ours is a name customers trust ...
>   C the dating agency for professionals ...
> 3 B Love is nearer than you think.
>   C Make it happen!
> 4 A Send a text message now and enter the fun!
>   C We'll give you the next three months absolutely free!
> 5 A You may find your perfect ... cell mate

Language note

'cell mate' usually means someone you share a prison cell with; here it is a play on the words 'cell phone' and 'mate', which means someone you share something with.

b *Focus on language.* Look at the language forms in turn and ask learners to find examples of each. Discuss why they are effective in promotional language. Check the meaning of:
 – rhetorical questions (= questions you don't expect to be answered)
 – inversion (= changing the order of the subject and verb).
 Possible examples:

> Imperatives: 'Send a text message'; 'Make it happen!'; 'log on to the dating agency'; 'Start a subscription'
> Rhetorical questions: 'How does it work, you ask?'; 'Not convinced by online love?'
> Conditional sentences: 'If you don't find that someone special ...'; 'You'd be a fool not to give it a try'
> Positive adjectives: 'brand new'; 'fun'; 'safe'; 'perfect'; 'personal'; 'unobtrusive'; 'exciting'; 'sure'; 'special'; 'great'; 'like-minded'; 'relaxed'; 'at ease'
> Inversion: 'ours is a name customers trust'
> Modal verbs: 'will' and 'may' in predictions

c Learners suggest other techniques that are used, e.g.
 – short sentences (which give a chatty style and the impression that the steps are simple).
 – words that emphasise simplicity and freedom of choice: *simple, immediately, anytime, anywhere*.

Alternative

👥 Learners work through **4a** and **4b** in groups and make notes of their answers. Then different groups report back the main things they noticed.

 You could use photocopiable activity 2B on the Teacher's DVD-ROM at this point.

How we met

LANGUAGE FOCUS *Say how you met someone*

Optional lead-in

Tell learners they will read a description of how two people met at a dating agency party. Ask what verb forms the person might use, and elicit these forms:
– to say what happened and how: past simple; past perfect; past progressive.
– to talk about things still going on now: present perfect; present simple; present progressive.
To focus on these forms, tell the class how you met someone, using examples of the above.

1 a Check that learners understand *testimonial* (= description of a positive experience, as a recommendation). Learners read the testimonial and fill the gaps.

> 1 says 2 saw 3 knew 4 was 5 'd seen
> 6 'd decided ('decided' is also possible) 7 was sitting
> 8 came 9 chatted 10 called 11 've been 12 have
> 13 work 14 are having 15 came 16 would have met

b Play recording **1.12** to check. Establish which verb forms are used and why. Write them on the board. If you introduced the verb forms earlier, check which ones were used in the testimonial. If necessary, remind learners that:
– you use the past perfect simple to 'go back' from the past to an earlier event (*I had seen*).
– you use the past progressive to talk about things going on at the time (*I was sitting ...; he came over*).
– you use the present perfect + *for / since* to talk about something that started in the past and is still going on (*We've been together ever since* = since that evening).

WRITING and SPEAKING

2 a To show how the game works, you could write the opening expressions on the board and use them to tell the class a story about how you met someone. Alternatively, make up a story together, writing opening expressions on the board and getting learners to suggest how it might develop.

👤 Learners write the beginning of the story on a piece of paper. They pass their paper to the person next to them, who continues it. Continue in this way until all the stories are complete.

b In turn, learners read out the completed stories.

Alternative

👥/👥👥 Learners write the sentences. After each stage, they pass their story to the next pair / group.

3 👥/👥👥 In turn, learners tell each other how they really met someone important to them. It could be a partner, a spouse, a close friend, a business colleague or a neighbour.

Round-up. Ask a few learners to tell you what their partner told them.

Unit 2 Self 33

2.3 Target activity: Promote yourself

Goals: use effective introduction strategies
promote yourself

Core language:
TASK LANGUAGE   Introduction strategies

Promote yourself

TASK LISTENING

1 a Look at images A and B. Point out that:
– facial gestures and body language are just as important as what you say.
– just introducing yourself isn't as important as *how* you introduce yourself (by smiling, shaking hands, looking interested or friendly).
– business training often includes practice in presenting yourself in a positive way. This will also be the focus of this Target activity.

b *Listening: bad model.* Tell learners they will hear three situations where people do not present themselves very successfully. Play recording **1.13**. Pause after each conversation and establish:
– the situation and what happened.
– what the candidate did not do successfully.

> Uri: *He has been unemployed and is now at a job interview. He's uneasy and hesitant; he doesn't give a convincing reason why he wants the job.*
> Sandy: *She is coming to a group interview after a long period of email correspondence. She talks too much without thinking; she says inappropriate (over-personal) things to the interviewer.*
> Carmelo: *She has arrived late for a group interview or an exam. She makes it obvious that she's nervous and that she doesn't know the name of the interviewer, who she has met before.*

c *Listening: improved model.* Tell learners they will hear the same conversations, but the candidates present themselves more successfully. Play recording **1.14**, pausing after each conversation to establish what they do better.

> Uri: *He sounds more confident. He introduces himself clearly, refers to his CV and background, gives a convincing, positive reason for wanting the job and plays up his own strengths without sounding too boastful.*
> Sandy: *She introduces herself clearly. She sounds open and friendly, without saying anything too personal. She conveys pleasure at being there.*
> Carmelo: *She sounds more confident and assured. She introduces herself clearly and covers up the fact that she can't remember the name by saying "I don't think we've been introduced". She doesn't refer to her nervousness (when asking to borrow a pen).*

TASK LANGUAGE Introduction strategies

> **Optional lead-in**
>
> *Books closed.* Brainstorm a few general strategies for presenting yourself successfully in an interview, e.g.
> – plan some of the things you might say.
> – respond to what the interviewer says.
> – expand on comments, so the interview isn't dominated by the interviewer.
> – (when using English) if you can't remember the precise word, paraphrase it or use other ways to get the point across.

2 a Read through the strategies and check that learners know what they mean. Point out the meaning of:
– *backtracking* (= going back and rephrasing what you said in a better way).
– *reformulating* (= saying the same thing again in a different way).
– *equivalent term* (= one that means the same).
– *keep the floor* (= keep the initiative in the conversation, be the one who's speaking).
– *handling interjections* (= responding when the interviewer interrupts with a question).

👤/👥 Learners decide which strategies are represented by the highlighted examples. Point out that the examples may represent a number of different overlapping strategies. Discuss the answers together. Possible answers:

> 1 b   2 a   3 c, e   4 c   5 e   6 d, f

b Compare the way the candidates introduce themselves. Discuss who seems to come across best. Point out that:
– Uri is quite formal and matter-of-fact; Sandy is more informal and 'chatty'.
– how formally you introduce yourself obviously depends on the kind of interview it is, the nature of the job, and on how you want to present yourself.

c Look at what the interviewers say and discuss how they put the candidates at ease. Point out that:
– in conversation A, the interviewer softens the opening question (*Would you like to tell me a little bit ...*) so as not to sound too aggressive or dominant.
– in conversation B, the interviewer comes across as friendly and welcoming (*It's nice to meet you*), and agrees with the candidate (*Yes, that's right*) to make her feel they are on the same side.
– in conversation C, the interviewer is welcoming (*It's really nice to ...*), and reassures the candidate about borrowing a pen (*Of course, no problem*).

TASK

3 *Preparation.* Give each learner a letter, A or B. The A learners will be candidates, Bs will conduct the interview. There should be twice as many interviewers as candidates, so that each candidate can be interviewed by an 'interview board' of two people. Learners read about the job which the interview will be based around. Student As look on p126 and Bs look on p134. They prepare what they will say or what they will ask.

> **Alternative: Pair or group preparation**
>
> 👥/👨‍👨‍👦 Candidates prepare for the interview together. Interviewers form 'interview boards' straight away and prepare what they will ask their candidates.

Interview. Interviewers form pairs (interview boards). They each interview one candidate. When the interview is finished, the candidates move to a new interview board and have a second interview.

Round-up. Interview boards decide which candidate they will accept for the job. Ask the boards and the candidates to comment on the interviews.

 You could use photocopiable activity 2C on the Teacher's DVD-ROM at this point.

2 Explore

Across cultures: Your cards

Goal: to make learners aware of different attitudes to using business cards or name cards

Core language:
business card, membership card, loyalty card, identity card; layout, font, texture

> **Optional lead-in**
>
> *Books closed*. To lead into the topic, discuss what kind of people use business cards. Ask learners if they have a card, and if so, what information it shows about them.
> In a mixed-nationality class, ask whether cards are important in the learners' own country.

1. a *Discussion.* Learners look at cards A–D and discuss what they say about the people who own them.

   b If you haven't already done so, discuss who uses business cards and whether learners use them.

   c *Pre-reading discussion.* Ask learners to imagine they are creating a business card for an individual or a company. Ask what features might be important to consider. Build up ideas on the board, e.g.
   – size, material, quality of the card.
   – layout, use of colour, font, style, logo.
   – information (e.g. name, company, phone number, job or position in the company).

2. a *Reading.* Learners read the article. Then establish which points are the same as those you discussed and which are different.

   Ask learners what kind of person they think wrote it. Ask whether learners agree with what it recommends and why or why not.

   b Learners look at the cards again and identify any features mentioned in the article.

3. a Consider each of the types of people in turn and discuss what image they might want to convey and what features their card might have. Try to bring out possible differences, e.g.
   – *a sales manager:* corporate card, the same as other people in the company, conventional, serious-looking, good quality, with company logo.
   – *a singer:* more individual, less formal, perhaps with a musical image.
   – *architect:* neat, simple design to reflect the job, stylish.
   – *yoga teacher:* might have a 'new age' or oriental look, perhaps tinted or with a yoga image.
   – *website designer:* clear and simple, stylish, elegant, to reflect the style of his / her work.
   – *furniture shop owner:* traditional-looking, good quality card, perhaps with a furniture image.

   b Pairs each choose one of the people and design a card. Go round to give help and suggestions, and check that learners consider details such as font, layout, logos or images, etc.

> **Alternative**
>
> Divide the class into pairs or groups at the start of 3a. Each pair / group chooses one of the people, discusses what the person's card might look like and designs a card.

   c Learners sit with others who designed a card for the same person and compare what they have produced. Alternatively, each pair or group shows their card to the class and summarises their ideas.

4. Discuss the questions together, or let learners discuss them in groups and then report back to the class.

> **Alternative**
>
> For question 4, ask learners to write a list of all the cards they have (e.g. credit cards, health insurance card, library membership card, name card). Then they compare with other learners.

Keywords: describing skill and ability

Goal: to describe skills, talents and abilities

Core language:
talent, skill, ability, capable

1. a *Focus on 'skill', 'talent', 'ability'.* Look at the examples together and discuss the questions.

   > a This could be part of an email about a student who has just gone to university (or school).
   > b A job ad in a newspaper or on a website, for a manager of a small company.
   > c This is probably a spoken commentary (on the TV or radio) about a football match.

   b Look again at the examples and discuss prepositions and verbs for the gaps.

   > a for learning
   > b in running
   > c to win

> **Language note**
>
> *Talent, skill* and *ability* can be followed by these structures:
> – *have a talent for* + noun or *-ing*
> – *acquire* (or *develop*) *skills in* + noun or *-ing*
> – *have an ability to* + infinitive

   c Ask learners to suggest sentences using *talented*, *skilled* and *capable*, and write the forms on the board. Possible answers:

   > a She seems to be a talented sportsperson ...
   > b We need someone who is skilled in business ...
   > c ... they are capable of winning the match in the last minute ...

2. a *Focus on collocations.* Learners write the collocations in two lists. Then go through the answers and build the expressions up on the board.

real talent	leadership skills
natural talent	academic skills
considerable talent	basic skills
	computer skills
	technical skills
	intellectual skills

   As you do this, ask learners to suggest a context for each expression, e.g.
   – *He shows <u>real talent for acting</u>* (= genuine)
   – *The CEO of a company needs to <u>have leadership skills</u>* (= be able to lead people)

Unit 2 Self 35

> **Language note**
>
> 1 *talent* is general underlying ability; *skills* are specific abilities to do something
> 2 You can use *talent* as:
> – an uncountable noun to talk about general ability (*He has considerable talent as a musician*).
> – a countable noun + *for* (*He has a natural talent for playing the piano*).
> 3 You can use *skill* as:
> – a singular noun (*She negotiated the deal with great skill*).
> – a plural noun (*She has very good negotiating skills*).

b Discuss which words could come before *ability* (all of them). Point out that *ability* is a general noun, meaning 'being able to do something', so it can be used in a wide range of contexts.

c Give an example of *talent* being used to refer to a person.
– *The company needs to bring in some new talent.*
(= talented new people)

Learners decide what the expressions might refer to and think of possible contexts. Possible answers and examples:

> 2 Both. 'The country has plenty of <u>creative talent</u>.' (= talented people); 'She has enormous creative talent.'
> 3 A person. 'There are well-established players in the team, but not much young talent.'
> 4 An ability. 'I have almost no athletic talent, but I enjoy swimming.'
> 5 An ability. 'Their children all have plenty of artistic talent.'

3 a *Pre-listening discussion.* Look at photos A–F together. Discuss what they show and what talent or skills they might illustrate. Possible answers:

> A a pop band (performing skills, talent for music)
> B a politician giving a speech (speaking skills, communication skills, leadership skills)
> C a piano lesson (musical talent, teaching skills)
> D a school class in Africa (basic reading skills, literacy skills, teaching skills)
> E a fashion model on a catwalk (creative talent, new talent, talent for design)
> F someone using a computer (computing skills)

> **Option**
>
> Learners look at photos A–F and brainstorm ideas. Then discuss them together and build up ideas on the board.

b *Listening.* Play recording **1.15**, pausing after each remark. Discuss answers to questions 1, 2 and 3.

> A real talent
> B leadership skills
> C natural ability
> D basic skills in reading and writing
> E new young talent
> F computational and technical skills

4 Give time for learners to think of someone and make a few notes.

Speaking. Learners describe the person to their partner.

Round-up. Ask a few learners what their partner told them.

> **Alternative: Mingling activity**
>
> Learners move freely round the class, telling other learners about their person.
> *Round-up.* A few learners tell you the most interesting description they heard.

Explore writing

Goals: write a cover letter
describe experience and ability

Core language:

ways of showing yourself in a positive light; expressions to describe ability and experience

> **Optional lead-in**
>
> *Books closed.* Write *MBA* on the board and ask the class what it means (answer: Master in Business Administration). Discuss what experience and qualifications you might need to be accepted for an MBA course.

1 a *Books closed.* Write the words in the box on the board. Learners imagine they are writing a covering letter / email to apply for an MBA course. Ask them how they might use the words in the letter. As learners make suggestions, add possible collocations on the board (e.g. *familiar with, aptitude for, accustomed to; relevant experience, respond to a challenge, computer skills*).

b *Reading and gap-filling.* Learners read the letter and complete the gaps.

> 1 application 2 specialty 3 relevant 4 accustomed
> 5 skills 6 familiar 7 aptitude 8 challenges 9 future
> 10 hesitate

> **Language note**
>
> *aptitude* = a natural or potential ability (*an aptitude for languages* = you could learn any language easily).
> *specialty* = the subject you specialise in.
> *relevant certificates* = certificates that are important for the application (the ones which are needed).
> *I am writing to ...* and *Please don't hesitate to ...* are standard expressions in letter writing.

2 a *Focus on style.* Discuss how you can identify the letter as US English. Show these US and British English equivalents:

US English	British English
specialty	speciality
grade	mark
resumé	CV

b Learners find expressions in the letter that show optimism and self-confidence. Possible answers:

> – I have received excellent grades
> – I'm on course to graduate with distinction
> – I honed my professional skills
> – my greatest strengths lie in ...
> – taking on whatever challenges come my way
> – I am able to take on the demands ...

c Learners cover the letter and complete the sentences. Go through the answers by focusing especially on the prepositions immediately following the given expressions.

> 1 an aptitude for (taking)
> 2 accustomed to (working)
> 3 familiar with (the banking world)
> 4 lie in (my ability)
> 5 available for (interview)

   d If necessary, learners check answers in the letter.

   e *Focus on function.* Discuss the function of each paragraph.

> **First paragraph:** *opening of the letter, says what it is about with a conventional opening (I am writing to ...).*
> **Second paragraph:** *gives academic experience and current course of study. It uses the present perfect to describe previous experience, and the present progressive to describe current activities.*
> **Third paragraph:** *describes work experience. It uses the present perfect and past simple, and expressions for describing familiarity (accustomed to, familiar with).*
> **Fourth paragraph:** *describes strengths and abilities. It uses expressions for talking about ability (abilities, I am able) and belief (I believe, I strongly believe).*
> **Final paragraph:** *finishes the letter. It uses standard formulae (I am available for interview; If you require ...; please don't hesitate ...; I look forward to ...).*

3 *Writing.* Organise the writing phase to suit the needs of your class. Either bring in a job advert that would be relevant to their qualifications, or give details of a course of study they could realistically apply for.

> **Alternative: group writing**
>
> Either give a different job advert to each group, or give them all the same advert. Working together, they write a covering letter, either giving real details about their experience and qualifications or (if they all have different backgrounds) inventing them. They should choose one 'secretary' to do the writing.
> *Round-up.* One person from each group reads out their group's letter.

2 Look again

GRAMMAR Verb tenses in narration

1 Ask learners what tenses were used in the story.

> – *Tenses used for narration (the story of how they met): past simple and progressive; past perfect simple*
> – *Tenses used to talk about things connected with the present (what happened since the time they met): present perfect simple*

2 Discuss the questions. Learners give examples from the story.

> | 1 Past progressive | 3 Past simple |
> |---|---|
> | 2 Past progressive | 4 Past perfect simple |

3 👥 / 👥👥 Learners decide on the best order for the pictures. Discuss the order together. Learners say what order they think the story happened.

> B D A C F E

4 👤 / 👥 Learners complete the story.

> 2 had been looking 3 hadn't found 4 changed 5 left
> 6 woke 7 took 8 struck 9 had done 10 had been travelling 11 waited 12 arrived 13 had happened
> 14 haven't gone / haven't been back

5 👤 Learners prepare a story. They should think about how they will use the tenses you have covered, noting down verbs they will use.

   👥 In turn, learners tell each other their story.

Round-up. A few learners tell their own or their partner's story to the class.

GRAMMAR Phrasal verbs; verbs + prepositions

6 a Look at the examples. Ask which are phrasal verbs and which are verbs + prepositions.

> *phrasal verbs:* 1, 2, 6
> *verbs + prepositions:* 3, 4, 5

> **Language note**
>
> Many verbs are followed by a preposition + noun or *-ing*. The preposition always comes just after the verb and before the noun:
> – *I have <u>worked in</u> the marketing area.*
> NOT *I have worked the marketing area in.*
> Other verbs are phrasal verbs (= two-word verbs) – they have a verb + a particle (a 'small word'). The particle can come before the noun, or it can come after it:
> – *Please <u>fill out</u> this questionnaire.*
> – *Please <u>fill</u> this questionnaire <u>out</u>.*
> The particle must come after a pronoun:
> – *Please <u>fill</u> it <u>out</u>.*

   b Learners complete the sentences. As you go through the answers, check that learners know what all the expressions mean. (PV = phrasal verb)

> 1 succeed in
> 2 lacking in (= I don't have enough)
> 3 look up (PV) (= find and see what it says about it)
> 4 benefit from
> 5 relied on (= made use of)
> 6 appealed to (= I liked the idea)
> 7 make out (PV) (= understand, hear)
> 8 opt for (= decide to do)
> 9 immerse yourself in (= be surrounded by it)

   c 👥 Learners experiment with saying the sentences using a different part of speech (e.g. changing the verb to a noun or an adjective).

Discuss the answers together. Possible answers:

> 1 I wasn't successful in ...
> 2 I have a lack of practical experience.; I lack practical experience.
> 3 –
> 4 It would be beneficial for me to ...
> 5 –
> 6 What I found really appealing was ...
> 7 –
> 8 I'd take the option of both working and studying ...
> 9 You need total immersion in ...

   d To demonstrate the activity, say a few sentence beginnings yourself and learners continue them.

   👥 Learners take it in turn to say sentence beginnings, and their partner continues them.

Round-up. Ask a few pairs to tell you their most interesting sentences.

VOCABULARY self-

7 Look at the examples and ask learners to suggest others.

> **Alternative**
>
> *Books closed*. Write the three examples on the board and learners say how they are different. Then learners suggest other examples of each type.

8 a Learners make adjectives from the box.

b As you go through the answers, learners explain what the expressions mean. Possible answers:

> *a self-evident idea* (= obvious)
> *a self-contained system* (= one that doesn't need anything coming in from outside)
> *a self-contained person* (= someone who doesn't need other people)
> *a self-contained flat* (= has everything you need, e.g. bathroom, kitchen)
> *a self-centred person* (= thinks mainly about him/herself)
> *a self-made person* (= someone who became successful through their own work, without outside help)
> *a self-sustaining system* (= keeps running by itself)
> *a self-fulfilling prophecy* (= because you predict something will happen, it does happen)

c Learners add expressions to the gaps.

> 1 self-contained   2 self-made   3 self-sustaining
> 4 self-evident   5 self-fulfilling   6 self-centred

9 a Learners add nouns to the gaps. As you go through the answers, check the meaning of the sentences.

> 1 self-esteem (= low opinion of yourself)
> 2 self-defence (= they were attacked)
> 3 self-discipline (= you need to make yourself work)
> 4 self-confidence (= belief in your own abilities)
> 5 self-interest (= what was good for him)
> 6 self-pity (= feeling sorry for yourself)

b Discuss which nouns have a negative connotation and which have equivalent adjective forms.

> negative: *self-interest, self-pity*
> adjectives: *self-disciplined, self-confident, self-pitying*

10 a *Preparation.* Give time for learners to think of a person and make a few notes.

b Learners describe the person to their partner.

Feedback. Ask a few learners what their partner told them.

> **Alternative: Whole-class activity**
>
> In turn, learners tell the class about the person they chose. The others listen and ask further questions.

VOCABULARY Reformulating what you say

11 a Look at the example and discuss other ways to reformulate the sentence. Build up ideas on the board.
– ..., *or rather*, why it appealed to me.
– *that is to say*, why it appealed to me.
– ... why it appealed to me, *that is*.
– *I mean*, why it appealed to me.

> **Language note**
>
> These expressions can come before the reformulated part, or at the end of it:
> – ..., *or rather*, why it appealed to me.
> – ..., why it appealed to me, *rather*.
> – ..., *that is*, why it appealed to me.
> – ... why it appealed to me, *that is*.

> **Optional practice**
>
> Give some simple sentences for learners to reformulate, using the expressions you have introduced. Indicate what they need to correct, e.g.
> – *We went to Paris (London).*
> – *I sent my resumé (my CV).*
> – *His name's Jack Rogers (Sir Jack Rogers).*

b Play recording **1.16**. Learners listen and identify the details that are changed.

> *a villa* → *an apartment*
> *a private beach* → *a public beach*
> *empty* → *busy at the weekends and in summer*
> *by the sea* → *10 minutes' walk* → *20 minutes' walk*

c Ask what ways of reformulating learners noticed in the recording. Play it again if necessary. Then let them check in the script on p148, and discuss the answers together. Write key expressions on the board.

> – *not really ..., more ...*
> – *when I say ..., I mean ...*
> – *not literally ...*
> – *that is to say ...*
> – *to be honest, ...*
> – *not strictly speaking ...*
> – *I should say ...*
> – *or well, ...*
> – *or perhaps ...*

12 a To demonstrate the activity, tell the class about someone you know and keep reformulating what you say, as in the recording. Then discuss together how your story changed.

Give learners a letter, A or B. Working alone, learners think of something or someone to talk about.

Learners take it in turn to tell each other their story / description, using the reformulating expressions given on the board.

b *Round-up*. Ask pairs what they talked about and which expressions they used. Ask which were easy to use and which were more difficult.

Self-assessment

To help focus learners on the self-assessment, you could read it through, giving a few examples of the language they have learned in each section (or asking learners to tell you). Then ask them to circle a number on each line.

Unit 2 Extra activities on the Teacher's DVD-ROM

Printable worksheets, activity instructions and answer keys are on your Teacher's DVD-ROM.

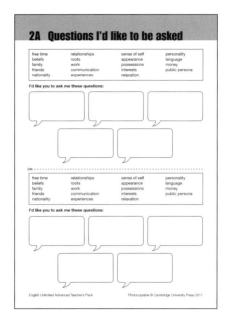
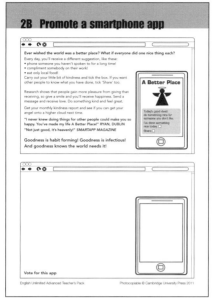
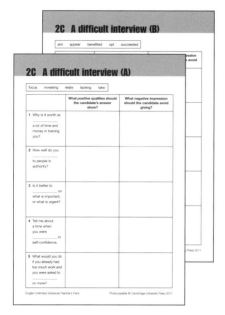

2A Questions I'd like to be asked

Activity type: Speaking – Interviews – Pairs

Aim: To improve fluency and language for talking about yourself

Language: Talking about identity – Coursebook p17 – Vocabulary

Preparation: Make one copy of the worksheet for each pair. Cut it in half along the dotted line.

Time: 25–30 minutes

2B Promote a smartphone app

Activity type: Speaking – Discussion – Groups

Aim: To practise understanding and writing promotional texts

Language: Promotional language – Coursebook p19

Preparation: Make one copy of the worksheet for each group.

Time: 30–40 minutes

2C A difficult interview

Activity type: Speaking – Discussion and role play – Pairs / Groups

Aim: To practise responding to difficult questions

Language: Using effective introduction strategies – Coursebook p20 – Target activity

Preparation: Make one copy of each worksheet for every pair.

Time: 20–30 minutes

Unit 2 Self-study Pack

In the Workbook

Unit 2 of the *English Unlimited Advanced Self-study Pack Workbook* offers additional ways to practise the vocabulary and grammar taught in the Coursebook. There are also activities which build reading and writing skills, and two pages which give your learners the opportunity to develop their skills in extended reading.

- **Vocabulary:** Talking about identity; *skill, talent, ability; self*
- **Grammar:** Verb tenses in narration; Phrasal verbs; verbs + prepositions
- **Explore reading:** Biographies and abstracts

On the DVD-ROM

Unit 2 of the *English Unlimited Advanced Self-study Pack DVD-ROM* contains interactive games and activities for your learners to practise and improve their vocabulary, grammar and pronunciation, and also their speaking and listening.

- **Vocabulary and grammar:** Extra practice of the Coursebook language and Keywords
- **Explore listening:** A lecture
- **Explore speaking:** Opening strategies

3 Language and literature

3.1

Goals: describe a book
give a personal response

Core language:
LANGUAGE FOCUS   Describe a book and its significance

Life-changing books

SPEAKING and READING

1 a *Discussion.* Check that learners know what the genres are. You could ask them to give examples of each, or tell you if they have recently read a book representing that genre. Point out that:
   - *fiction* is a general category that includes adventure and romantic novels (i.e. books with imaginary characters and events).
   - the opposite is *non-fiction* (= books about facts, real people, etc.).
   - *current affairs* = events happening in the world at the moment, especially political issues.

   b 👤 / 👥 Learners cover the summaries and discuss which genre each book might belong to and what each might be about.

   c *Reading to check.* Learners read the summaries. Then discuss what the genres are.

   > How to heal a broken heart in 30 days: *self-help guide*
   > What I talk about when I talk about running: *autobiography*
   > Slaughterhouse–Five: *fiction*
   > Farthest North: *adventure, autobiography*
   > The flying carpet to Baghdad: *current affairs*
   > 365 penguins: *children's fiction, humour*

   Learners discuss which books they think would be bestsellers.

   > **Alternative**
   >
   > 👤 / 👥 Learners each read different summaries. Then they report back to the class what genre the book is and what it is about.

   Ask learners which books they think would be most worth reading and why. Alternatively, they choose two books to read on a journey, explaining their choice.

LISTENING

2 a *Listening for main points.* Tell learners they will hear explorer Ian McDonald talking about a book which has some significance for him: *Farthest North*. Play recording **1.17**. Learners listen and note down only the main points.

   b 👥 Learners compare to see if they noted the same points. Then discuss this together and build points up on the board in note form. Possible notes:

   – he was 12
   – Nansen – 19th century
   – Arctic – ship stuck in ice
   – dog-sled and kayak – tried to reach North Pole
   – very brave
   – very long
   – about science
   – re-read it as an adult – boring, disappointed

   c Establish what the sentences mean and focus on key words and expressions.

   > 1 socially awkward, probably spent a lot of time alone, reading
   > 2 the things they did were daring – they took huge risks, came close to death and survived
   > 3 it was difficult to read (because of the length and the style)
   > 4 it influenced him (he became an explorer himself)
   > 5 it described science in action (observations on their journey)

   d Discuss whether learners think it would be an interesting book to read and why / why not.

LANGUAGE FOCUS Describe a book and its significance

3 a Look at the sets of words and discuss how they are different.

   > A They describe the book itself.
   > B They describe Ian's feelings about the book and its effect on him.

   b 👤 / 👥 Learners try making expressions from the words, either the ones the speaker used or other possible expressions.

   Discuss the expressions together and write possible collocations on the board.

   c Play recording **1.17** again, pausing from time to time to check. Focus on any new items.

   > A
   > an <u>obscure</u> book (= not well known)
   > an <u>account</u> of an attempt to reach the North Pole
   > a very <u>daring</u> book
   > the stuff they did was <u>unbelievably</u> brave
   > <u>enormously</u> long / <u>detailed</u> / <u>discursive</u>
   > Ian read a <u>condensed</u> <u>version</u> (= shorter)
   > B
   > I <u>vividly</u> <u>remember</u> ... (= clearly)
   > it really <u>meant</u> a lot to me
   > I was absolutely <u>fascinated</u>
   > I liked the <u>idea</u> of ...
   > It gave me an <u>interest</u> in maps
   > I was <u>amazed</u> that I'd read it as a teenager
   > I was <u>depressed</u> by how boring it was
   > ... are always going to be a <u>disappointment</u>
   > an <u>outright</u> <u>embarrassment</u> (= complete)

SPEAKING

4 a Each learner chooses a book and creates two word clouds.

> **Option**
> To demonstrate this, talk about a book yourself and build up word clouds on the board as you speak.

b Learners show their word clouds to each other and see if their partner can interpret them. They ask and answer questions to find out more about the book.

> **Option**
> Add a second pair or group stage: learners show their word clouds to a new partner.

Round-up. Ask a few learners to tell you (or the rest of the class) about their partner's book. Then ask the partner to add further information.

5 Discuss the question with the class, getting learners to give examples of books they read as a child. To give this more focus, ask learners to think of a book they read as a child and write down its name, then use this as a basis for discussion.

3.2

Goals: talk about languages and ways to learn them
describe experiences of language learning

Core language:
LANGUAGE FOCUS   Language learning

Learning a language

LISTENING

1 a Discuss the photos with the class, or let learners do this in pairs or groups and then discuss the answers together. Possible answers:

> - *learning online (using a language programme on the Internet); using an interactive DVD-ROM*
> - *listening to an audio recording; carrying out pronunciation practice*
> - *going on holiday in a foreign country; chatting to people*
> - *watching TV in a foreign language with subtitles*

Ask learners which of the methods they think are successful, or which they have experience of themselves.

b Discuss the question together. Ask learners if they think people from their own country are good at learning languages, and why / why not. Try to bring out different factors, e.g. education, seeing TV and films in the original language, whether the language of the country is widely spoken, contact with people from other countries, differences between generations, etc.

2 *Pre-listening.* Look at the questions. Before playing recording **1.18**, learners guess what they think Norman might say.

Listening for main idea. Play recording **1.18**. Then check answers to the questions.

> 1 He learned basic English at school in Germany, then had contact with British and American people when he studied (probably abroad).
> 2 People are expected to speak basic English when they leave school; Germans are quite international.
> 3 To find work and to talk to people from other countries who live in Germany.

3 Read the questions about Pilar, then play recording **1.19**. Check answers together.

> 1 They both probably lived in an English-speaking country; they both speak very good English. Norman learned English at school in Germany. Pilar started learning when she came to England.
> 2 a She knew almost no English.
>   b They were friendly, they helped her to learn, they came from different parts of Britain.
>   c She didn't have much contact with French people; she didn't master French; she didn't try so hard.

LANGUAGE FOCUS Language learning

4 a Learners try to complete the sentences. If they can't remember exactly what the people said, they should try to imagine what expressions could go in the gaps.

b Discuss the answers together. Play recording **1.20** to check.

> 1 to get to grips with; get by   2 exposure to
> 3 express myself   4 being immersed in
> 5 have a basic conversation   6 took up; get to grips with

c Discuss the answers together.

> 1 get to grips with; take up
> 2 have exposure to; be immersed in
> 3 get by in; express myself in; have a basic conversation

> **Language note**
> Use the answers to focus on these expressions:
> – *get to grips with* a language = really start to use it, begin to master it.
> – *get by in* a language = to speak enough to do the things you need.
> – *have exposure to* a language = to hear it or read it a lot, so you become familiar with it.
> – *be immersed in* a language = you hear it and use it all the time, it's all round you.
> – *take up* a language = start learning it.

> **Optional discussion**
> To activate these expressions, ask a few questions round the class, e.g. *What languages can you get by in? How much exposure have you had to English? Have you ever been immersed in an English-speaking environment? Would you like to take up another language?*
> Do not go into too much detail, as learners will also talk about this in **4d**.

d Learners list the languages they know. The list should include English and also languages they only know a few words of.

/ Learners tell each other about the languages in their list, using the expressions in **4b**.

Discuss the questions with the class. Encourage learners to talk about their own experience and people they know. Focus on particular questions, e.g.
- *How perfect does pronunciation have to be?*
- *How much do grammar mistakes matter?*
- *Is it important to correct mistakes?*
- *Should you take risks when speaking a foreign language, or keep to what you know well?*
- *What do you think of the way Norman and Pilar speak English?*

> **Alternative: Group discussion**
>
> Learners discuss the questions in groups and try to agree on a point of view. Then ask a learner from each group to summarise their point of view and give reasons.

 You could use photocopiable activity 3A on the Teacher's DVD-ROM at this point.

READING and SPEAKING

5 a *Pre-reading.* Discuss the questions together. If necessary, expand on these slightly to make them clearer:
1 someone goes to live in an English-speaking country and develops a different 'personality' when using English from their personality in their own language.
2 there are certain ideas or feelings you can express in your own language that you can't exactly express in English.
3 the way you speak your own language is an expression of your personality, so this should also be true when you speak a foreign language.

Give learners time to think about these questions or talk about them in pairs before you discuss them together.

b *Reading for general idea.* Learners read the extracts. Discuss how they reflect the statements and what the novels seem to be about. Possible answers:

> *A (Reflects the second statement.) The structure of Chinese is different from English, and expresses meanings in different ways. The novel is about a Chinese woman coming to live in Britain and falling in love.*
> *B (Reflects the first statement.) The writer feels she is being 'invaded' by the foreign language, that it's taking her over. This is an autobiography of an American woman who went to live in France.*
> *C (Reflects the third statement.) The writer feels that gradually she is making the new language part of herself, and she's learning to express herself through the new language. This is the true story of a Polish girl who emigrated to Canada at the age of 13.*

6 a *Reading for detail.* / Learners read the extracts again and identify the points in the lists.

Discuss the answers together and ask learners what words indicate the answer. Possible answers:

> *1 A ("no verb-change usage, no tense differences")*
> *2 B ("a counter language")*
> *3 C ("I gradually making them mine")*
> *4 B ("likely to be set off at any time")*
> *5 B ("it was holding me up"); C ("invade me")*
> *6 A ("English language is boss of English user"); C ("I do not yet possess them, they possess me")*
> *7 B ("the new muscles in my mouth"); C ("lending me their modulations, intonations, rhythms")*

b To guide the discussion, learners choose any two points from **6a** that correspond to their own experience of learning a new language. Then ask learners what points they chose and why.

3.3 Target activity: A plan to improve your English

Goals: talk about languages and ways to learn them (3.2)
describe experiences of language learning (3.2)
discuss plans and priorities

Core language:
3.2 LANGUAGE FOCUS Language learning
TASK LANGUAGE Plans and priorities

A plan to improve your English

TASK LISTENING

1 / Learners look at the advertisements and discuss the questions. Then discuss the questions together, and ask learners which advertisement they think is the most effective.

2 a *Pre-listening discussion.* Learners mark the areas they think they most need to work on. Go through the items together. Build up the most frequently mentioned areas on the board, but don't go into too much detail at this point as learners will discuss the areas in more detail later.

b *Listening for general idea.* Play recording **1.21**. Establish which areas she talked about and what she says about them.

> *1 speaking fluently – no problem, because she's talkative*
> *2 writing accurately – she doesn't check what she's written*
> *3 listening comprehension – she can't understand regional accents*

TASK LANGUAGE Plans and priorities

3 a Learners complete the expressions in the table.

> **Option**
>
> To make this more personal, tell the class about a language you are learning, using the expressions to talk about your strengths and weaknesses. Then learners complete the sentences for themselves.

Round-up. Different learners round the class read out some of their sentences.

42 Unit 3 Language and literature

b Play recording **1.21**. Learners identify the expressions they hear.

> **Language note**
> 1 We say *work on, focus on, concentrate on* + noun or *-ing*:
> – *I need to concentrate on verb tenses.*
> – *I need to concentrate on using verb tenses correctly.*
> 2 Expressions 8–15 can all have nouns or *-ing* forms in the gaps:
> – *I'd really benefit from spending a month in Britain.*
> – *I've considered taking a course in business-letter writing.*
> 3 *It's worthwhile* means 'it's a good way to spend your time'. We can also say *It's worth* + *-ing*:
> – *It's worth going on a summer course in Australia.*

TASK

4 a *Preparation.* Learners complete the questionnaire on p127. As they do this, circulate and give suggestions where necessary.

  b *Discussing plans.* Learners exchange plans with their partner. In turn, they 'talk through' what they have written and get feedback from their partner.

  Round-up. Learners summarise the most important point they discussed and what suggestions their partner gave.

 You could use photocopiable activity 3B on the Teacher's DVD-ROM at this point.

3 Explore

Across cultures: Attitudes to English

Goal: to make learners more aware of different attitudes to studying English

Core language:
attitude (to); is seen as, is viewed as, is perceived as, is regarded as; is considered (to be)

1 *Books closed.* Ask learners what they know about the Philipines. Ask:
  – *Do you know where it is?*
  – *What kind of country is it?*
  – *What languages are spoken there?*

  Open books. Read the background information to check. Then look at the images. Ask what they show and what their 'message' is.

> *They're photos of students learning English, and slogans to encourage people to learn English.*
> *The message: English is the language of the future. If you learn English, you will have more opportunities.*

Learners read the information accompanying the images and discuss the questions.

> 1 a True
>   b False (an elite language)
>   c False (young people don't speak English so well)
>   d False (they speak Filipino but not English)
>   e True
>   f False (they don't see it as important)
> 2 Reaction against US influence; Filipino is more useful for communicating within the country; unusual because in many countries, English is seen as an international language, and a way of increasing opportunities.

2 Learners look at the information and identify the verb.

> *is perceived as*

3 Learners identify the verbs. Write them on the board.

> *is seen as*
> *is viewed as*
> *is regarded as*
> *is considered (to be)*

> **Language note**
> All these are passive forms (= *people perceive it as*, etc.). Notice that we say *is regarded as* but *is considered (to be)* (without *as*):
> – *English is regarded as essential.*
> – *English is considered (to be) essential.*

4 *Discussion.* Learners decide if they think each question in **3** applies to their country or not (they could mark each one with a tick, a cross or a question mark).

  Learners form pairs or groups and compare their answers, explaining why they answered as they did.

  Learners discuss the other questions.

  Round-up. Discuss the questions together. Ask further questions, e.g.
  – *Why is English so important at work?*
  – *Do you think this has changed over the last few years?*
  – *What do you think older people's attitude to English is? What do you think of that?*
  – *In what ways do people see it as enriching their life? Do you think it really has that effect?*
  – *Why do you think people see English as threatening? What kinds of people see it in that way?*

> **Mixed-nationality classes**
> 1 Learners from the same country work in groups together. Then get feedback from each group about their own country.
> 2 Learners work in groups with learners from different countries. Then in the feedback stage, ask learners what differences and similarities they discovered between their countries.

Keywords: *worth, worthwhile*

Goal: to use expressions with *worth* and *worthwhile* to recommend courses of action

Core language:
worth, worthwhile

1 *Focus on 'worth' + -ing or noun.* Look at the examples together and establish the meaning of *worth* (= it has some point, it's a good thing to do).

  Establish that *worth* can be followed by a verb + *-ing* or by a noun:
  – *It's worth trying.*
  – *It's worth a try.*
  – *It's worth going there.*
  – *It's worth a visit.*

Unit 3 Language and literature 43

2 a 👥 Learners complete the sentences.

Go through the answers and focus on the use of the definite or indefinite article. Ask what each sentence is about and where you might find it. Possible answers:

> 1 worth the wait (about a computer program or a film)
> 2 worth the risk (about steroids in sport)
> 3 worth a visit, worth a trip (about a restaurant)
> 4 worth a try, worth a shot (about an application for a job)
> 5 worth the risk, worth the trouble, worth the hassle (about where to invest your money)
> 6 worth a look (about a website)
> 7 worth the trouble, worth the hassle, worth the effort (about visiting somewhere by car or by public transport)

Language note
a shot = a try
hassle = trouble
Both are mainly used in conversational English.

b Write on the board:
It's _____ worth the trouble.

Ask learners to suggest suitable words to go in the gap. Possible answers:

> definitely, certainly, really; not really, hardly

c Go through the sentences again and ask learners to change the noun to an *-ing* form. Possible answers:

> 2 worth risking (it); worth taking the risk
> 3 worth visiting; worth going there
> 4 worth trying; worth having a shot
> 5 worth taking the risk
> 6 worth having a look at; worth visiting
> 7 worth making the effort; worth bothering (with)

3 a *Focus on 'worthwhile'.* Read the examples and discuss what *worthwhile* means in each case.

> 1 a good thing to do
> 2 a good cause, one that it's good to give money to
> 3 it wouldn't be a good way to spend my time
> 4 a good idea

Language note
worthwhile means 'it's a good way to spend your time' or 'it's a good thing to do'
worthwhile can come on its own or before a noun:
– It's really worthwhile.
– It's a worthwhile cause.
worthwhile can also be 'split' by a possessive:
– It's not worth my while.
– Is it worth his while to do it?

b Look at photos 1–4 and ask learners to guess what the people might say.

c Play recording **1.22** to check and establish what the people are talking about.

> 1 The Grand Canyon in the USA. It's really worthwhile going there.
> 2 A speech. He had nothing worthwhile to say.
> 3 The World Wildlife Fund. They're a very worthwhile organisation.
> 4 The stock market. It's worth your while if you're investing over a long period.

4 a *Speaking.* Give time for learners to think of four examples and prepare what to say.

Optional activity
To show what to do, write an item for each category on the board yourself. Then get the class to ask you about each one. Either recommend it or not. E.g.
– Paella. It's the national dish of Spain.
– Is it worth trying?
– Yes, definitely. But it can be quite expensive.
– So, is it worth the money?
– If it's cooked properly, yes, it's definitely worth it.

b 👥 Learners exchange items and ask each other about them, using expressions with *worth* or *worthwhile*.

Round-up. Ask a few learners what their partner told them.

Explore speaking

Goal: use strategies for communicating effectively
Core language:
Using paraphrase, repetition and fillers
Using emphasis to keep interest

1 a Give learners time to read the summary of the novel. Ask them to imagine they picked this book up in a bookshop. Would they want to read it? Why / Why not?

Note
If some of your learners have read the book, ask them to briefly tell the class what happens in it and what they thought of it.

b *Reading.* Learners read the extract from the novel on p126. Discuss what is unusual about it. Point out that:
– it's written as if the writer cannot speak good English.
– the way the book is written matches the author's own situation (arriving in Britain without speaking English).
– the chapter starts with a dictionary entry that refers to the topic of the chapter.

c *Listening for main points.* Play recording **1.23** and answer the questions.

> 1 Everything was exciting and new, she had to learn a lot of things.
> 2 The author made up her own 'Chinese English', using *-ing* instead of tenses and verb forms, to convey the feeling of someone who didn't speak English well.
> 3 Chinese doesn't have verb forms or tenses. Because Chinese has symbols, it can represent ideas and feelings more visually.

2 *Focus on speaking strategies.* Play the extracts in recording **1.24** and let learners follow in the book.

👥 Learners match the examples with the strategies Sze uses to communicate.

Discuss the answers together. Possible answers:

> a 4 wonderful
> b 1 when I came here
> c 5 she makes a picture (= visualise)
> d 3 I guess; I mean
> e 2 past; future

3 a Play recording **1.23** again while learners follow in the script. Then discuss which parts are more and less coherent, and why.

44 Unit 3 Language and literature

b Learners mark the strategies they think they use when they speak (in their own language and in English). Find out which strategies learners use most and whether they use them consciously.

4 a Working alone, learners choose a topic and prepare what to say, making brief notes and planning to use some of the strategies in **2**.

b *Speaking.* In turn, learners talk about their topic and answer their partner's questions.

Feedback. Ask a few learners how much they 'stretched' themselves and what strategies they used.

Speaking. Learners form new pairs and talk about their topic again.

Round-up. Ask a few learners whether they expressed themselves differently the second time.

3 Look again

GRAMMAR Present verb forms

1 a Ask learners to identify the present tense verbs.

> is pokes fun explores is captured (is) sent invade enter make

b Match the examples with the uses.

> 1b 2a 3c

Point out that we often use the present tense to talk about events in stories (in telling stories). The use of the present makes the events seem more immediate (as if they were happening now).

2 Learners discuss the questions.

Discuss the sentences together. Possible answers:

> 1 A weather forecast (future = will continue)
> 2 From a newspaper article or book about the 1980s (past = broke out)
> 3 A conversation – two people going out (future = will leave)
> 4 Someone talking about a wedding or a celebration (past = told)
> 5 An anecdote (e.g. an accident) (past = we were waiting)
> 6 Someone asking about a holiday (past = I've heard)
> 7 Someone (e.g. in an office) letting a colleague know dates (future = I will leave)
> 8 A formal letter, to someone who entered a competition (present = I am writing)
> 9 Instructions on how to send an email attachment (present = every time)
> 10 Someone has just lost their wallet (past/present = He has lost his wallet before, and it often happens)

Use the examples to highlight these uses of the present:

Present simple:

– 'historic' present, to make a narrative more immediate (2)
– in particular expressions (*I hear …*; *he tells me …*) (4, 6)
– to talk about a scheduled event in the future (3)
– in formal expressions in letters (*I write, I attach …, I enclose …*) (8)

Present progressive:

– 'historic' present progressive, to make a past description more immediate (5)
– to talk about something that's definitely arranged in the future (7)
– to say something happens too often or too much (expressing irritation) (10)

3 a Look at the first example together, and establish that:
– in **1a**, *think* describes a state (= *I believe, my opinion is …*). It's in the present simple (= in general)
– in **1b**, *think* describes an activity (= *what's going on in his head*). It's in the present continuous (= what's happening around now).

Learners discuss the other sentences.

b Discuss the answers together.

> 2a = I understand
> b = we're meeting
> c = she's going out with him
> 3a = I imagine, probably
> b = I think it will probably happen
> c = she's waiting for them
> 4a = probably, I think
> b = think something's happening (but it isn't)

GRAMMAR Adverbs

> **Optional presentation**
>
> *Books closed.* Write on the board:
> – *The stuff they did was _____ brave.*
> Ask where this sentence comes from (*answer:* Ian McDonald said it in 3.1), and what word could go in the gap. Use this as a basis for discussing the questions in **4a**.
> You could introduce **4b** with books closed in the same way, by writing on the board:
> – *I am _____ happy with my level of English.*
> Ask what adverbs would make the adjective stronger (*extremely, very, completely*), and which would make it weaker (*fairly, reasonably, moderately*).

4 a Look at the example and discuss the questions:
– *unbelievably* is an adverb; it comes before the adjective *brave*, it intensifies the adjective (= makes it stronger).
– other possible adverbs: *incredibly, extremely, fantastically, amazingly.*
– other adjectives the speaker used: *enormously (long), absolutely (fascinated).*

b Discuss the sentence together:
– *unbelievably* increases the strength of *brave*
– other adverbs with the same meaning include: *very, incredibly, remarkably.*

5 Learners add adverbs to the sentences.

> 1 highly questionable; extremely questionable
> 2 fully aware (= completely)
> 3 extremely disappointing
> 4 generally happy
> 5 practically impossible (= nearly impossible)

Point out that these are common collocations that naturally belong together.

6 a Learners match the adverbs with the verbs. Several answers are possible, but common collocations are:

> vividly remember
> strongly believe; strongly agree
> thoroughly enjoy; thoroughly agree; thoroughly regret
> deeply regret
> entirely agree

   b Learners write sentences.

   c Learners read out the last part of their sentence and their partner guesses the first part.

   d Learners write sentences, and compare with others.

> **Alternative: Mingling activity**
> Learners move freely round the class, saying the last part of their sentence and seeing if other learners can guess the first part.

7 a Learners suggest a suitable adverb. Possible answers:

> absolutely, definitely; possibly, probably

   b Read through the sentences together. Learners suggest suitable adverbs. Point out these possible additional responses:

> 2 totally (= yes, they're totally corrupt)
> 3 vividly, vaguely

   Learners take it in turn to say the sentences and respond.

VOCABULARY Expressions with *language*

8 a Write the categories on the board and brainstorm examples for each. Or you could let learners do this in groups first, then elicit expressions from each group and build them up on the board. Possible answers:

> A take up, master, pick up, get by in, learn
> B language teacher, language learning, language practice, language school, language course
> C foreign language, second language, native language
> D be immersed in, have exposure to, get to grips with

   b Learners complete the sentences. Then discuss the answers together.

> 1 command (D), picked up (A)   5 master (A), exposure (D)
> 2 grasp / command (D)   6 barrier (B)
> 3 common (C)   7 preserve (A)
> 4 skills (B)   8 second (C), get by in (A)

> **Language note**
> – *language barrier* = people are unable to communicate because they don't speak the same language
> – *a common language* = the language everyone can understand

   c In turn, learners say an expression and give a sentence based on it.

   Feedback. Ask learners to tell you a few things they found out from their partner.

VOCABULARY Idioms about speaking

9 a *Books closed*. Write the sentence on the board. Ask who it refers to (Chinese speakers of English) and what *get your message across* means (*answer*: communicate what you want to say).

   Learners match the idioms with the definitions and the cartoons.

> 1e 2d 3a 4c 5b
> Cartoon A: tongue tied
> Cartoon B: beating about the bush

> **Alternative exercise**
> Do this with books closed. Say each example in turn (possibly giving more of a context, e.g. *He called me last night to ask my advice, but I couldn't get a word in edgeways.*). Ask learners what they think the idiom means.

   b Play recording **1.25**, pausing after each speaker to establish what the recording is about.

> 1 Commenting on an ineffective presentation.
> 2 Advice to a politician giving a speech.
> 3 Commenting on a salesman (possibly on the phone).
> 4 Someone talking about being nervous in an oral exam.

   c Play the recording again. Practise saying the idioms.

 You could use photocopiable activity 3C on the Teacher's DVD-ROM at this point.

Self-assessment

To help focus learners on the self-assessment, you could read it through, giving a few examples of the language they have learned in each section (or asking learners to tell you). Then ask them to circle a number on each line.

Unit 3 Extra activities on the Teacher's DVD-ROM

Printable worksheets, activity instructions and answer keys are on your Teacher's DVD-ROM.

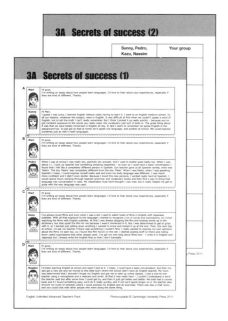

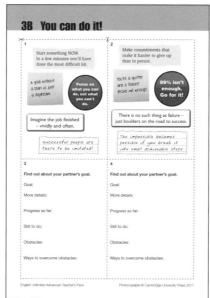

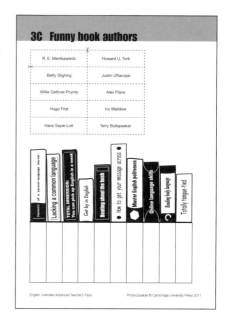

3A Secrets of success

Activity type: Reading and Speaking – Jigsaw reading and discussion – Groups of four

Aim: To practise reading and speaking on the subject of language learning

Language: Language learning – Coursebook p28 – Vocabulary

Preparation: Make one copy of worksheet 1 for each group. Cut worksheet 1 into four along the dotted lines. Make two copies of worksheet 2 for every group. Cut into two along the dotted line.

Time: 20–25 minutes

3B You can do it!

Activity type: Speaking – Discussion – Pairs / Whole class

Aim: To practise planning and prioritising for goals

Language: Plans and priorities – Coursebook p30 – Target activity

Preparation: Make one copy of each worksheet for each pair. Cut the worksheet along the line into four cards.

Time: 30–40 minutes

3C Funny book authors

Activity type: Speaking and pronunciation – Matching – Pairs

Aim: To play with language

Language: Vocabulary from the unit – Coursebook Unit 3

Preparation: Make one copy of the worksheet for each pair and cut along the dotted lines.

Time: 10–15 minutes

Unit 3 Self-study Pack

In the Workbook

Unit 3 of the *English Unlimited Advanced Self-study Pack Workbook* offers additional ways to practise the vocabulary and grammar taught in the Coursebook. There are also activities which build reading and writing skills, and a whole page of tasks to use with the DVD-ROM video, giving your learners the opportunity to hear and react to spoken English.

- **Vocabulary:** Describing a book and its significance; *language*; Plans and priorities
- **Grammar:** Present verb forms; Adverbs
- **Explore writing:** Job adverts and letters of interest
- **DVD-ROM Extra:** Visual poem – *Forgetfulness*

On the DVD-ROM

Unit 3 of the *English Unlimited Advanced Self-study Pack DVD-ROM* contains interactive games and activities for your learners to practise and improve their vocabulary, grammar and pronunciation, and also their speaking and listening. It also contains video material (with the possibility for learners to record themselves) to use with the *Workbook*.

- **Vocabulary and grammar:** Extra practice of the Coursebook language and Keywords
- **Explore listening:** Significant books
- **Explore speaking:** Adverbs in replies
- **Video:** Visual poem – *Forgetfulness*

4 World

4.1

Goals: interpret maps and facts
make comparisons and talk about changes

Core language:
LANGUAGE FOCUS   Differences and changes
LANGUAGE FOCUS   Interpreting meaning

Maps of the world

READING

1 a Learners cover descriptions B and C and look only at the maps. Point out that Map A is a 'normal' map of the world (it shows land area). Discuss what maps B and C show. Lead learners towards the answer by asking additional questions, e.g. *What do you notice about India? What about Europe? So it doesn't show land area – what else might it show? What's bigger in India than in Russia?*

   b *Reading.* Learners read the descriptions to check.

   > Map B: *distribution of the world's population*
   > Map C: *distribution of the world's wealth*

   Check that learners understand *Gross Domestic Product* (= a country's economic output, the total value of everything it produces).

   c *Discussion.* Look at maps B and C in turn and discuss the questions. Make a list of countries that are shown especially large or especially small on each map.

   Ask questions to draw attention to some of these points:

   Map B:
   – India, Bangladesh, and most of South-east Asia are huge, showing they have a very large population.
   – China is a large country but in population is shown even larger. Russia appears tiny, and so does Australia.
   – in the Middle East, Egypt looks much larger than Saudi Arabia.
   – West African countries like Nigeria and Ghana take up most of north Africa; countries in the Sahara almost disappear.
   – most of Latin America is quite small (because of large areas of unused land, e.g. the Amazon), but Mexico is larger.

   Map C:
   – the USA and Western Europe look 'bloated' as if they had too much to eat!
   – in East Asia, Japan and South Korea are huge; China and India are closer to their real size (but would probably be shown bigger on a map produced now).
   – Africa almost disappears, and about half of what is shown is South Africa.
   – surprisingly, Australia is not particularly big, perhaps because it has large areas of unproductive land.

   Focus on the learners' own country or countries and discuss what the maps show.

Alternative: Pair or group work

Learners work through the questions together and make notes. Then discuss the questions together and ask each group to tell you their main conclusions.

Optional language focus

Use the discussion to focus on vocabulary for regions of the world (e.g. the Middle East, the Far East, Western Europe) and particular countries that cause difficulty.

LANGUAGE FOCUS Differences and changes

2 a Learners choose words that could replace the highlighted items. Then check the answers together and discuss how the changes affect the meaning (in brackets below).

   > 1 huge (not so strong as 'vast'); dramatic (= large and sudden); massive; enormous
   > 2 easily; far and away (more conversational expression)
   > 3 considerably (= much); significantly (= much, also it's important); far (= much); marginally (= very slightly; you hardly notice it)

Language note

All the words make the meaning stronger.
The adjectives in 1 come before a noun and all mean 'very large'.
The adverbs and expressions in 2 are used with a superlative:
– *easily the best; by far the most interesting*
The adverbs in 3 are used with a comparative:
– *far richer; marginally easier; considerably more useful*

Optional practice

Give sentences and ask learners to add a suitable word to make them stronger, e.g.:
– *There are a number of unemployed people.*
– *There was a drop in temperature.*
– *The new iPhone is faster.*
– *It's the most exciting film at the festival.*

   b Learners write sentences about the maps.

   c Learners read out their sentences. Ask other people if they agree that the sentence is true.

 You could use photocopiable activity 4A on the Teacher's DVD-ROM at this point.

SPEAKING

3 a *Pre-reading discussion.* Learners discuss the questions. Talk briefly about each idea together, getting ideas from different pairs/groups.

   b *Jigsaw reading.* Give learners a letter, A or B. They look at their map and read the description.

   In turn, learners tell their partner what their map shows, without showing the map. After they have explained it they show the map to their partner.

   They discuss the questions together.

48   Unit 4 World

Alternative: Reading in pairs or groups
Give pairs or groups a letter, A or B. They look at their map together and discuss the questions. Then learners form new pairs or groups. They tell their new partner(s) about their map and discuss the questions.

Feedback. Look at each map in turn with the whole class, and ask what conclusions they came to.

LANGUAGE FOCUS Interpreting meaning

4   *Listening for main idea.* Play recording **1.26**, pausing after each speaker to establish the main point of what was said.

> 1 Nothing has changed. The rich countries are still rich and the poor countries are still poor.
> 2 The map doesn't tell us much about people's quality of life at that time.

5   a   *Language focus.* Learners fill the gaps with suitable expressions. They could either do this from memory or guess what words could go in the gaps.

   b   Go through the answers by playing recording **1.26** again to check.

> 1 is apparent   2 as the maps show   3 the significance of
> 4 indicate about   5 reveal much about   6 means that
> 7 doesn't necessarily mean

Language note
reveal, *indicate* and *show* are synonyms (*reveal* = show something that was hidden or not obvious). *It doesn't necessarily mean* = it doesn't have to mean ... , it may not mean ... *is apparent* = it's clear, we can see it

SPEAKING

6   a   Together, learners imagine a map showing wealth in 2050. They choose one 'secretary', who either makes notes or sketches out a map.

   b   One learner from each group presents their ideas to the class.

Optional language preparation
To prepare for the feedback stage, elicit the expressions from **5a** with books closed and write them on the board. Then learners present their ideas to the class.

WRITING

7   To prepare for the writing, look at each category and quickly brainstorm a few ideas.

   Learners choose one imaginary map and write a description like those in **1b**, explaining what their 'map' shows.

   A few learners read out their descriptions and see if the rest of the class agree with what they say.

Note
You can find the maps at www.worldmapper.org. If possible, you could show them to the class at the end of the activity.

4.2

Goals: talk about diet and nutrition
discuss changing trends

Core language:
LANGUAGE FOCUS   Types of food
LANGUAGE FOCUS   Changes and trends

What the world eats

LANGUAGE FOCUS Types of food

1   a   *Discussion.* Look at the photos and discuss the questions together. Bring out these main points:

> 1 The Brown family spends far more on food.
>   They eat more processed and packaged food, and a lot of meat.
>   The Ahmed family eat more fresh food.
> 2 The Browns: *probably a supermarket.*
>   The Ahmed family: *probably local markets and shops.*
> 3 The Browns: *meat dishes, maybe sausage, bacon and eggs, cereal and milk for breakfast.*
>   The Ahmed family: *probably traditional Egyptian dishes (stewed vegetables with meat and rice, or with bread).*

   b   Learners look at the pictures and note down one other interesting thing that strikes them.

2   a   *Focus on food and drink words.* Learners write the words in three lists. Emphasise that they should decide if the word normally collocates with *food*, *drinks* or both: for example, we talk about *bottled drinks*, but not normally about *bottled food*.

There may be some discussion about where the words go, but expected answers are:

Food	Drinks	Food / Drinks
dried	bottled	nutritious
GM	fizzy	take-away
packaged	soft	locally produced
raw		sugar-free
refined		canned
processed		diet
convenience		
low-fat		
wholemeal		

As you go through the answers, focus on the meaning of any new items, e.g.
– *GM food* = genetically modified
– *soft drinks* = cold drinks without alcohol
– *fizzy drinks* = drinks with carbon dioxide (e.g. cola)

   b   Ask which words are similar in meaning, and get examples from the class. Possible answers:

> 1 packaged food (= in a carton, or wrapped in plastic)
>   processed food (= treated with chemicals to preserve it, e.g. processed cheese)
>   refined food (= made purer, e.g. white sugar)
>   convenience food (= food that you can cook quickly or eat immediately, e.g. frozen meals, pizzas)
>   take-away food (= you can buy it to eat in the street or at home, e.g. burgers, pizzas)
> 2 low-fat food, sugar-free food, diet food
> 3 bottled drinks, canned drinks, fizzy drinks, soft drinks

c Discuss the words together, and learners give examples.

> *Types of food:*
> *pulses (beans, lentils, dried peas, ...)*
> *cereals (wheat, maize, rice, and also breakfast cereals such as cornflakes)*
> *dairy products (milk, butter, cheese, eggs ...)*
> *Contained in food:*
> *roughage, or fibre (= the part that you don't digest, e.g. raw vegetables contain fibre)*
> *protein (contained in meat, nuts, fish)*
> *carbohydrate (it is contained in flour, sugar, potatoes)*

d To introduce this part, tell the class what you eat and drink and whether you think you have a healthy diet, e.g. whether you drink a lot of soft drinks or fizzy drinks, how much packaged food you eat, how often you eat take-away or convenience food. Encourage learners to ask you questions.

Learners find out from each other how much of each type they eat and drink.

Feedback. A few learners tell you whether their partner seems to have a healthy diet.

3 a Give each group a letter, A or B. They look at their own photo and discuss the questions.

b A learner from each group in turn tells the class about their photo.

> **Alternative: New groups**
> Learners form new groups, so that each group contains at least one person from the original groups A or B. They show their photo and say what they thought about it.

 You could use photocopiable activity 4B on the Teacher's DVD-ROM at this point.

SPEAKING

4 a *Preparation.* Learners imagine a photo of their own family's food, and make notes. They should try to imagine it as a visual image (e.g. the room, the people, how the food is arranged).

> **Optional activity**
> To help learners visualise this, they imagine a scene in various stages. Ask them:
> *Imagine the room in your house. Where is it?*
> *Who is in the photo? Are you standing or sitting?*
> *Now imagine the table with food on it. What's on the table?*
> *What's in the centre of the photo?*
> *What drinks are there? Are they in bottles or cartons?*

b Learners describe their 'photo' to their partner.

Round-up. A few learners say how their and their partner's photo were similar or different.

Nutrition transition

READING

1 a *Pre-reading.* Learners cover the article. Look at each topic in turn, and ask learners what they think it might say about it. Try and get a few different ideas, e.g.:
– *new technologies*: they make food cheaper, people no longer eat traditional food, they help food to stay fresher for longer.

b *Reading for main points.* Learners read the article and check what it says about each topic.

Discuss the answers together.

> new technologies: *allow food to be eaten long after it was grown; foods can be eaten a long way from where they were produced; people eat previously unknown types of food*
> seasonal food: *people used to eat only seasonal food, now they no longer need to.*
> malnutrition: *some people don't have enough to eat, while others have too much.*
> food for convenience: *people eat more convenience food (and food prepared by others)*
> processed food: *food can be transported and eaten long after it was produced; people now eat more processed food*
> obesity: *rates of obesity are rising rapidly, especially in industrialised countries*

2 a Learners match the developments and the examples. Go through the answers by discussing the connection between them.

> 1 e (ketchup is made of preserved tomatoes, so the tomatoes can be eaten years later)
> 2 c (oranges can now be transported to far-away places e.g. Bhutan)
> 3 d (pasta is a processed form of flour and eggs, so it keeps much longer)
> 4 b (it used to be unknown, but is now drunk all over the world)
> 5 a (through marketing, there is a worldwide demand for it)

b Discuss what 'nutrition transition' means (*answer:* the change from not having enough to eat to eating too much).

LANGUAGE FOCUS Changes and trends

3 a Look together at the highlighted words and build them up on the board in two lists.

> 1 evolve, replace, change
> 2 develop, rise

b Learners give the noun forms. Write them on the board.

> 1 evolution, replacement, change
> 2 development, rise

c Look together at the article. Learners replace the verbs with nouns. Discuss what changes would be necessary. Possible answers:

> 1 There has been an evolution in response to ...
> 2 Changes take place in the way they eat.
> 3 This involves a replacement of grains and beans in their diet with foods ...
> 4 This leads to the development of heart disease ...
> 5 There has been a rapid rise in rates of obesity ...

50 Unit 4 World

4   *Introduction.* Tell the class that they will have a discussion about the way technology has changed food habits. To introduce this, briefly discuss what the arguments for and against food technology might be (but without actually discussing the issues at this point).

👤 *Preparation for roleplay.* Give learners a letter, A or B. Tell learners their roles: A learners are farmers, B learners are environmentalists. Working alone, they turn to p128 or p135 and prepare their arguments.

👥 Learners discuss the issue.

Round-up. Ask different pairs what points they made and whether they convinced each other.

> **Alternative: Preparation in pairs**
> Learners work in pairs for the preparation stage. Give each pair a letter, A or B: they will both take the same role. Together, they look at their instructions and prepare what they will say. Learners form new pairs, so each pair has one A and B. They have a discussion.

4.3 Target activity: Say how a town or a country has changed

Goals: make comparisons and talk about changes
discuss changing trends
talk about result

Core language:
4.1 LANGUAGE FOCUS   Differences and changes
4.2 LANGUAGE FOCUS   Changes and trends
TASK LANGUAGE   Result

TASK LISTENING

1   *Pre-listening.* Look at the photos together. Ask learners if they can identify any of them and discuss how they might be connected with changes or developments in Britain.

2 a *Listening for main points.* Play recording **1.27** and answer the question. Possible answers:

> *Before Britain joined the EU, people used to bring back Italian pasta or French cheese. Joining the EU made these available.*
> *This led to new cookery writers like Jamie Oliver.*
> *People now eat better food.*

   b Discuss any questions you haven't already answered. If necessary, play the recording again.

> *He thinks things have got better.*

TASK LANGUAGE Result

3 a *Focus on 'result' expressions and collocations.* To introduce the idea of result, write on the board:

   People cooked French and Italian food.
   → .... *a new style of British cooking.*

   Ask how we can begin the second sentence to show it is the *result* of the first. (Possible answer: *This gave rise to ..., This led to ...*)

   Look at the expressions and elicit the prepositions.

   b Learners match the expressions with the endings.

   Go through them together by discussing what different answers are possible (likely alternatives are shown here in brackets).

   c Play recording **1.28** to check.

   Make these points:
   – expressions 1–5 are used to talk about the *result* or consequence of something (X caused Y).
   – expression 5 (*was a consequence of*) is used to talk about the *cause* of something (Y was caused by X).
   – as the alternative answers show, *gave rise to*, *led to* and *resulted in* all mean roughly the same.

> **Note**
> Other expressions for talking about cause and effect are introduced in **Look again**, p45.

TASK

4 a 👤 *Preparation.* Learners think about changes to their town, region or country, and make notes on how they have affected people.

   b 👥 / 👥👥 *Talking about changes.* In turn, learners tell the others what they think. If learners come from different countries, they answer further questions from their group. If they come from the same country, they see if the others in the group agree with them or not.

   Round-up. Ask each group to report back on some of the things they talked about.

4 Explore

Across cultures: Restaurants

Goal: to make learners more aware of the approach and attitudes to different cultures' foods

Core language:
cuisine, decor, stereotypical, misconception, cliché

1 a Learners look at the photos. Discuss what kind of restaurants they are and what kind of food they might serve. Possible answers:

> 1 Chinese take-away restaurant. Stir-fried meat and vegetables, rice, noodles, soup.
> 2 a traditional café, probably in France or Belguim. Coffee, drinks, light meals.
> 3 American-style fast-food restaurant. Burgers, pizza, chicken wings, pizzas.

Ask how learners decided on their answers (they may have used clues in the photos, or their own knowledge and experience of similar restaurants).

b Learners match the names to the restaurants and decide what nationality they are.

> A Jade Dragon (Chinese)
> B Café Quentin (Belgium)
> C Ben's Chilli Bowl (USA)

c Discuss which were easiest to identify and why.

2 *Discussion.* Learners discuss restaurants where they live. To make this more focused, they could write a list of types of restaurant in their town (e.g. Indian, Japanese ...), and use this as a basis for discussing what decor and atmosphere they have.

Feedback. Ask each group to tell you some types of restaurant they discussed and what they said about them.

Mixed-nationality classes

Either: Let learners from the same country work in groups together. Then get feedback from each group about their own country.
Or: Make sure each group has learners from different countries. They tell each other about their own country. Then in the feedback stage ask learners what differences and similarities they discovered between their countries.

---

3 a *Pre-reading.* Learners write down three things they associate with Mexican culture and cuisine. Use this as a basis to brainstorm ideas. You could write key expressions on the board.

b *Reading for general idea.* Learners read the blog quickly. Then ask:
– What is wrong with the restaurant, in his view?
(*answer:* the food is bad and not authentically Mexican)
– What does he object to in general?
(*answer:* Mexican restaurants in the USA give a stereotyped view of Mexican culture)

Reading for detail. Learners read the blog again and underline the negative words. Possible answers:

> sad, candy-flavoured, stale, wrong, nothing but, stereotypical, tired of, deafening (= very loud), disappointed, clichés

Ask learners what images they associate with the sentences. Present any new expressions, e.g.:
– *cardboard tortilla* = it looks and tastes like cardboard
– *outlet* = part of a chain of restaurants
– *candy* = sweets (because it was sweet and not at all hot)
– *makes your mouth water* = looks (or smells) good to eat
– *teary-eyed* = you have tears in your eyes because there is so much chilli
– *serenade* = play music for your pleasure
– *deafening* = so loud they make you deaf

4 *Discussion.* Learners exchange ideas about how their cuisine is represented abroad, what the 'stereotypes' of their country are, and how they feel about them.

Feedback. Ask groups what conclusion they came to, and see if other groups agree.

Mixed-nationality classes

Either: Let learners from the same country work in groups together. Then get feedback from each group about their own country.
Or: Make sure each group has learners from different countries. Then get feedback from individual learners about their country.

Note

If the cuisine of your learners' country isn't well known abroad, they could:
Either: talk about what other stereotypes people have about their culture (e.g. music, dress, lifestyle, drinks), and whether they think that is positive or negative.
Or: choose a country close to their own whose cuisine is better known abroad.

Keywords: *get, become*

Goal: to use *get* and *become* to describe changes that lead to a situation

Core language:
get, become

1 a *Focus on 'get'.* Read the examples to focus on *get* or *got* being used to express the idea of change from one situation to another:
– *It was quite wealthy before. Later it was very wealthy.*
→ *It got wealthier.*
– *People weren't in the habit of eating well. Now they are.*
→ *They've got into the habit of eating well.*

Discuss the questions.

> 1 Comparative adjectives and expressions (wealthier, bigger) and expressions with prepositions ('get into the habit').
> 2 Only before an adjective; 'become' can't be followed by a preposition, only by an adjective or a noun:
> – She became rich.
> – She became president.
> 3 We often use the present perfect to talk about changes (from past to present), so it naturally occurs with 'get'.

b 👤/👥 Learners think of ways to complete the sentences. Possible answers:

> 1 ... gets cold
> 2 ... got through it; ... got it finished
> 3 ... I got to like it; ... I got used to it
> 4 ... get locked out
> 5 ... I've got behind; ... I got delayed

c Point out that:
– you often use *get / got* with a past participle:
   get lost, get stuck, get drunk, get locked in / out
– instead of *gets cold* you could say:
   ... before it goes cold.

You can also say:
– *He's gone bald, the food has gone bad, Have you gone crazy?*

For a gradual change, you can also use *grow / grew*:
– *The difference between rich and poor has grown bigger.*

2 a 👤/👥 *Pre-listening.* Learners think of situations for the remarks. Then discuss possible answers.

b *Listening to check.* Play recording **1.29**, pausing after each remark to check the answers to **2a**. Possible answers:

> 1 part of a weather forecast.
> 2 a nurse talking to someone with a cut or a wound.
> 3 someone's first day at work. The boss or a colleague is reassuring them.
> 4 a TV discussion of a race (probably athletics).
> 5 police interviewing a man who may have attacked someone; or a judge at a trial.

3 a *Focus on 'become'.* Discuss the examples together. Establish that:
– the adjectives are used in a fairly formal style (could be spoken or written), so *become* is used rather than the less formal *got*.
– *got* could also be used in example 6, which is less formal than the others.

b Discuss what the sentences are about and where you would find them. Possible answers:

> 1 to someone applying for a job (spoken, or an email). (= becomes free)
> 2 part of a lecture, a newspaper article or a book about political history. (= people connect it with the political right)
> 3 government information about becoming a citizen of a country (= before you can become a citizen)
> 4 speech or news item about an airport (= became clear)
> 5 someone talking about an appliance, e.g. a vacuum cleaner or washing machine. (= they are no longer made)
> 6 newspaper article or review about a writer or poet.

4 a *Speaking.* To show what to do, think of an example yourself and say a few things about it. Learners think of an example for each of the items. They could make brief notes to help them prepare.

b 👥 Learners tell each other their examples, asking and answering further questions.

Feedback. A few learners tell you their most interesting example.

Alternative: Mingling activity

Learners move freely round the class, telling their examples to other people.
Round-up. A few learners talk about the most interesting example they heard.

---

5 👥/👥👥 *Extension.* Learners look at photos A–D and think of sentences to describe the people. They could either talk about it together or write down sentences.

Feedback. Learners tell you a few of their sentences for each photo.

Explore writing

Goals: write captions
write economically
Core language:
vivid adjectives and expressions

Optional lead-in

Books closed. Write *Mumbai* on the board. Brainstorm what learners know about it and add words and phrases on the board.
Alternatively, ask learners to write down adjectives and phrases that come into their mind when they think of 'Mumbai' or 'India'.

---

1 *Reading.* If you didn't introduce this earlier, check that learners know where and what Mumbai is (it's a port on the west coast of India – India's largest city).

Give time for learners to read the introduction and the caption. Then discuss the questions together.

Alternative

Learners read the introduction and the caption alone, then work through the questions in pairs.

Possible answers:

> 1 It's huge, there are very rich and very poor areas, it's changing very fast, it's full of life day and night.
> 2 'transformed': completely and suddenly changed (appropriate for India, which is changing very fast) 'elephant': very big, powerful, difficult to control; also the symbol of India.
> 3 They don't really understand what's happening, because it's changing so fast.
> 4 They cover a large area, they're disorganised, they cover the ground with low-rise buildings.

2 a 👤/👥 *Focus on descriptive language.* Learners compare the two descriptions. Discuss how they are different.

> The caption: *two sentences; five adjectives and two-word expressions; two verbs*
> The extended description: *five sentences; three adjectives, no two-word expressions; eight verbs*

Unit 4 World 53

b Ask what this tells us about the language used in the caption and why it is more effective.

- the aim of the caption is to convey information as economically as possible.
- it uses adjectives and two-word expressions to give a more condensed, vivid description.
- the extended description relies more on complete sentences, so uses verbs rather than adjectives and expressions.

3 a *Reading.* Learners read the captions and match them with photos A–C.

1A 2C 3B

b *Focus on vocabulary.* First discuss what kind of word might go in each gap (a noun, a verb or an adjective). Then ask learners to suggest a suitable word for each gap.

1 famous
2 hangout (= place to stay)
3 snooze (= sleep for a short time)
4 stunted (= short, not growing properly)
5 carnival
6 screaming
7 squat (= half sit, with legs bent)
8 enormous
9 grimy (= with a layer of dirt on everything)
10 pristine (= very clean)
11 exquisite (= beautiful)
12 chill out (= relax)
13 softly lit
14 sophisticated (= in touch with culture and fashion)
15 fancy (= smart and expensive)

Alternative

Learners discuss this in pairs. Then go through the answers together.

Discuss the effect of the captions.

- they convey the atmosphere vividly by using descriptive language.
- they complement the photos by filling in the background to the visual information.

4 *Writing.* Working together, each group chooses one of the photos on p128. They discuss what their caption might say about it and write a caption together.

Editing. Learners look at what they have written and think of ways to make the writing more vivid and more economical. Encourage learners to use dictionaries to find suitable descriptive words.

Round-up. In turn, one person from each group reads out their caption to the class. The others listen and identify the photo the caption goes with.

4 Look again

GRAMMAR The future

Optional lead-in

Write an example of the future on the board:
– *The exhibition will open next week.*
Learners suggest different ways of expressing the future instead of *will* (e.g. *is going to, is opening, opens, is due to, should, might, is likely to*).

1 Learners read the example and underline ways of expressing the future.

are likely to
will be + -ing
will
are set to
is due to

2 a Discuss how the expressions in the table are used.

1 is about to; is on the point / verge / brink of.
2 is due to, is set to; is sure to, is bound to, is certain to, is to

Language note

1 *Is due to* and *is set to* and *is to* are used for planned or predictable events:
– *The work is due to be completed next summer* (this is the plan)
– *The prime minister is to give a speech tomorrow.*
– *The population is set to double by the end of the century* (if the current trend continues)
2 *On the point / verge / brink of* can be followed by a noun or *-ing*. They mean 'it could happen at any minute':
– *This job is so frustrating, I'm on the verge of giving up.*
– *We're on the point of a major breakthrough in cancer research.*

b Learners suggest ways of expressing uncertainty. Write these on the board in three lists:

= probably	= maybe	= probably not
will probably	may	probably won't
is likely to	might	is unlikely to
should	could	

3 Learners re-write the sentences. Then go through the answers together.

2 The president is set to arrive here at 5 p.m.
3 Eating organic food is bound to be a trend for some time.
4 The new mp3 players are on the point of arriving.
5 The trial is due to take place on 23 May.
6 I'm on the verge of turning down that job. (or I'm on the verge of making a decision.)
7 Life is unlikely to be so different in 2050.

4 a To introduce the activity, write three sentences on the board (they could include events in your own life and world events). Get the class to ask you further questions about them.

Working alone, learners write three sentences.

b Learners tell each other their sentences and ask further questions.

Round-up. Ask pairs or groups to tell you the most interesting sentence they talked about.

54 Unit 4 World

GRAMMAR Comparisons involving different verbs and times

5 a Look at the photos. Elicit possible continuations and write them on the board.

> A It wasn't nearly as impressive as ... I expected (it to be).; ... I thought it would be.;
> B I don't go out as much as I ... used to.; ... usually do.; ... would like to.
> C It's much safer than it ... used to be.; ... was before.

b Play recording **1.30** to check. Ask which words are repeated, and establish these points:
– the verb *be* is repeated in the comparison: ... *wasn't; ... would be; It's ... used to be.*
– other verbs are either not repeated or are replaced by a form of *do*: *go out ... used to; ... go out ... usually do.*
– you can't say '~~I don't go out as much as I used to go~~'.

6 Learners change the sentences and think of different ways to express the same comparison. Discuss the answers together. Possible answers:

> 1 You don't do as much exercise as you ought to. You should do more exercise than you do at the moment.
> 2 It wasn't nearly as dangerous as I was expecting (it to be). I was expecting it to be much more dangerous than it actually seemed to be.
> 3 This year the exam was harder than it usually is. The exam isn't usually as difficult as it was this year.
> 4 I haven't managed to do as much work today as I'd hoped (I would). I'd hoped I would get more work done today than I actually managed to do.
> 5 As it turned out, she was even angrier than I'd expected (her to be). I hadn't expected her to be quite as angry as she turned out to be.
> 6 He turned out to be much older than I'd imagined (him to be). I'd imagined him to be younger than he turned out to be.
> 7 He helped a lot less than he promised (to do). He promised to help a lot more than he actually did.

> **Optional lead-in**
>
> *Books closed*. Write *The film was much more exciting ...* on the board. Elicit possible continuations and add them on the board. Then check with the sample answers in the book.

7 Discuss what the sentences might be about and how they might continue. Try to get a number of different answers each time.

Possible answers:

> 2 ... as I was hoping it would be. / ... as everyone expected.
> 3 ... as it has been this week. / ... as it was last year.
> 4 ... than people say he is. / ... than he seems to be from a distance.
> 5 ... as much as she used to. / ... as easily as she did when she was younger.

VOCABULARY Changes

8 a Elicit possible adjectives and adverbs and build them up on the board.

> 1 a slowly, steadily, progressively, naturally
>   b slow, steady, progressive, natural
> 2 a quickly, fast, dangerously, alarmingly, precipitously
>   b sudden, dangerous, alarming, precipitous

> **Note**
>
> You wouldn't say *a quick rise*, as this would imply that it lasted for a short time and is now over.

b, c Learners look at the sentences and discuss the questions.

Discuss the answers together and ask for alternative adjectives. Possible answers:

> a 1 description of a city, e.g. Mumbai. Could be part of a travel guide, or a feature article in a newspaper, or could be a caption accompanying a photo.
>   2 transformation (= fast, dramatic change)
>   3 better (positive words: 'remarkable', 'glittering')
>   Other adjectives: 'amazing', 'astonishing', 'impressive'
> b 1 news report on a political speech, e.g. by a UN leader
>   2 transition (= slow, gradual change)
>   3 better (positive words: 'importance', 'smooth')
>   Other adjectives: 'successful', 'gradual', 'safe'
> c 1 travel guide or brochure about a historic site (direct, persuasive language: 'If you ...', 'stop off')
>   2 evolution (= slow, gradual development)
>   3 better (they have become more complex)
>   Other adjectives: 'gradual', 'architectural'
> d 1 news report about anti-government protests
>   2 collapse (= sudden change)
>   3 probably worse (negative words: 'paralysed', 'collapse'), but it depends on the writer's point of view
>   Other adjectives: 'complete', 'irreversible'
> e 1 feature article about the way music is produced and distributed
>   2 revolution (= fast, dramatic change)
>   3 probably better (positive words: 'quietly', 'putting it in the hands of'), but depends on the writer's point of view
>   Other adjectives: 'grassroots', 'popular', 'unstoppable'
> f 1 instruction leaflet about a necklace, or an advice website on how to look after jewellery (direct instructional language: 'your pearls', 'don't')
>   2 deterioration (= slow change for the worse)
>   3 worse (tells you how to stop it happening)
>   Other adjectives: 'slow', 'steady'
> g 1 report on a medical trial, probably for a general reader (language not technical)
>   2 improvement (faster change than expected)
>   3 better
>   Other adjectives: 'remarkable', 'noticeable', 'significant'
> h 1 newspaper report on a sports team (probably football), or could be radio or TV commentary
>   2 decline (= in this case, a fast change for the worse)
>   3 worse
>   Other adjectives: 'sudden', 'irreversible', 'terminal'

9 a Learners choose a topic and write a few sentences. If necessary, you could think of suitable topics and give them out as a list to choose from.

b In turn, learners read out their sentences. Ask other people in the class if they agree.

> **Alternative**
> Learners read out their sentences, but without mentioning the name of the place, person, etc. (they could replace it by X or *this person / place*).
> Other learners listen and identify what they are describing.

VOCABULARY Cause and effect

10 a Look at the sentences and discuss what they mean.

> 1 A caused B
> 2 A influenced B
> 3 B was caused by A

b Ask which sentences the expressions could go in and whether they would change the meaning.

> generated 1
> had an effect on 2
> resulted in 1 (= this happened after a time)
> brought about 1
> influenced 2 (less strong than 'had an impact on')
> resulted from 3 (less immediate)
> stemmed from 3 (less immediate / direct)
> was caused by 3 (more direct cause)
> triggered 1 (= it happened suddenly)
> had its origin in 3 (= indirect, long-term cause)
> had an influence on 2 (less strong than 'had an impact on')

11 Learners choose the best expression.

Check the answers and ask learners to give reasons for their choice.

> 1 influence ('effect' would mean 'emotional effect')
> 2 has its origin in ('led to' doesn't fit the context)
> 3 trigger (= a sudden, unexpected effect)
> 4 brought about (= cause, not influence)
> 5 stemmed from ('resulted in' doesn't fit the context)

12 a To introduce the activity, give one or two sentences about yourself and invite learners to ask you further questions.

Learners write sentences about themselves. As they do this, circulate and give help with ideas if necessary.

b Learners use their sentences to tell their partner about themselves and answer further questions.

Round-up. Ask a few learners what they found out about their partner.

 You could use photocopiable activity 4C on the Teacher's DVD-ROM at this point.

Self-assessment

To help focus learners on the self-assessment, you could read it through, giving a few examples of the language they have learned in each section (or asking learners to tell you). Then ask them to circle a number on each line.

Unit 4 Extra activities on the Teacher's DVD-ROM

Printable worksheets, activity instructions and answer keys are on your Teacher's DVD-ROM.

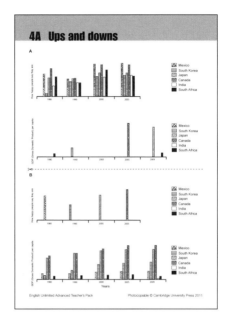
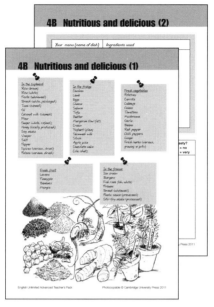

4A Ups and downs

Activity type: Speaking – Information gap and discussion – Pairs / Whole class

Aim: To practise describing and reacting to information in graphs

Language: Differences and changes – Coursebook p37 – Vocabulary

Preparation: Make one copy of the worksheet for each pair. Cut it along the dotted line to make parts A and B.

Time: 20–25 minutes

4B Delicious and nutritious

Activity type: Speaking – Discussion – Pairs / Small groups

Aim: To practise speaking on the subject of food, cooking and health

Language: Types of food – Coursebook p38 – Vocabulary

Preparation: Make one copy of each worksheet for each pair.

Time: 20–25 minutes

4C Life-changing experiences

Activity type: Speaking – Find someone who – Whole class

Aim: To practise speaking about important events and changes in your life

Language: Cause and effect – Coursebook p45 – Vocabulary

Preparation: Make one copy of the worksheet for each learner.

Time: 20–25 minutes

Unit 4 Self-study Pack

In the Workbook

Unit 4 of the *English Unlimited Advanced Self-study Pack Workbook* offers additional ways to practise the vocabulary and grammar taught in the Coursebook. There are also activities which build reading and writing skills, and two pages which give your learners the opportunity to develop their skills in extended reading.

- **Vocabulary:** Types of food; Differences and changes; Cause and effect
- **Grammar:** The future; Comparisons involving different verbs and times
- **Explore reading:** Travel writing

On the DVD-ROM

Unit 4 of the *English Unlimited Advanced Self-study Pack DVD-ROM* contains interactive games and activities for your learners to practise and improve their vocabulary, grammar and pronunciation, and also their speaking and listening.

- **Vocabulary and grammar:** Extra practice of the Coursebook language and Keywords
- **Explore listening:** Vegetarianism
- **Explore speaking:** Describing food

Concepts of space

5.1

Goals: describe spaces in cities
describe how spaces are used

Core language:
LANGUAGE FOCUS   Describing spaces

Post-it city

READING

1   a   *Pre-reading.* Learners cover the four captions, then look at photos A–D and say what cities they think they show and why.

   b   Discuss in more detail what each photo seems to show. Focus on these points:
   – photo A seems to show graves or a cemetery, but with washing hanging up.
   – photo B shows a street stall; the woman seems to be selling something to eat or drink.
   – photo C shows small houses and gardens between railway tracks.
   – photo D seems to show a disused stadium with tents or a market.

   Ask what the photos have in common, and lead learners towards the idea that they are all ways of using space in a city and they are all improvised (set up by people themselves).

2   *Reading for main idea.* Learners read captions 1–4 and match them with photos A–D.

   | 1D   2B   3A   4C

   Check that learners understand *allotments* (= small pieces of ground in a city for growing vegetables).

   Note
   Photo A shows the 'City of the Dead', a cemetery outside Cairo. The buildings were once used by families who came to visit the graves, but many are now occupied by poor families.

3   *Reading for details.* Learners read and answer the questions. As you go through the answers, ask learners to expand on them, e.g.
   1 There's now a football stadium on the site.

   | 1 Jarmark   2 the cemetery   3 the allotments
   | 4 the cemetery   5 the allotments   6 Jarmark
   | 7 the street stall

LANGUAGE FOCUS Describing spaces

4   a   Learners find adjectives in the captions.

   | a overcrowded   b abandoned   c makeshift
   | d open-air   e precarious   f provisional

   b   Discuss the question and bring out these points:
   – some of the adjectives (*abandoned, overcrowded*) are negative ways to describe a city, suggesting bad urban planning.
   – others (*precarious, makeshift, provisional*) are negative ways to describe a home, suggesting they are not properly built.
   – in both cases, they give the impression that people have no choice or are doing their best, so we sympathise with them.

5   a, b   Learners write the adjectives in three lists and mark any that are new to them.

   As you go through the answers, discuss whether each adjective has a positive or a negative connotation (shown here as P or N). Expected answers:

Cities	Buildings	Both
restful (P)	claustrophobic (N)	quaint (P)
desolate (N)	ramshackle (N)	run-down (N)
bustling (P)		glitzy (P)
vibrant (P)		imposing (P)
		futuristic (P)
		picturesque (P)
		stylish (P)
		soulless (N)
		seedy (N)

   Focus on the meaning of any new items, e.g.
   – *desolate* = sad and empty (e.g. a square, car park)
   – *bustling* = full of busy activity (e.g. a street, market)
   – *vibrant* = exciting, full of life (atmosphere)
   – *ramshackle* = badly built, likely to fall down (e.g. a hut)
   – *quaint* = old-fashioned and pretty (e.g. a cottage, village)
   – *run-down* = not looked after (e.g. an apartment block)
   – *glitzy* = fashionable, showy (e.g. a restaurant, shopping centre)
   – *soulless* = dead, without human feeling (e.g. a building, street)
   – *seedy* = dirty and neglected (e.g. a hotel, an area)

   c   Together, learners choose a place and think of suitable adjectives to describe it. It could be either a building or a public space.

   d   Pairs describe their places in turn. Other learners listen and guess what or where it is.

    You could use photocopiable activity 5A on the Teacher's DVD-ROM at this point.

LISTENING

6 a *Pre-listening; vocabulary task.* To show what to do, look at the word *property* together and ask what word from the second column goes with it (*answer: developers*). Ask what *property developers* are (= people who build new houses and flats).

👥 / 👥👥 Learners make collocations from the words. Then check the answers and write collocations on the board. Common collocations are:

> property developers
> urban/city developers (= people who develop towns/cities)
> urban/city dwellers (= people who live in towns/cities)
> urban/city planning (= planning towns/cities)
> urban space (= open space in towns, e.g. squares)
> public space (= space available to the public, e.g. parks)
> basic needs (e.g. water, housing, food)
> living organism (= animals, plants, insects, etc.)
> living space (= areas where you can live)

Note
You can say:
– *urban / public space* = open space in general that isn't built on.
– *urban / public spaces* = particular open areas, e.g. parks.

b *Listening for main ideas.* Read through the questions, then play recording **2.1**. Learners listen and answer the questions. If necessary, play the recording a second time, pausing after each section. Establish how the speaker uses each collocation.

> 1 The exhibition ('project') views the city as a *living organism*.
> It explores the ephemeral (= short-lived) occupation of *public spaces*.
> It promotes informal models of urban planning (i.e. it shows how planning can be informal and left to individuals).
> City dwellers make alternative uses of the city (i.e. different from those that were planned).
> People find ways to adapt environments to their *basic needs*.
> 2 Public spaces: People often use *public spaces* differently from the way they were planned and for different purposes.
> 'Alternative' urban spaces: People often take over spaces that are not used or abandoned and use them for an alternative purpose which matches their own needs (often because of poverty).

Discuss question 3 together (*possible answer:* they are temporary, informal, home-produced; they disappear as soon as they are no longer needed; they appear between the planned urban areas, like Post-its in a book).

For question 4, discuss the lecturer's attitude to urban planning, and bring out these points:
– he seems to approve of 'alternative' urban spaces; he sees them as an expression of people's needs. He uses positive words to describe them (*living organism, flexible, innovative, transform*)
– he is critical of 'official' urban planning (he uses negative words like *dictate, prescribed*)
– he emphasises positive things that people have created (e.g. reclaiming land, creating gardens, making homes).

You could also ask learners to give their own views about what the lecturer says.

c *Vocabulary focus: adjectives.* Ask what adjectives learners noticed and build them up on the board.

d Play recording **2.1** again, pausing occasionally to check. Alternatively, learners could check in the script on p150.

> unpredictable, ephemeral, alternative, unexpected, makeshift, innovative, informal, temporary, spontaneous

SPEAKING

7 a 👤 *Preparation.* Learners think about areas that have been reclaimed or transformed, either officially through urban planning or informally through people finding an alternative purpose for them. They write a list, and also note down a few ideas about them.

b 👥 / 👥👥 *Discussion.* Learners talk about the spaces on their list and discuss whether they think they are a good idea or not.

Mixed-nationality classes

Learners either talk about the place where they are studying (if they know the area fairly well), or they tell each other about spaces they know of in their home town.

Feedback. Ask each pair or group to tell you some of the conclusions they came to.

Surveillance

5.2

Goals: talk about crime and surveillance
comment on experiences

Core language:
LANGUAGE FOCUS   Legal and illegal activities
LANGUAGE FOCUS   Commenting on experiences

READING

1 a Learners cover the article and look at images A and B. Discuss what they show (*answer:* A is a view of a shopping mall through a surveillance camera; B is a street with a large number of surveillance cameras). Use this to teach *surveillance* (= watching people for security purposes) and *CCTV* (= closed circuit television).

b Discuss the questions together and also ask:
– *Do you see surveillance cameras as protecting you, or as threatening or interfering, and why?*
– *Do you think there are too many (or not enough) surveillance cameras in your country?*
– *Do you think these cameras should be clearly visible, or hidden?*

2 a *Reading for main idea.* Learners read the article and find answers to the questions. When they have finished, they could compare answers with a partner. Discuss the questions together. Possible answers:

> 1 He's in a surveillance control centre in Manchester, watching CCTV screens. He's a journalist finding out how surveillance works.
> 2 Probably useful (he mentions successful operations against football hooligans and gangs). Not sinister (the operators don't work for the police).
> 3 The first paragraph gives the impression they are efficient and successful; the second paragraph suggests that they don't succeed in catching many criminals, and appears less enthusiastic.
> 4 Manchester council (but they pass information to the police). It means the police don't have complete power over surveillance.

b *Vocabulary focus.* Find out if learners know the highlighted words or can guess them from the context, and discuss other ways to express the same idea. Possible answers:

> 1 = put his hands in his pocket (awkwardly, trying to find something; he searches in his pockets for tobacco)
> 2 = unaware (he doesn't seem to notice the camera was there)
> 3 = calmed (he stopped feeling suspicious)
> 4 = sharpened, made perfect (he's become very good at spotting suspicious behaviour)
> 5 = running and being violent (running through the city centre, causing damage)
> 6 = has the characteristics of (seems / feels more like)

3 *Reading for main idea.* Learners read the rest of the article on p129, then discuss the answers with their partner. Discuss the questions together. Bring out these points.

> – The last part of the article puts the viewpoint of critics of CCTV cameras.
> – They say surveillance cameras have very little effect on crime (less than good street lighting).
> – The reason there are so many CCTV cameras in England is that money has been made available for them.

LANGUAGE FOCUS Legal and illegal activities

4 a Check what the words mean and focus on any new items. Point out that:
– *mugging* = attacking someone in the street and stealing something from them (e.g. money).
– *robbery* = taking something (e.g. money) from someone (or a bank) by force.
– *burglary* = breaking into someone's home or car to steal something.
– *pick-pocketing* = stealing from someone's pocket (without them noticing).
– *shop-lifting* = stealing things from shops.
Other possible new words:
– *busking* = playing street music
– *sleeping rough* = sleeping in the street, in a park, etc.
– *squatting* = living in an unoccupied house / flat that belongs to someone else.

As you go through the words, elicit the verbs and the nouns for the people who do the activity. Write important items on the board, e.g.

Activity	Verb	Person
mugging	*mug*	*mugger*
writing graffiti	*write graffiti*	*graffiti artist*
burglary	*burgle*	*burglar*
busking	*busk*	*busker*
begging	*beg*	*beggar*
vandalism	*vandalise*	*vandal*
robbery	*rob*	*robber*
pick-pocketing	*pick ... pocket*	*pick-pocket*
hooliganism	–	*hooligan*

Alternative
To save time, give these to the learners on a handout.

c *Discussion.* Groups choose five of the activities and discuss the questions.

Feedback. One learner from each group reports their conclusions about one of the topics they discussed. Ask if other people in the class agree.

Security

LISTENING

1 *Pre-listening.* Look at photos A–D and discuss what they show.

> A speed camera (to check that you're keeping to the speed limit)
> B airport security (x-ray scanner) (to check that you're not carrying anything dangerous)
> C chip and pin (credit card) machine (so that you can buy goods safely with a credit card)
> D traffic lights (to control traffic)

2 *Listening for main point.* Read through the questions, then play recording **2.2**. Pause after each speaker and answer the questions.

> Jane: D Mixed feelings (thinks they're important, but she shouldn't have been fined)
> Uri: A Against them (he thinks they serve no purpose)
> Patrick: B Mixed feelings (thinks they're necessary, but too restrictive)
> Tina: C In favour of them (thinks they're a sensible idea, but you have to remember your PIN)

LANGUAGE FOCUS Commenting on experiences

3 a Learners try to complete the sentences. They can remember what the speakers said, or they could guess what could go in the gaps.

b Go through the answers together for each section, then play recording **2.2** to check.

> 1 a bit over the top (= exaggerated)
> 2 It's not as if
> 3 no purpose whatsoever
> 4 quite ludicrous
> 5 they're probably necessary; out of proportion
> 6 ridiculous; talk about
> 7 a very sensible idea
> 8 really embarrassing

SPEAKING

4 a *Discussion.* Discuss the four security measures with the class. Try to elicit ideas about:
  – whether they're essentially a good idea.
  – why they're important or necessary and what they achieve (if anything).
  – what bad points they have, or how they inconvenience people.

You could also ask learners what they would say to each of the speakers in the recording.

b *Preparation.* Learners think about positive or negative experiences they have had with security measures (either those in the unit or others they can think of). They make a few notes to help them prepare.

Discussion. In turn, learners talk about their experiences and ask and answer questions.

Round-up. Ask each group to summarise the most interesting experience they talked about.

5.3 Target activity: Plan a city square

Goals: describe spaces in cities
outline problems
discuss and suggest solutions

Core language:
5.1 LANGUAGE FOCUS   Describing spaces
TASK LANGUAGE   Outlining problems

TASK PREPARATION

1 a Learners cover the report and look at the photos and plan. Ask what the square seems to be like and what it would be like to live there. Bring out ideas such as:
  – it would probably be quite noisy, as there are main roads with buses and cars.
  – the buildings look quite grand so the flats would probably be nice to live in, but there's no outside space.
  – it's probably a convenient place to live: there are buses and there are probably shops and cafés.

b *Reading for main idea.* Learners read the report and find out if it confirms what they thought or not. Discuss any problems you haven't mentioned already, including:
  – there is a lot of traffic and narrow pavements, so it's noisy and dangerous for children.
  – it is probably difficult to park.
  – it is probably not easy to cross the road.
  – cycling might be quite dangerous as there are no cycle tracks.

TASK LANGUAGE Outlining problems

2 *Listening for main points.* Play recording **2.3**. Pause after the first part and discuss answers to the first question.

> 1 shops: *it is difficult to go from one shop to another because they are cut off by the square*
> traffic: *flows all round the square*
> the middle: *you can only get to it through the underground station, so no-one uses it*
> buildings: *very beautiful, from the turn of the century*

Play the second part. Learners listen and make notes on the main points.

Learners compare their notes. Then discuss these together and build up points on the board, e.g.
  – road area reduced, but keep flow of traffic
  – short-term parking for shoppers
  – access to buses (bus stops)
  – pedestrians and cyclists
  – aim: high-quality urban space that people will use

3 a *Books closed.* To introduce the two patterns, write the following expressions on the board.
  – *a lack of*
  – *cut off*

Learners suggest sentences with each expression to talk about the square's problems and add them on the board.

Look at the table. Point out that there are two ways to talk about problems, using either a noun or an adjective.

Learners complete the sentences.

> 2 no access to (= you can't get there easily)
> 3 a lack / shortage of (= not enough)
> 7 inaccessible
> 8 inadequate
> 9 congested
> 10 overcrowded

Point out that *there's a lack of* and *there's a shortage of* mean the same. We can also say:
  – The square <u>lacks</u> (or <u>is lacking</u>) *parking spaces.*
  – The square <u>is short of</u> *parking spaces.*

b Discuss which sentences apply to the square at Harras (*answer:* 1, 2, 3; traffic flow isn't a problem, and not enough people use the square at present)

c Learners re-phrase the sentences.

> *There's a problem getting to the post office.*
> *There's a problem with access to the post office.*
> *There's a problem finding a parking space.*

Language note

After *problem* you can say:
– *with* + noun
  There's a problem with parking spaces.
– verb + *-ing*
  There's a problem finding a parking space.
You could also say:
There's a problem with finding a parking space

TASK

4 a *Role-play.* Put learners into groups of four. In each group, give learners a letter: A, B, C or D. They read their role on p129.

Learners discuss the issues in their group and try to agree on a solution, then draw their solution on the blank plan provided. You could also make copies of the plan beforehand and give one to each group.

Optional preparation
Before dividing the class into groups, give each learner a letter: A, B, C or D. Working alone, they read their role on p129 and prepare ideas and suggestions that would match their interests. Then learners form groups of four to have the discussion.

b *Reporting.* Groups choose one person to represent them. In turn, that person reports the group's solution to the class.

c *Round-up.* Play recording **2.4**. Learners listen and look at the drawing and plan on p138. Compare what the planner says with the learners' solution, and discuss which ideas are better and why.

 You could use photocopiable activity 5B on the Teacher's DVD-ROM at this point.

5 Explore

Across cultures: Privacy

Goal: to make learners aware of different cultural attitudes towards privacy

Core language:
privacy, introverted, extroverted, have a sense of privacy, invade someone's privacy

1 a Look at photos A–F. Discuss what learners think they show and how they are connected with the idea of privacy. Use this to introduce the key expressions:
– *have a sense of privacy* (= feel privacy is important)
– *invade someone's privacy* (= enter someone's personal space)

b Learners discuss the question. Focus on what the images show and why the titles are appropriate. Possible answers:

> A 1 – Symbolises the way the internet invades our privacy, as if someone is watching us.
> B 2 – It might be someone's makeshift home, because they have nowhere else to live; or perhaps a temporary shelter while someone is building a house; or perhaps a shelter after an earthquake; they've managed to give themselves a minimal amount of privacy by putting a screen round their 'home'.
> C 6 – The card gives the user security, but it also invades privacy (his personal details are stored).
> D 4 – The photo respects the girl's privacy by not showing her face, while showing the beauty of her arm and her jewellery.
> E 3 – The people in this apartment block appear to have very little privacy.
> F 5 – Someone doesn't want the baby to be photographed, so this could be what they say.

> **Note**
> Learners might choose different answers. If so, ask them why they chose them and encourage discussion. There is no 'right' or 'wrong' answer.

2 *Discussion.* Talk together about what 'privacy' means and whether it means different things to different people. To make this more focused, ask learners to write down three words or expressions that they associate with 'privacy'.

3 *Listening.* Read through the questions, then play recording **2.5**. Learners listen and answer the questions.

> 1 Having time to himself or with his girlfriend.
> 2 David has a close relationship with his girlfriend; he's sociable, but he's introverted. He spends a lot of time at home, he needs time on his own. He's lived in Egypt; now he lives in England.
> 3 Egypt: less sense of privacy; people did more together
> England: people are shut away in their own homes; a negative image.

Ask whether the learners' own country is more like Egypt or more like England, and in what ways.

4 Learners note down answers to the questions.
Learners interview their partner.
Check the questions together and find out if learners gave the same answers. You could also build up a 'majority' answer on the board.

> **Alternative**
> Write a line on the board to represent 'privacy'. At one end write *very important*, at the other end write *not at all important*. Learners copy the line and mark an 'X' to show their position.
> Then learners ask each other the questions. They find out if their partner would make a mark in the same place on the line as they did themselves.

5 *Discussion.* Discuss the questions together. Ask learners if they have any experiences from visits to other countries which showed something about people's sense of privacy.

Keyword: *need*

Goal: to use *need* to describe things which have to be done

Core language:
need (verb): *need to, need + -ing*
need (noun): *a need for, no need to, in need of*

1 a Read the example and ask what words could go in the gaps. Establish that *need* can be followed by:
– a noun:
  it needs a new concept, a new design, a lot of work, improvement
– a verb + *-ing*:
  it needs improving, reorganising, widening
– *to* + passive infinitive:
  it needs to be improved, to be redesigned, to be reduced

b *Listening to check.* Play recording **2.6** and check what the planner actually said.

> 1 reorganising
> 2 a new concept
> 3 to be reduced

62   Unit 5 Concepts of space

c 👤/👥 *'Need' as a verb / noun.* Learners read the examples and answer the questions.

> 1 As a verb: noun, verb + '-ing', 'to' + passive infinitive
>   As a noun: 'for' + noun, 'to' + infinitive, 'of' + noun (in the expression 'in need of')
> 2 urgent / urgently
>   desperate / desperately
>   Also: dire, great / greatly, real / really, bad / badly
> 3 Possible answers:
>   a The traffic needs complete re-organisation.
>   b More discussion is necessary / required ...
>   c The whole building is in urgent need of redecoration.
>   d We urgently need more qualified staff. / We're desperately short of qualified staff.
>   e It's OK – you don't need to panic.
>   f Many people in the area desperately need financial support.

2 a *Collocations with 'need'.* Discuss the expressions together and establish what they mean.

> a complete overhaul: *a system (= it needs completely changing)*
> repair: *a building (e.g. if the windows are broken)*
> renovation: *a building (= it's old, some things need replacing)*
> medical treatment: *a person (= to see a doctor or go to hospital)*
> a break: *a person (= he / she has been working too long)*
> food and shelter: *a person (= food and a place to live)*
> a change: *a person (= he / she has been doing the same thing for too long); a system (= it has stayed the same for too long)*
> assistance: *a person (= to help someone, e.g. a disabled or sick person)*
> an upgrade: *a system (= it's out of date and not good enough, e.g. computer software)*

b 👤/👥 Learners make sentences about photos 1–4 using expressions from **2a**.

Discuss possible answers together. Try to elicit a few different ideas.

c Play recording **2.7** and check the answers.

> 1 in need of a complete overhaul (a rail network)
> 2 in need of repair (a school)
> 3 in desperate need of food and shelter (flood survivors)
> 4 in need of assistance (the poor and the elderly)

3 a 👤/👥 Learners continue sentences 1–6. As they do this go round and check, but don't go through the answers together at this point. Possible sentences:

> 1 They need replacing. / They urgently need repairing.
> 2 You don't need to pay it back immediately.
> 3 They badly need food and shelter. / We need to provide more homes.
> 4 It needs a new concept. / It needs to be redesigned.
> 5 They need to be made more effective. / We need to reconsider them.
> 6 You don't need to shout. / There's no need to speak so loud.

b In turn, learners read out a continuation. Other learners guess the first sentence.

4 a *Speaking.* Give time for learners to make notes.

b 👥 Learners use their notes to exchange ideas.

Feedback. Ask a few learners which topics they talked about.

> **Alternative: Mingling activity**
> Learners move freely round the class, exchanging ideas with three or four other people.

Explore speaking

Goal: give a presentation with images
Core language:
structuring a presentation
showing and referring to slides

1 a Look at photos A–K and ask learners what they think the presentation will be about. Try to elicit some of these points:
  – it will be about a tourist resort, probably on a Caribbean island.
  – it will mention accommodation (in huts), beaches, a nearby town.

b *Listening for main idea.* Play recording **2.8**. Learners listen and mark the photos in order. Alternatively, pause at each 'beep' and learners identify the photo.

> 1I 2K 3E 4D 5H 6A 7F 8G 9C 10B 11J

c Discuss the questions and elicit ideas from different learners:

> 1 an island in the eastern Caribbean; not very big; covered in forest; tropical; one main town (St. Georges)
> 2 a collection of chalets, simple style, one-story; surrounded by palm trees, by the sea
> 3 not a private beach, fisherman use it
> 4 fresh, good; fresh fish every day

2 a *Language focus: structuring the presentation.* Learners close their books. To introduce this exercise, learners consider how the speaker structured the presentation. Ask what the main stages were and what kind of language Len had to use. Establish that he used expressions for:
  – introducing the topic.
  – referring to the slides he was showing.
  – moving from one topic to the next.
  – finishing the presentation.

👤/👥 Learners complete the gaps. They can either remember what the speaker said or guess which expressions go in each gap.

b Discuss the answers together and play each section on recording **2.9** to check. For each item, discuss what else Len could have said (shown here in brackets).

Unit 5 Concepts of space 63

1 I'd just like to (I just want to; I'd like to take this opportunity to)
2 I'd just like to (I want to; just to; I'll begin by giving you)
3 I'll talk about the hotel (We'll come back to this; I'll give you more details)
4 first I'd just like to give (to start with, I'm going to give)
5 let's go on now to (let's move on to; let's have a look at; now we're going to talk about)
6 I hope I've given you some idea of (I hope you've got a picture of; I hope now you can see)
7 If anyone would like to ask (If you have; If anyone has)
8 I'd be very happy to (I'd be delighted to; I'll try to; I'll do my best to)

3 a *Language focus: presenting visual information*. To introduce this, give the situation (e.g. you're pointing at a slide of the market) and ask what you could say (e.g. *as you can see here*). Look at the expressions. Learners suggest alternative words.

> A Here's a shot of / a glimpse of ...
> Here's a close-up / different / general view of ...
> Let's just home in on / focus on ...
> B As you can tell form this photo ...
> You can tell that ...

Focus on these expressions:
– *zoom in on* and *home in on* = get a closer view
– *a shot of* = a photo of
– *a glimpse of* = a quick look at
– *you can tell from* = it's clear from

b Learners choose one photo from the presentation and practise presenting it, using expressions from the table. You could give a different photo for each pair to work on.

Pairs in turn present their photo to the class. After each one, look at the script or play part of the recording to compare.

4 *Preparation*. Learners prepare a presentation. They rehearse what they will say. They should practise:
– introducing the presentation.
– referring to their slides.
– moving from one topic to the next.
– giving a conclusion.

Speaking. In turn, learners give their presentation. The others listen and ask questions afterwards.

Options

1 Learners think of a place they know well (e.g. a holiday place, a tourist site, a town, a museum or gallery). For homework, they find suitable images which they could show as slides (or print out to show in their presentation). They give their presentation in the next lesson.
2 Learners imagine slides they could show and make notes of the order they would show them in. They give their presentation, referring to their imaginary slides.

5 Look again

GRAMMAR Passive reporting verbs

Optional presentation

Books closed. Write on the board:
People reckon that CCTV operates in around 500 British towns.
Ask learners how we could say this sentence using a passive form, and elicit:
– *It is reckoned that CCTV operates ...*
– *CCTV is reckoned to operate ...*
You could introduce the other examples in the same way.

1 a Look at the examples and discuss the questions.

> 1 You can use verbs representing speech or thought in the same way, e.g. 'say', 'think', 'claim', 'believe', 'hope', 'consider', 'understand', 'prove', 'feel'.
> 2 Example a refers to the present; it is followed by the infinitive ('to operate').
> Example b refers to the past; it is followed by the past infinitive ('to have been spent').
> Example c refers to the present; it is followed by the present simple ('street lighting is ...').
> 3 a = People think (reckon) that ...
> b = People say that ...
> c = Experiments / trials show that ...

Language note

You use these structures, especially in writing, to create a 'distance' from what you are reporting (= it's not my point of view but I'm reporting what other people say or what many people think).
To report something in the past, we use a reporting verb + past infinitive (*to* + *have* + past participle).

b Learners rewrite the sentences. Possible answers:

> 1 It is said that CCTV cameras don't deter ...
> CCTV cameras are said not to deter ...
> 2 It is calculated that there are ...
> There are calculated to be ...
> 3 It is believed that the use of CCTV cameras hasn't had ...
> The use of CCTV cameras is believed not to have had ...
> 4 It is said that speed cameras have reduced ...
> Speed cameras are said to have reduced ...
> 5 It has been shown that ...
> Most security checks at airports are shown to be ...
> 6 It is felt by many people that ...
> Security checks at airports are felt by many people to be ...

c Ask how these constructions are expressed in the learners' own language. The aim of this is to give insight into the way English typically uses the passive as a 'distancing' device when reporting.

2 a *Writing*. Learners write sentences. As they do this, go round and check.

b In turn, learners from each pair read out their news item. The others listen and identify which of the photos A–E is being talked about.

VOCABULARY Describing places

3 Read the example and discuss the questions. Establish these two ways to describe a space in a town:
– by describing the shape (e.g. *unusual, triangular*).

64 Unit 5 Concepts of space

– by describing features (using adjectives or participle expressions, e.g. *surrounded by*).

> **Alternative**
> Look again at the photos of the square at Harras on p50 and cover the report. Ask learners to describe its shape, and elicit *triangular* and *surrounded by buildings*. Then read the example in **3**.

To focus on other shapes, draw them on the board and elicit the noun and adjective forms:

Noun	Adjective
square	*square*
circle	*circular / round*
rectangle	*rectangular*
oval	*oval*

4 a Check the meaning of the highlighted expressions and identify which can be matched with photos A–D.

> A 5   B 4   C 2   D 1

Focus especially on these expressions:
– *the focal point* (= the centre, the most important place).
– *is bounded by* (= they mark the boundary).
– *look out over / overlook* (= have an immediate view of).
– *just off* (= close to).

b To show what to do, discuss sentence 3 together. Ask learners to imagine the scene: *What does the road look like? What's the atmosphere like? What country is it? What are people doing? What about traffic?* etc.

Learners discuss the other sentences in the same way.

Feedback. For each sentence, elicit ideas from different pairs.

5 a To demonstrate the activity, choose a place yourself and say a few sentences about it. Find out if the class can guess what place it is.

Learners write sentences.

b Learners read out their sentences. Other learners guess what place they are describing.

6 Learners choose a place that they think could be improved. This could be a street, a square, a shopping centre, a park, a suburb, etc.

Learners tell each other about the place they chose and find out if their partner agrees.

Pairs choose one of their two places and discuss it with the rest of the class.

> **Alternative: Mingling activity**
> Learners move freely round the class and talk about the place they chose with three or four other people in turn. *Round-up.* Learners say what place they chose, what they think about it, and whether the people they spoke to agreed with them.

VOCABULARY Solutions to problems

7 a *Listening.* Play recording **2.10**, pausing after each speaker to establish what they are talking about. Ask learners what words and expressions indicate what the topic is (shown here in brackets).

> 1 redesigning a city square (central space, bus stations)
> 2 a war (ceasefire, conflict)
> 3 an industrial dispute (dispute, workers, equipment)
> 4 immigration (global problem, border controls)

b *Language focus: expressions with 'solution'.* Ask which speaker uses each expression.

> 1 a practical solution
>   our proposed solution
> 2 an interim solution
>   a diplomatic solution
> 3 a mutually agreeable solution
>   a long-term solution
> 4 a global solution
>   partial solutions

c Learners discuss what the expressions mean. Discuss the answers together and focus on any new items.

> 1 partial solutions
> 2 a global solution
> 3 an interim solution
> 4 a practical solution
> 5 a diplomatic solution
> 6 our proposed solution
> 7 a long-term solution
> 8 a mutually agreed solution

> **Alternative**
> Elicit the meaning of the expressions as you go through the answers to **7b**.

d *Language focus: verbs.* Brainstorm ideas with the class and write verbs on the board. Possible answers:

> come up with
> propose
> find
> suggest
> look for
> provide
> search for
> work towards

e Play recording **2.10** to check.

> 1 come up with
> 2 provide, find
> 3 search for
> 4 require, suggest

8 *Preparation.* Learners think of a problem and make notes.

Discussion. In turn, learners discuss their topic with the others.

Round-up. Ask each group to report back on the topic they found most interesting to talk about.

 You could use photocopiable activity 5C on the Teacher's DVD-ROM at this point.

Self-assessment

To help focus learners on the self-assessment, you could read it through, giving a few examples of the language they have learned in each section (or asking learners to tell you). Then ask them to circle a number on each line.

Unit 5 Extra activities on the Teacher's DVD-ROM

Printable worksheets, activity instructions and answer keys are on your Teacher's DVD-ROM.

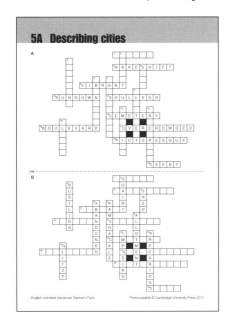

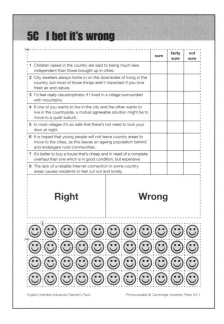

5A Describing cities

Activity type: Speaking – Crossword – Pairs

Aim: To consolidate knowledge of vocabulary for describing cities

Language: Describing spaces – Coursebook p47 – Vocabulary

Preparation: Make one copy of the worksheet, cut into two, for each pair.

Time: 20–25 minutes

5B Your solutions wanted

Activity type: Speaking – Discussion – Small groups

Aim: To practise speaking about appropriate punishments for minor crimes

Language: Outlining problems – Coursebook p50 – Target activity

Preparation: Make one copy of the worksheet for each learner.

Time: 30–40 minutes

5C I bet it's wrong

Activity type: Speaking – Correct sentence identification – Pairs

Aim: To discuss language from the unit

Language: Vocabulary from unit 5 – Coursebook, unit 5

Preparation: Make one copy of the worksheet for each pair. Cut along the dotted lines to make one table and several counters. Count 16 for each pair. Keep the others aside.

Time: 20–25 minutes

Unit 5 Self-study Pack

In the Workbook

Unit 5 of the *English Unlimited Advanced Self-study Pack Workbook* offers additional ways to practise the vocabulary and grammar taught in the Coursebook. There are also activities which build reading and writing skills, and a whole page of tasks to use with the DVD-ROM video, giving your learners the opportunity to hear and react to spoken English.

- **Vocabulary:** Describing spaces; Outlining problems; Describing features of places; *need*; Legal and illegal activities
- **Grammar:** Passive reporting verbs
- **Explore writing:** Reports
- **DVD-ROM Extra:** Documentary – *Iconic buildings*

On the DVD-ROM

Unit 5 of the *English Unlimited Advanced Self-study Pack DVD-ROM* contains interactive games and activities for your learners to practise and improve their vocabulary, grammar and pronunciation, and also their speaking and listening. It also contains video material (with the possibility for learners to record themselves) to use with the *Workbook*.

- **Vocabulary and grammar:** Extra practice of the Coursebook language and Keywords
- **Explore listening:** A presentation
- **Explore speaking:** Addressing an audience
- **Video:** Documentary – *Iconic buildings*

6 Appearances

6.1

Goals: describe appearance and changes to appearance
discuss photos and images
talk about aim and intention

Core language:
LANGUAGE FOCUS Altering physical features
LANGUAGE FOCUS Expressing aim

The camera never lies?

LISTENING

1 a Look at images A and B. Ask learners to suggest ways that image A has been changed. Build up ideas on the board. Do not focus particularly on the verbs at this point.

b *Listening.* Play recording **2.11** to check.

1 skin is smoother	6 lips are redder
2 teeth are whiter	7 longer eyelashes
3 eyes are whiter	8 spots are removed
4 face is thinner	9 eyebrows are thinner
5 lines are removed	10 background is lighter

As you check the answers, present any new words for facial features, e.g. *eyebrows, eyelashes*.

c *Focus on verbs.* Learners read the script on p151 and discuss the questions.

Check the questions together and bring out these points:
– the speaker is describing changes from the past to the present (how the image is different now from before), so he uses the present perfect.
– the focus is on what has happened or what has changed, not on who made the changes; so most verbs are in the passive (*has been* + past participle).
– some of the verbs mean 'make thinner', 'make redder', etc., so they are formed from adjectives:
  white → *whiten*
  thin → *thin (down)*
  red → *redden*.

READING

2 a Learners read the article. When they have finished, they work with a partner to discuss what the highlighted words mean.

> **Optional reading task**
> Give learners an initial reading question: *What is the main point the writer makes?*
> Then discuss this briefly before learners focus on the highlighted words (*answer:* all fashion photos are digitally enhanced nowadays).

Discuss the words together. Possible answers:

| 1 the things they use, their weapons |
| 2 shape of face (= beautiful faces) |
| 3 absolutely perfect, without any flaws |
| 4 without any control |
| 5 retouched without any limit, far too much |
| 6 reflect accurately |
| 7 it doesn't make the model look good |
| 8 it doesn't have any, it's completely lacking |
| 9 they know enough about the world |

You could explore other contexts in which we use:
– *arsenal* = a stock of weapons (e.g. *nuclear arsenal*)
– *with abandon*: dance with abandon (= *wildly*)
– *... to death*: scared to death; sick to death (of); worried to death; work yourself to death

b Discuss the questions. Bring out these points.
– It gives both sides of the argument: he quotes people who are both critical and positive.
– It's more critical than positive: more space is given to critical quotes, the quotes are longer and say more.
– The people's attitudes are:
  1 too much is manipulated these days.
  2 airbrushing removes life and individuality from the images.
  3 photos of models aren't intended to be real but to create an image.
  4 people realise that images are digitally enhanced and accept this.

Ask learners if they agree with the writer and why. You could also ask if anyone has used software to digitally alter images, and how they feel about it.

LANGUAGE FOCUS Altering physical features

3 a *Focus on nouns.* Learners write a list of words from the article.

Go through the answers together by writing the words on the board.

| 1 bone structure   2 pimples   3 wrinkles |
| 4 thighs   5 lines   6 chins |
| All except 4 refer mainly to the face. |

b Learners brainstorm other physical features that can be digitally altered and write a list.

c Look at the list of verbs and check the meaning of any new items (e.g. *enhance* = make better, clearer or stronger; *alter* = change slightly).

Learners talk about the items on their lists and use the verbs to say how they can be changed (e.g. hair can be lightened, darkened, removed, added).

> **Note**
> Verbs beginning and ending in *en* are focused on in **Look again**, p65.

 You could use photocopiable activity 6A on the Teacher's DVD-ROM at this point.

Unit 6 Appearances 67

Fake photos

LANGUAGE FOCUS Aim and intention

> **Optional lead-in**
> *Books closed.* Write *fake* on the board and ask learners what it means. They give examples of fakes and discuss what different things can be fakes (e.g. paintings, photos, identity).

1 a Give learners time to look at the photos and discuss what they think is the fake element in them. Make sure they *do not* look at the back of the book!

Discuss the photos together. Elicit different ideas from the class but do not tell them the answers at this point.

b Look at the highlighted expressions. Learners add words to the gaps. Then go through the answers by writing the expressions on the board.

> 1 so as to   2 in order to   3 so that
> 4 hoping to   5 with the aim of

Point out that the expressions are all similar in meaning: they are all ways of describing the *aim* of something.

> **Note**
> Expressions with *aim* are focused on in **Keywords**, p62.

c Look at the sentences again and find out if learners can guess which photos they go with, or if they help them to interpret what the fake element is. Again, do not tell them the answers at this point.

READING and SPEAKING

2 *Jigsaw reading.* Give each learner a letter: A or B. Learners look only at their own information and photos.

Learners form pairs. In turn, they explain the fake element in their photo and then show the original photo to their partner.

3 a *Language practice.* Learners match the sentence halves, using linking expressions from **1b**. Possible answers:

> 1b The pyramids were moved closer together so as to fit the vertical format of the magazine.
> 2d They changed his face to make it darker than it really was with the aim of making it look more menacing.
> 3a ... extra smoke rising from the buildings in order to make it look more dramatic.
> 4c ... inserting a black student in a crowd of white football fans, hoping to emphasise the diversity of their students.

b *Discussion.* Focus on each of the fakes in turn. Ask learners if they think it is ethical and why/why not.

Genuine fakes

6.2

Goals: talk about fakes and forgery
convince people and express doubt

Core language:
Fakes and forgery

LANGUAGE FOCUS Fakes and forgery

1 a *Vocabulary focus.* Look at the expressions together. Ask what they mean and give simple examples if necessary.

> 1 not genuine, illegally printed
> 2 making money illegally from investing (e.g. tricking people into investing, then disappearing with the money)
> 3 not genuine (looks like the real thing, but it isn't)
> 4 using fake credit cards to get money or buy things (they appear to be genuine, but they aren't)
> 5 deceiving someone into e.g. giving you their money
> 6 not genuine but looks exactly like the original
> 7 get money from the government that you aren't entitled to (e.g. find ways not to pay tax, electricity bills, etc.)
> 8 someone who can't help telling lies

b Discuss the other forms of the highlighted words and build them up on the board.

verb	noun	adjective
forge	*forgery*	*forged*
–	*scam*	–
fake	*fake*	*fake*
–	*con*	–
counterfeit	*counterfeit*	*counterfeit*
cheat	*cheat*	*cheat*
lie	*lie / liar*	*lying*

c *Discussion.* Learners discuss the questions and make brief notes of their answers. Possible answers (1–3):

> 1 documents, credit cards, paintings, a signature
> 2 jewellery, designer clothes, fur, a smile
> 3 find ways not to pay bills, don't pay enough tax, get expenses they aren't entitled to

READING

2 a *Pre-reading discussion.* Discuss the questions together or let learners discuss them in pairs first and then ask them what they decided. Elicit possible ways to find out if a painting is genuine, e.g.:
– look at the signature.
– do a chemical test to find out the age of the painting.
– compare the style with other paintings by the same artist.
– find out if there is a record of the painting.
– find out who was the last owner.

b Look on p128 and read the information.

3 a *Reading for main idea.* Look at the photo of John Myatt. Ask learners whether they think he looks honest and whether they would buy a painting from him.

Learners read the article and decide if the statements are true or false. When they have finished, they compare answers with a partner.

Discuss the answers together. Ask learners to say why they think each statement is true or false.

> 1 T – He's honest about his failings, he thought his own landscapes were dull.
> 2 F – They were laughably amateurish, he painted them in emulsion.
> 3 T – John Drewe created false provenances (= historical records) for the paintings.
> 4 T – The paintings were amateurish but they 'fooled the experts'.
> 5 F – He was only in prison for four months.
> 6 F – He feels he has nothing to apologise for and he's now painting fakes legally.
> 7 T – He found it easier to paint fakes than develop his own style and he was able to 'churn out' fakes.

b Discuss what kind of person John Myatt is, focusing on the adjectives and presenting any difficult items e.g. *devious* (= clever but not to be trusted), *daring* (= ready to take risks). Possible answers:

> He's devious, daring, clever.
> He doesn't seem to be ashamed.
> He's quite modest about his paintings, considering his success.

c *Focus on language.* Learners suggest possible verbs.

> 1 produced
> 2 pretending they are
> 3 intend
> 4 found, arrested

d Discuss what 'mental image' each phrasal verb has. Use this to help focus on the precise meaning.

> 1 suggests producing things quickly in large quantities: churn = stir liquid around quickly
> 2 suggests giving them out to people quickly (like someone distributing leaflets in the street)
> 3 suggests starting on a course in life; you set out on a journey
> 4 suggests that he was running away or hiding; you catch up with someone who is walking ahead of you

e Check that learners understand the sentence. Explain that it signals the double meaning of *forge*: you forge (= start, create) a career, but John Myatt is a forger.

Discuss other points that reveal the writer's attitude, e.g.:
– *disarmingly honest, had high hopes* (the writer seems to like Myatt and feels sympathetic towards him).
– *master forger, 'the biggest art fraud of the 20th century'* (the writer seems impressed by his achievements).

Optional pair or group activity
Let learners work through the article and answer all the questions in **3** in pairs or groups, then go through the answers afterwards.

LISTENING

4 Read through the questions and ask learners what they think John Myatt might say for each one.

Play recording **2.12**. Learners listen and answer the questions.

> 1 He was a single parent and he needed to work from home and earn money.
> 2 He bought paintings from him.
> 3 John Drewe sold one of his fakes as a genuine painting for £25,000, then offered to split the profits with him.
> 4 It would be too obvious that they were fakes.

SPEAKING

5 *Role-play.* Give learners a letter, A or B. They look at the instructions on p130 or p138 and prepare what they will say.

Learners form A/B pairs and have a conversation.

Round-up. Ask some of the art dealers whether they persuaded their customer to buy the painting. Then ask some of the customers whether they bought the painting, and why or why not.

Alternative: Preparation in pairs
Give each pair a letter, A or B: they both have the same role and they prepare for the conversation together. Learners form new pairs, so each pair has one A and one B, and have the conversation.

6.3 Target activity: Interview someone and present a profile

Goals: describe appearance
conduct a personal interview
describe someone's life, achievements and attitudes

TASK READING

1 a *Pre-reading.* Learners say what they know about Paulo Coelho.

b *Reading for main idea.* Focus on the structure of the profile. Learners read the interview and answer the questions. When they have finished, they discuss the questions with a partner.

Discuss the answers together. Possible answers (1–4):

> 1 He's small and delicate.
>   He wears black and has long hair in a rat's tail.
>   He's mystical; he's good at communicating; he seems to be self-contained.
> 2, 3 Things he said: paras 1, 3 (present simple)
>   Setting: paras 2, 3 (present simple)
>   Past life: para 1 (past simple)
>   Achievements: paras 1, 4 (present perfect)
>   Promotion: para 5 (past simple, present simple)
> 4 Para 1: a short mention of his past life to arouse interest
>   Para 2: the setting to establish the mood of the interview
>   Para 3: a quote to give a personal feel
>   Para 4: achievements – the main 'body' of the profile
>   Para 5: marketing: gives unusual/surprising information about him

TASK

2 *Preparation.* Give each learner a letter, A or B. B will interview A first. Working alone, they follow the instructions and prepare for the interview. Emphasise that the interview is in a typical setting, so the interviewees should choose an imaginary setting and suitable clothes to wear. As part of the preparation, A tells B what the setting is and what he / she is 'wearing'.

Unit 6 Appearances 69

3 *Interview.* B interviews A and makes notes.

4 *Preparation and interview.* Repeat stages 2 and 3. This time A interviews B, and B chooses a setting and what to wear for the interview.

5 In turn, learners present an oral presentation of their partner, based on their notes from the interview.

Note
Learners will write a profile of their partner in **Explore writing**, p63.

 You could use photocopiable activity 6B on the Teacher's DVD-ROM at this point.

6 Explore

Across cultures: Piracy

Goals: to make learners more aware of different attitudes towards pirating material

Core language:

piracy, copyright, file-sharing, royalties

1 a *Pre-reading.* Look at the images and the news and discuss what the news stories might be about. Or, ask learners to close books, and write the headlines on the board.

 b *Reading and discussion.* Learners read the news stories. Briefly discuss which they think is the most serious offence and why, but don't get involved in too much discussion of issues at this point.

2 *Discussion.* Learners discuss each activity in turn. They could make brief notes of their conclusions.

Discuss the activities together. Encourage learners to consider specific issues, e.g.
– why the people are doing it.
– whether they could afford to do the same thing legally.
– whether there is a difference between corporate and individual crime.
– whether other people suffer from the activity.

Alternative
1 Give each pair or group one of the topics to consider. 2 Discuss each topic with the class. First get feedback from the pair / group that discussed it, then find out if other groups agree or disagree.

3 a *Preparation.* Learners consider each statement and note down their opinion about it.

 Discussion. Learners compare their opinions.

 Feedback. Look at each opinion in turn, and ask different pairs or groups what they said about it. You could write a 'majority opinion' for each on the board.

Alternative: mingling activity
Give each learner one opinion to consider. They decide their own opinion about it, then move freely round the class and discuss it with three or four other people. *Round-up.* Ask learners whether most of the people they talked to agreed with them.

b *Class discussion.* Discuss the questions together. In a single-nationality class, find out if everyone agrees about the answers. In a mixed-nationality class, find out what the situation is in different learners' countries and what they think about it.

Keywords: *aim, purpose*

Goal: to use *aim* and *purpose* to describe purpose.

Core language:

expressions with *aim* and *purpose*

1 a *Focus on 'aim'.* Read the texts and learners add expressions in the gaps.

> 1 is aimed at   2 aims to   3 is aiming for

Language note

is aimed at usually refers to a target audience:
– *The book is aimed at children.*
aim for and *aim to* usually refer to a goal:
– *She's aiming for a job in the City.*
  (She's aiming to get …)
– *We're aiming for 1 million sales a year.*
  (We're aiming to sell …)

Ask where the stories might appear and what they seem to be about.

> 1 Film review, about the film 'Avatar'.
> 2 Website information about a graphic design course.
> 3 Newspaper report about an athlete who may have won medals under suspicious circumstances.

 b Learners discuss the questions. Go through the answers by writing them on the board.

The adverbs 'specifically', 'primarily', 'solely' and 'mainly' can be used in either 1 or 2. They can come before or after the verb: – *The film is <u>specifically</u> aimed at …* – *The film is aimed <u>specifically</u> at …* *The adverbs 'clearly' and 'apparently' can only be used in 1. They are more likely to come before the verb:* – *The film is <u>clearly</u> aimed at …*

 c *'Aim' as a noun.* Discuss the sentence together, then ask learners to find it. (*answer:* p127 – the text about Abraham Lincoln).

 d Learners complete the gaps.

> 1 The aim of   2 the aim of

Use these examples to show that *the aim* is most commonly followed by *of*.

2 a   Learners think of possible continuations.

 b Go through the answers and try to get a range of suggestions from different learners. As you do this, play recording **2.13** item by item to compare.

3 a *Focus on 'purpose'.* Discuss the examples together.

> 1e   2b   3c   4f (or b)   5a   6d

Focus on these common expressions with *purpose*:
– *the purpose of* + noun.
– *the purpose behind* + noun (= the underlying purpose).
– *for the purpose of* + *-ing* (= in order to).
– *have a purpose in life* (fixed expression).

b Discuss how you could express the sentences using *aim*. Possible answers:

> 1 The aim of this meeting is ...
> 2 This paper aims to analyse ... / The aim of this paper is to analyse ...
> 3 ... any aim in life.
> 4 ... with the aim of developing ...
> 5 The primary aim of the club ...
> 6 ... art exists with the aim of putting ...

Language note

aim and *purpose* mean almost the same, and can often be used interchangeably:
– *purpose* can mean 'the reason why something exists', so it is more likely than *aim* in sentence 6.
– you say *with the aim of* but *for the purpose of*.
– *aim* can also be used as a verb (*aims to*).

4 Learners make notes about their aims for the future.

Learners tell each other about their aims and ask further questions

Feedback. A few learners tell you their partner's aims.

Explore writing

Goals: use written and spoken styles appropriately
appreciate written and spoken genres

Core language:
Features of written and spoken language

1 Look at photos A–E and discuss what kinds of writing or speaking they show and what style they involve.

Alternative: Pairwork

Learners discuss the photos in pairs first. Then talk about them together.

Possible answers:

> A writing a contract. Formal written style, clearly organised structure.
> B giving a lecture (or a speech). Probably a formal style with rhetorical devices, maybe read from notes.
> C chatting on the phone (to a friend). Very informal, with frequent interaction and interruptions.
> D doing homework. Formal written style (for an essay), careful punctuation and structure.
> E an Internet posting (a tweet). Informal, short sentences, condensed structure.

Discuss spoken and written styles.

Language note

Written styles tend to be more carefully structured (punctuation, paragraphs, linking devices, expressions for showing logical connections) and to use more formal words and expressions.
Spoken styles usually involve more repetition, hesitation, checking with the listener, and is less carefully structured. They are also more likely to use informal words and expressions.
There are also formal spoken styles, e.g. lectures, speeches, professional presentations; and informal written styles, e.g. text messages, emails to friends.
Emails and text messages are often more similar to spoken than to written styles (they are spontaneous, and punctuation and spelling are less important).

2 a *Focus on written and spoken styles.* Look at the two extracts, and make it clear that:
– the spoken versions are from the recording of John Myatt from p59.
– the written versions convey the same information, but as if part of a written autobiography or memoir.

Learners compare the two pairs of extracts.

b Learners compare their answers. Then discuss the answers together. Focus on these points:

> 1, 3 In the spoken version, the speaker strings together main clauses joined together with 'and'. In the written version, the information is more condensed, so there are fewer main verbs and more phrases (e.g. 'with very small children'; saying 'Genuine fakes').
> 2 The spoken version is full of 'fillers' allowing the speaker time to think. These don't appear in the written version, which is more carefully structured.
> 4 The spoken version has informal and imprecise expressions ('and she wasn't coming back', 'and there were two ...'; 'one of the things that cropped up was this idea'). These are 'tidied up' in the written version, made more precise and less conversational ('had left home for good'; 'One idea I had').
> 5 The spoken version has direct quotes ('he said to me would I be interested ... and I said yes'). In the written version, these are in reported speech ('he asked me if I would be interested ... I accepted').

3 a *Writing from notes.* Learners expand the notes they made for their partner's profile in lesson 6.3. As they do this, go round and check and give help where necessary. Make sure learners pay attention to the structure of and style and express the ideas coherently.

b Learners read out a few sentences from their profile. Then ask them to convey the same information in an informal spoken style, as if they were just chatting. The others listen and comment on what features are different.

Alternative

Learners choose an extract from their profile and write an informal 'spoken' version of it, as if part of a play or film in which someone is chatting about the person.
Then a few learners read out their written and spoken versions.

4 *Discussion.* Learners discuss the questions.
Round-up. Ask each group what ideas they had. Bring out these points:
– as people write emails and texts rather than letters, language has become less formal and conversational.
– people write less than they used to (e.g. most people don't write letters, keep personal diaries) and they write more quickly (on a computer rather than by hand). Because of this, people pay less attention to handwriting, punctuation, sentence structure, etc.

6 Look again

GRAMMAR Present perfect simple and progressive

1 a Learners look at the examples of the present perfect simple and match the highlighted verb forms with the uses.

> 1b 2a 3c

b Learners look at the examples of the present perfect progressive and match the highlighted verb forms with one of the two uses.

> 1b 2a

c Learners read the four sentences. Discuss whether the activity or feeling has stopped, or whether it is still continuing.

> a stopped b continuing c stopped d continuing

Learners discuss ways in which the sentences could continue. Possible answers:

> a ... have you been?
> b ... with no luck unfortunately. I'll keep on trying.
> c ... it stopped half an hour ago.
> d ... the new proposals with my colleagues.

d Learners read the sentence beginnings and write down ways in which they could continue.

Learners compare their sentences.

GRAMMAR Present participle expressions

2 Read through the examples.

> **Alternative**
> Books closed. Write the complete sentence from p60 on the board one expression at a time. After each expression, learners guess (or remember) what comes next. Then open books and read the examples.

3 a Learners match the expressions with the topics.

> 1 a woman's eyes
> 2 the lights of a farmhouse
> 3 a woman at an airport
> 4 people in an office
> 5 people by the sea

b Learners suggest a scene for each expression, e.g.:

1 a romantic dinner, in which a man proposes to his girlfriend (*she slipped on the ring, her eyes sparkling in excitement*); or a woman about to go on her first parachute jump (*she put on her parachute, her eyes sparkling with excitement*).

c Play recording **2.14**. Learners listen and compare with their own answers.

4 a Learners think of a scene for each sentence and add a participle expression.

b Go through the sentences together by eliciting several ideas for each one. Then turn to p130 and read the original examples.

> **Alternative**
> After discussing each sentence, read out the original version from p130.

5 *Writing game*. Pairs build up descriptions, following the instructions. Continue this for four or five rounds.

In turn, learners read the descriptions.

VOCABULARY New crimes

6 *Books closed*. Write on the board *new crimes*. Establish what this means and ask learners how many they remember from the unit. Possible answers:

> credit card fraud
> illegal downloading
> illegal photocopying

7 a *Open books*. Look at images A–D and ask what crimes they show.

b Learners read the pieces of advice and match them with the words and images A–D.

> 1 credit card theft (image B: the person is concealing his PIN)
> 2 phishing (image A: the criminal is 'fishing' in the computer)
> 3 identity fraud (image D: the criminal is 'stealing' the person's online identity)
> 4 hacking (image C: shows 'trojan horses' round a computer. A 'trojan' = a type of virus that can hack into a computer)

c Learners match the sentences.

> 1c 2d 3b 4a

 You could use photocopiable activity 6C on the Teacher's DVD-ROM at this point.

VOCABULARY Verbs with -en and en-

8 a Read through the examples.

> **Alternative**
> Books closed. Write on the board:
> – make whiter
> – make redder
> – make better
> Learners give verbs with the same meaning. Write them on the board.
> Then look at the examples to check.

b Establish what the verbs mean.

> make black(er)   make shorter   make stronger
> make deeper   make longer   make harder   make wider
> put into danger   make softer   put something round
> make larger   make lighter   make more alive
> make tougher   make darker   make thicker
> make weaker   make straight(er)

Establish that the verbs have these different forms:
– adjective + -en
   black → blacken, thick → thicken
– noun + -en
   strength → strengthen, length → lengthen
– en- as a prefix
   danger → endanger, large → enlarge

72 Unit 6 Appearances

c Discuss which adjectives could be used to talk about each noun. Possible answers:

> a road: *straighten, widen*
> a bridge: *widen, strengthen*
> a room: *enlarge, lengthen, widen, enliven*
> a skirt: *lengthen, shorten, widen*
> a canal: *widen, deepen*
> a sauce: *thicken*
> a photo: *enhance, enlarge, darken, lighten, enclose (in a letter)*
> health: *endanger*
> feet: *toughen, soften*

9 a Learners discuss the sentences.

b Check the answers. After each sentence, play recording **2.15** to compare. Contexts in the recording:

> 1 *At a trial (= tried to destroy my reputation, said bad things about me).*
> 2 *Someone refusing to eat (or buy) tuna (= they could becoming extinct)*
> 3 *In a letter of application for a job.*
> 4 *A football coach speaking after a match.*
> 5 *Someone choosing slides for a presentation.*
> 6 *Someone has been made redundant, and was given money to make things seem better.*

10 a To show what to do, write a sentence on the board and learners guess what it is about.

Learners write two or three sentences. They could also do this together in pairs.

b In turn, learners read out their sentences. The others guess what they are about.

Self-assessment

To help focus learners on the self-assessment, you could read it through, giving a few examples of the language they have learned in each section (or asking learners to tell you). Then ask them to circle a number on each line.

Unit 6 Extra activities on the Teacher's DVD-ROM

Printable worksheets, activity instructions and answer keys are on your Teacher's DVD-ROM.

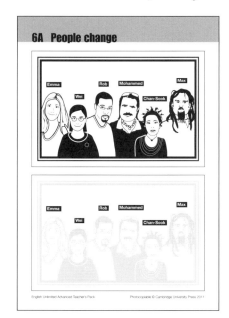
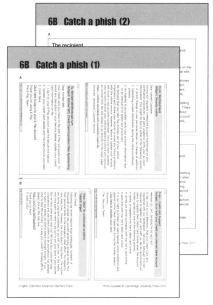
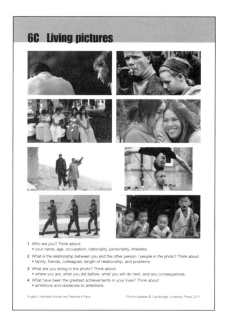

6A People change

Activity type: Speaking – Describe and draw – Pairs

Aim: To describe changes in people's appearance

Language: Altering physical features – Coursebook p57 – Vocabulary

Preparation: Make one copy of the worksheet for each learner.

Time: 15–20 minutes

6B Catch a phish

Activity type: Reading and speaking – Collaborative task – Pairs / Groups of four

Aim: To recognise features of scam emails

Language: Fakes and forgeries – Coursebook p58 – Vocabulary

Preparation: Make one copy of each worksheet for each group of four. Cut each worksheet along the dotted lines.

Time: 30–40 minutes

6C Living pictures

Activity type: Speaking – Image-based roleplay – Pairs / Groups of four

Aim: To speculate and talk about other people's lives.

Language: Describe someone's life – Coursebook p60 – Target activity

Preparation: Make one copy of the worksheet for each pair.

Time: 30–40 minutes

Unit 6 Self-study Pack

In the workbook

Unit 6 of the *English Unlimited Advanced Self-study Pack Workbook* offers additional ways to practise the vocabulary and grammar taught in the Coursebook. There are also activities which build reading and writing skills, and two pages which give your learners the opportunity to develop their skills in extended reading.

- **Vocabulary:** Fakes and forgery; Verbs with *-en* and *en-*; Altering physical features; *aim, purpose*
- **Grammar:** Present participle expressions
- **Explore reading:** Comparing news articles

On the DVD-ROM

Unit 6 of the *English Unlimited Advanced Self-study Pack DVD-ROM* contains interactive games and activities for your learners to practise and improve their vocabulary, grammar and pronunciation, and also their speaking and listening.

- **Vocabulary and grammar:** Extra practice of the Coursebook language and Keywords
- **Explore listening:** A news report
- **Explore speaking:** Written / spoken styles

7 Health

7.1

Goals: talk about health problems and treatment
describe and comment on an exhibition or a show

Core language:
LANGUAGE FOCUS Health problems and treatment
LANGUAGE FOCUS Descriptive participles

Cradle to grave

READING

1 a *Pre-reading*. Check that learners understand what an *art installation* is (= objects which are set up, but which are also a work of art).

Cover the text and look at the photos. Find out if learners can see what they show. Try to elicit:
– why it's called 'Cradle to Grave' (= the whole of your life, from birth to death).
– what it shows (a collection of pills and tablets in a long piece of cloth with photos beside them).
– what the point of it is (learners will probably guess that these are the pills people take during their life, so the cloth represents a person's life).

b Reading for main idea. Learners read the text and answer the questions. When they have finished, they discuss the answers with a partner.

Check what the installation is, if learners didn't guess this from the photos. Then go through the questions.

> 1 Prescribed drugs, not drugs bought, e.g. at a pharmacy without prescription.
> 2 Man: he has good health till he's 50; he smokes but gives up when he's 70; he dies of a stroke.
> Woman: she has a healthy life; suffers from arthritis and diabetes in middle age.
> 3 Possible answers: that we rely heavily on drugs and medicine; that we don't realise how many pills we take.

LANGUAGE FOCUS Health problems and treatment

2 a *Focus on vocabulary*. Learners read the text again and write the words and expressions in two lists.

> Illnesses: *arthritis, diabetes, asthma, hay fever, chest infection, high blood pressure, heart attack, stroke*
> Treatments: *prescribed drugs, pills, injection, immunisation, antibiotics, painkillers*

Check that learners understand:
– *injection* (treatment using a needle or syringe).
– *vaccination* (injection to prevent you getting a disease).
– *immunisation* (routine vaccination given to e.g. all children).

b Focus on pronunciation. Check which words are the same in learners' own language. Play recording **2.16** to focus on any differences in pronunciation.

c *Discussion*. Learners consider the health problems and treatments in their lists, and relate them to their own country.

Round-up. Ask each group to summarise the main points they discussed. You could extend this into a discussion of:
– how much people rely on prescription drugs to keep healthy and whether this is a good idea.
– whether there is a tendency to move away from reliance on drugs.
– what alternatives learners think there are to conventional medical treatment.
– to what extent the illnesses shown in the installation are a result of lifestyle and whether this is also true of learners' own country.

> **Mixed-nationality classes**
> *Either:* Let learners from the same country work in groups together. Then get feedback from each group about their own country.
> *Or:* Make sure each group has learners from different countries. Then in the feedback stage, ask learners what differences and similarities they discovered between their countries.

> You could use photocopiable activity 7A on the Teacher's DVD-ROM at this point.

Audio guide

LISTENING

1 a To introduce this, ask learners whether they use audio guides when they visit art galleries, museums or famous buildings, and why or why not.

To prepare for taking notes, learners could write the six headings on a piece of paper. Emphasise that they should only note down information not given in the reading text, and should make notes on main points only (not individual examples).

Play recording **2.17**, pausing after each main section to give learners time to make notes.

Discuss the answers together. Build up ideas on the board. Possible answers:

> 1 Pharmacopia: a textile artist, a video artist, a GP (= doctor)
> 2 composite lives: four men and four women
> 3 fine, pale grey net, 13m x 0.5 m
> 4 different shapes and colours, arranged in groups, blocks of colour
> 5 from different sources, family photo albums, show various stages of life

b Learners put the items in order and discuss what they relate to.

c Discuss the answers together and build up an order of 'age' on the board. Then play recording **2.17** again to check, pausing after each item to check what was referred to.

> 1 footprint: baby's ID form
> 2 syringes: childhood vaccinations
> 3 kitchen cupboard: photo of a toddler (= child who can just walk)
> 4 gas and air mask: photo of woman in childbirth
> 5 silver blade: artificial hip
> 6 ashtray: full of cigarette ends (high blood pressure)
> 7 coffin: photo of a funeral
> 8 rolled-up fabric: the woman's life hasn't ended

2 a, b Discuss the question together, then learners look at the script. Bring out these points:
– the audio guide focuses on it mainly as a work of art (describes the colours and patterns of the pills; it gives a precise description of the arrangement of the objects and photos; it uses the present simple to give the impression we are looking at the details).
– it mentions the significance ('It explores our approach to health in Britain today') but says very little about it; it just describes what the installation shows, not the significance of it.
– it says nothing about how it was produced.

LANGUAGE FOCUS Descriptive participles

> **Optional presentation**
> Books closed. To introduce the idea of passive participles, write this sentence on the board:
> – *The artist has arranged the tablets in patterns.*
> Then learners change this to a passive sentence:
> – *The tablets are* (or *have been*) *arranged in patterns.*
> Then write:
> – *There are 14,000 tablets, arranged in patterns.*
> This uses just the past participle (*which are* is left out)

3 a *Focus on passives and participles.* Look at sentence 1 together (*answer:* wrapped in).

Learners complete the other sentences.

b Learners check the answers in the script on p152.

> 1 sewn into
> 2 wrapped in
> 3 interspersed with (= alternating)
> 4 arranged in
> 5 intermingled with (= mixed together)

4 Learners add expressions to the sentences. Discuss the answers together. Possible answers:

> 1 She sat close to the fire, wrapped in a blanket. (or ... with a blanket wrapped round her)
> 2 The old houses in the street are interspersed with newer houses.
> 3 ... an ID card sewn into the lining of his jacket.
> 4 ... are now intermingled with other groups.
> 5 ... are arranged in a circle.

SPEAKING

5 a *Discussion.* Learners discuss the questions. Then ask what ideas they had. Alternatively, discuss the questions together with the class. You could ask follow-up questions, e.g.
– *How important do you think art is? What kind of art do think is worth spending money on? Think of examples of art in your town that is / isn't worth spending money on or going to see.*
– *If you went to a museum, what would you expect to see? Would you think an installation like 'From Cradle to Grave' would be worth looking at? Why do you think it is in a museum, not an art gallery?*

b *Preparation.* Learners choose something they have seen and make notes: it could be an exhibition, an art installation, a show, a sculpture, an urban space, a garden or a park. They should try to include participle expressions to make their description more precise.

Then learners think about their opinion of it and plan a few things to say.

Speaking. In turn, learners describe what they chose to the others and say what they think about it. If any of the others have also seen it they can add their comments; if they haven't they can ask further questions.

Feedback. Ask each group what they talked about and which things seemed the most worth seeing.

7.2

Goals: describe a process or experiment
discuss implications and significance
Core language:
LANGUAGE FOCUS   Describing processes and experiments

Mind over matter

SPEAKING and LISTENING

1 a Discuss the questions with the class, or let them discuss them in pairs or groups first. Focus on these words and expressions, which feature in the listening:
– *alert* = awake, quick to notice things.
– *cognitive abilities* = ability to think, process information, etc.
– *motor skills* = ability to do things automatically (e.g. movement, co-ordination).
– *jittery* = shaking because you are nervous.
– *placebo effect* = you think you've taken medicine, so you get better; but in fact you've only taken a sugar pill (a placebo).

2 *Listening for main idea.* Play recording **2.18**. Learners listen and answer the questions. Discuss the answers together. Possible answers (1–3):

> 1 it does you no harm (so the experiment is harmless); it's something most people drink and know the effects of; it's easy to set up.
> 2 it tested volunteers' cognitive abilities and motor skills; it asked them what they thought the effect of caffeine would be; it gave them de-caffeinated coffee (but pretended it was real coffee); it tested their cognitive abilities and motor skills again.
> 3 if you think you have drunk caffeine, it will have the effect you expect, even though you haven't drunk it. So the placebo effect works.

At this point, ask learners if they (or people they know) have any experiences of the placebo effect.

3 Ask how the images relate to the experiment. Possible answers:

> A a volunteer doing a test, probably of cognitive abilities
> B a coffee machine producing the coffee used in the experiment
> C paying snooker (or pool) illustrates motor skills

LANGUAGE FOCUS Describing processes and experiments

4 a *Focus on collocations.* Learners make collocations with two or three words.

Go through the answers by building up useful collocations on the board. Possible answers:

> devised an experiment / a test / tasks
> measured ability / performance
> tested ability / performance
> measured / assessed ability
> (there was) a significant correlation
> (people) report various effects of caffeine
> proved the placebo effect
> tested co-ordination skills

b *Speaking.* Learners practise summarising the experiment using the collocations until they feel they could talk about it effectively.

Feedback. Ask learners to tell you about the experiment, giving a sentence each round the class.

> **Alternative: Role-play**
> After practising in pairs, learners form new pairs. A takes the role of an interviewer and B takes the role of the scientist explaining the experiment.

 You could use photocopiable activity 7B on the Teacher's DVD-ROM at this point.

The 'nocebo' effect

READING

1 *Pre-reading.* Discuss the photos and establish that:
– Photo A shows a *voodoo doll*, which might be used by a *witch doctor* to cast a *spell* on someone (or put a *curse* on someone).
– Photo B shows an amulet (worn round your neck) to give you *protection* against the *evil eye* (or a curse).

You could ask learners if they have similar objects or customs in their own culture.

> **Note**
> Voodoo dolls were used in West Africa and some Caribbean countries. They could be used to put a curse on a person (e.g. by sticking pins in them, or burning them).
> Photo B shows a 'nazar stone'. These are common in Mediterranean countries and the Middle East (often sold to tourists). If someone envies you or your possessions, some people believe they may put the 'evil eye' on you (and so bring you misfortune). The stone protects against this.

2 a *Reading for main idea.* Learners read the article and think about the questions. Then discuss them together. Possible answers:

> 1 Yes.
> 2 Yes.
> 3 Yes, but not the main point of the article. (Patients may suffer harmful side effects if they are told to expect them.)
> 4 No. It mentions this, but not a serious point.
> 5 Yes (it hasn't been studied much).

b *Vocabulary focus.* Learners underline five words in the article.

Learners compare their words and discuss how useful they would be.

Feedback. Find out what words learners chose and which they felt would be useful. You could write the most useful words on the board and check that everyone knows what they mean.

c Learners find examples for each type. Discuss the examples together. Possible answers:

> 1 numerous documented instances; have established beyond doubt
> 2 the most remarkable thing
> 3 may be examples; are more likely to; it seems that; can produce; what we do know suggests; if it exists; may represent
> 4 may seem far-fetched

SPEAKING

3 a *Discussion.* Learners discuss the scenarios and give each one a ranking from 0 to 10.

Discuss the scenarios in turn and find out what ranking most learners gave each one. For each one, ask:
– whether anyone has had an experience of this kind.
– whether they think this was an example of the 'nocebo' effect or whether there were other factors involved.

b *Discussion.* Discuss the questions, or let learners discuss in pairs or groups first, then talk about them together.

> **Language note**
> *Placebo* is Latin for 'I will please'. *Nocebo* means 'I will harm', and so describes the opposite effect. It might be interesting to point this out to the class.

Unit 7 Health 77

7.3 Target activity: Global issues

Goals: discuss implications and significance
discuss an issue

Core language:
7.1 LANGUAGE FOCUS   Health problems and treatment
TASK LANGUAGE   Discussing issues

TASK LISTENING

1 a Look at the advert and discuss the questions. Possible answer:

> it shows a mosquito as a very large threat

2 *Pre-listening discussion.* Learners brainstorm what they know about malaria. They could write two lists: one of things they know, one of things they don't know or are not sure of.

Elicit quick feedback to establish what the class knows and doesn't know.

Learners read the fact sheet on p131. Go through the questions and establish what the answers are.

3 a *Listening for main idea.* Read through the questions, then play recording **2.19**. As the listening is quite long, you could pause after each main section to check answers to the questions that relate to it.

> 1 people see malaria as dangerous
> 2 people with no immunity (e.g. tourists); children, babies, pregnant women; poor people with no access to health care
> 3 expensive anti-malarial drugs; mosquito nets
> 4 in the short-term: mosquito nets, cheaper drugs in the long-term: vaccinations

b Discuss what the doctor sees as the most important issue (*answer*: education, changing people's attitudes).

TASK LANGUAGE Discussing issues

4 a Read through the sentences and ask learners what words they think go in the gaps.

Play recording **2.19** again. Learners listen and complete the sentences.

b Go through the answers and play the excerpts from recording **2.20** to check.

> 1 factor in this
> 2 a health issue
> 3 a question of
> 4 don't necessarily
> 5 a lot to do with
> 6 a big issue
> 7 the main problem
> 8 the only long-term solution
> 9 attitudes are changing

TASK PREPARATION

5 a Discuss the question together and bring out these points:
– It's an economic issue because it involves providing funds, providing infrastructure (roads, distribution systems, hospitals); also because it involves producing affordable drugs.
– It's a political issue because it involves dealing with governments, overcoming corruption, educating people and changing attitudes.

b Learners match the issues with the examples. Then discuss the answers together with learners giving reasons for their choice. Possible answers:

> 1 a social issue, a global issue, an educational issue
> 2 a global issue, an environmental issue, a moral issue, a political issue, an economic issue
> 3 a global issue, a cultural issue, an educational issue, a political issue
> 4 a health issue, a social issue, a moral issue
> 5 a health issue, a cultural issue, an economic issue

TASK

6 a Introduction. Before you start, agree on one of the issues in **5b** to discuss. You could ask the class to vote.

b *Group discussion.* Divide the class into groups (between three and five groups, depending on the size of the class). They discuss the issue in their group and try to agree on what they think the problems are and what they see as possible solutions. They could make brief notes.

7 *Panel discussion.* Groups choose one person to represent them on the panel. Conduct a panel discussion, with each speaker giving his / her group's point of view in turn and agreeing or disagreeing with what other speakers have said. After each speaker, open the discussion up for members of the audience to make comments or ask questions.

 You could use photocopiable activity 7C on the Teacher's DVD-ROM at this point.

7 Explore

Across cultures: Health campaigns

Goal: to make learners more aware of different attitudes towards health issues

1 a *Listening for main idea.* Look at the photo and read the questions. Ask what they think Percy might say about mosquito nets. Before you play the recording, explain that Percy's English is quite hard to follow, so learners should just try to catch in general what he is talking about. Play recording **2.21**. Learners listen for answers to the questions.

> 1 They are hot.
> 2 People leave them loose, so the mosquitoes get inside them.
> 3 Total house netting. It's a like a big tent round the room. It's cooler.

78   Unit 7 Health

b Read the sentences and find out if learners can remember (or guess) what words go in the gaps.

Play recording **2.21** again, pausing occasionally to check the answers.

> 1 poor   2 hot   3 attitude   4 World Health (= World Health Organisation)   5 distributed   6 set them up   7 hanging   8 covering   9 set it up   10 ventilation

c Discuss the variety of English Percy speaks. Establish that:
– he is a native speaker of English. You can tell this by his idiomatic use language e.g. *set them up*, *defeats the whole purpose, nooks and crannies* (= every corner); also that he speaks perfect grammatically correct English.
– he speaks a West African (Ghanaian) variety of English. Point out especially that it has a different rhythm from British English (much less difference between stressed and unstressed syllables, vowels not reduced, *-ing* pronounced as *-in*, *th* pronounced as *d*.
– he is in fact bilingual and also speaks a local Ghanaian language (Akan).

You could play the recording a third time and let learners follow in the script on p153.

2 a *Discussion: campaign adverts.* Look at the posters and discuss the questions. Bring out these points:
– A *message:* don't shake hands; instead of a handshake use an 'airshake'.
– B *message:* the sign says, in Nigerian pidgin English, 'Don't let malaria steal your child'.

b, c *Discussion: health issues.* Learners discuss the questions.

> **Optional preparation**
>
> To give this more focus, learners suggest diseases or health problems that are important and widely discussed in their country (e.g. diabetes, obesity, AIDS). Build these up on the board and use them as a basis for the group discussion.

Ask each group what health problems they talked about and what they said about campaigns and their effectiveness.

Keywords: *consist, include*

Goals: to describe what things consist of, comprise or include

Core language:
consist, comprise, include, involve, contain

> **Optional presentation**
>
> Give a few simple sentences with the verbs and ask learners what they think they are about, e.g.
> – It includes service (= a bill).
> – It contains liqueur chocolates (a box).
> – It consists of two rooms and a kitchen (an apartment).
> – It comprises 500 houses, two shops and a church (a village).
> Use this to focus on the meaning of the verbs.

1 a *Focus on verbs.* Learners read the examples and answer the questions. Use this to present the basic meanings of the highlighted words:
– X contains Y = it has Y inside it:
The jar contains pills.
– X comprises / consists of Y = it is made up of Y
The package comprises an mp3 player, a set of headphones, and a USB lead.
– X involves / includes Y = Y is part of it
Include is more often used for physical objects, *involve* for activities:
The bill includes 17% VAT.
My job involves being polite to customers.

> **Language note**
>
> Instead of *comprises*, we can also say *is comprised of*. This has the same meaning.

b Learners choose the correct verb.

> 1 include = it isn't part of it (a jar would contain pills)
> 2 involved (an activity = work was part of it)
> 3 contains (photos appear in the installation)

2 a Learners think of continuations for the sentences.

Discuss possible answers together. Try to elicit more than one suggestion for each.

b As you go through each answer, play recording **2.22** to check and establish what the news report is about.

> 1 the problem of how to attract women to motor racing events, so that can market their cars to them
> 2 changes in how people travel
> 3 part of a travel feature about Havana, Cuba.
> 4 problems with expanding an airport.
> 5 new regulations for travellers to the US.

3 a *Writing sentences from notes.* Learners write sentences based on the notes.

> **Optional lead-in**
>
> Books closed. Write the first two sets of notes on the board. Ask the class how you might expand them into complete sentences using verbs from **1a**, and write them on the board. Then learners do the rest of the exercise.

b Discuss the answers together. Then play recording **2.23** to check and compare answers.

c *Role-play: selling a product.* Look together at photos A–C and establish what the products are (breakfast cereal; a skiing holiday package; a computer package). Discuss how you might use *contain* or *include* to describe the products, and brainstorm ideas from the class. Possible answers:

> A   *It contains only organic fruit and nuts.*
>   *It contains added fibre and minerals.*
>   *Each packet contains a children's toy.*
> B   *It includes a week's free ski pass.*
>   *It includes a full breakfast and evening meal.*
> C   *It includes a three-year guarantee.*
>   *It includes thousands of apps.*

Together, learners choose one of the products and practise 'selling' it. They should work out together what they might say to make it appealing.

  Learners form new pairs. In turn, they try to 'sell' their product to their new partner.

  Round-up. Ask learners whether they agreed to buy their partner's product, and why / why not.

d Ask learners what verbs in their own language are equivalent to those in this section. The aim of this to give learners insight into differences between English and their own language.

Explore speaking

Goals: take turns in a discussion
give opinions in an extended conversation

Core language:
Ways of agreeing and disagreeing
Ways of interrupting and 'turn taking'

1 Look at the cartoon and discuss the questions. Try to elicit these points:
   – The old lady sees 'taking turns' as a nice thing to do, but the man is talking about children fighting.
   – Parents encourage their children to take turns playing with toys, playing on swings, using a computer, etc., because it helps then learn to be less selfish.
   – Other situations when you take turns: driving, taking food for yourself at meals, using a cash machine (you wait your turn).
   – You also 'take turns' in conversation: you wait until the other speaker pauses or has finished before speaking or replying.
   – the opposite is *interrupting*.

   Tell the class that the focus of this lesson is on ways to interrupt politely and take turns in a conversation.

2 a *Reading for gist*. Give time for learners to quickly read the conversations. They should read for general idea, not try to understand the details.

   Ask what the people are talking about (*answer: a recent ban on smoking in cafés, bars and restaurants. They disagree about whether it has been effective*).

  b *Focus on language strategies*. To show what to do, look at the first conversation and consider the first strategy together (*find a way to interrupt and stop A talking*). Learners suggest things the speaker might say, and build these up on the board, e.g.:
   – *Just a minute.*
   – *Yes, but ...*
   – *No, that's not true.*
   – *Stop, I want to say something.*
   – *Wait a minute.*

   Learners try out the remarks to see which sounds best and would be most successful (*answer: probably Just a minute* or *Wait a minute*, because they are polite, but effectively signal that you want to interrupt).

   Learners discuss the other strategies in the same way. They should note down the remarks they think would be successful in each case.

  c *Listening to check*. Taking each strategy in turn, ask groups for their ideas, then play recording **2.24** of the conversation to check.

   Discuss how effective the speakers were and why they interrupt each other. Ask learners if they would interrupt in this way themselves. This may lead into a discussion of cultural differences in 'turn-taking'.

3   Learners choose an issue to talk about (they can either use the same issue for all three conversations, or they can discuss a different issue each time). In their group, they practise turn-taking, following the instructions.

4 Groups choose a different topic. In turn, they have discussion about it, with the rest of the class listening. After each conversation, ask the others to comment on how successfully the group took turns.

Alternative
Instead of a spontaneous discussion, each group repeats one of their rehearsed conversations in front of the class.

7 Look again

GRAMMAR Passives and participles

Optional presentation
Books closed. Write the examples on the board, with the highlighted items gapped out. Ask if learners can complete the gaps, and use this as a way to focus on the passive and participle forms.

1 Look at the examples. Learners find other examples in the script.

drawn from	are arranged in
wrapped in	intermingled with
unwrapped	are indicated by
sewn into	are placed alongside
taken from	is rolled up

2 a   Learners discuss what they think each example is about.

  b Learners match the expressions with photos 1–4.

  c Go through the answers and ask what each example in **2a** is about. Then play recording **2.25** to check.

a 3 a parking ticket   b 1 CDs
c 2 a calendar   d 4 houses

  d Elicit synonyms for each participle. Possible answers:

a taped, placed
b piled, heaped
c stuck, glued, nailed, taped
d scattered, built, spaced

3 Elicit the participle forms.
     /   Learners add participles to the sentences.

1 parked   2 buried   3 hidden   4 stuck
5 arranged   6 gathered

4 a To introduce the activity, write a sentence of your own with the participle missing, and find out if learners can tell you what it is.

     Together, pairs write two or three sentences.

80   Unit 7 Health

b Learners form new pairs. They show each other their sentences and guess the missing participle.

> **Alternative**
>
> Do this stage with the whole class. Learners read out their sentences in turn and other learners guess the missing participle.

GRAMMAR Referencing and substitution

5 a Learners cover **5b**. Look at each example in **5a** in turn and ask what it refers to.

> 1 malaria
> 2 the 'Cradle to Grave' installation
> 3 providing mosquito nets
> 4 a placebo effect experiment
> 5 the witch doctor's curse

b Point out that the extracts in **5b** are the sentence before those in **5a**. Learners match them together.

> 1d 2e 3a 4c 5b

6 a Point out that the highlighted words all refer back to another word or an idea, and are used to avoid unnecessary repetition. Look at each one in turn, and establish what word it replaces.

> 1 killed
> 2 the man and the woman
> 3 providing good mosquito nets
> 4 a test
> 5 when he was in hospital

b Use the question to establish common words used to refer back to previous words or ideas:
– *a* + noun → *one*
– plural noun or uncountable noun → *some*
– *the* + noun → *it*, *him*, *her*
– *the* + plural noun → *they*, *them*
– main verb → *do* / *did*
– complete idea → *this*, *which*
– time phrase → *then*

You could elicit these by giving examples, e.g.
– *I'm making coffee. Do you want some?*

> **Language note**
>
> For further examples, see Grammar Reference, p143.

7 a 👤 / 👥 Learners rewrite the conversation.

b Discuss the answers together. Possible answers:

> A ...
> B ...
> A Oh, I hope you don't have to have one ... for your sake.
> B I hope I don't have to, too!
> A Well, if not, what's the other option?
> B I don't know. I think convalescence is much longer. I have to go the clinic tomorrow and wait there all morning for tests and then he'll tell me the results.

VOCABULARY Tests

8 a Ask what kinds of test the people did in the caffeine experiment (*possible answers:* a co-ordination test, a motor skills test, a cognitive test, a performance test).

Look at the types of test in the box and discuss the questions. Possible answers:

> placement test: *before starting a course, to find out if you are suitable and what class you should be in*
> eye test: *to find out if your eyes are healthy, or if you need glasses*
> literacy test: *children going to school, to find out how well they read and write*
> driving test: *so that you can drive*
> IQ test: *out of interest, or before getting a job, to find out how intelligent you are*
> typing test: *to get a job as a typist or computer operator*
> hearing test: *to find out how well you can hear*
> a DNA test: *a suspected criminal, to find out if you committed a crime*
> personality test: *probably for fun (in a magazine), to find out what kind of person you are.*

b Discuss the questions.

> – you usually 'do' / 'take' a test where you are more active (e.g. you write something, drive a car): placement, driving, literacy, IQ, typing, personality
> – we usually use 'have' with a test where you are more passive (someone does things to you): eye, hearing, DNA
> – other possible verbs: take part in, pass, fail, get through, volunteer for; undergo, be given

c 👥 Learners note down the tests that they have done or had. They tell their partner about them and ask or answer further questions.

Feedback. Ask a few learners which tests both they and their partner have done.

VOCABULARY All-purpose nouns

> **Optional lead-in**
>
> To introduce the idea of all-purpose nouns, ask learners to imagine they overhear this remark: *I think it's a really important issue.*
> Discuss what it might be about, and establish that *issue* is an 'all-purpose' word that can be used in a wide range of contexts.

9 👤 / 👥 Learners read the extract and identify the all-purpose nouns.

> 1 qualities
> 2 questions
> 3 aspects
> 4 thing
> 5 concern
> 6 factor

Discuss what other words could be used instead of each noun.

> 1 features, characteristics
> 2 issues, decisions
> 3 features (of), events (in), developments (in)
> 4 point, conclusion
> 5 issue, factor, topic
> 6 issue

Unit 7 Health 81

10 a 👤/👥 Learners choose the best noun.

b Go through the answers. Learners give reasons for their choice and suggest other possible nouns.

> 1 characteristic; quality
> 2 approach; technique
> 3 process; system
> 4 question
> 5 elements; features

Optional exercise

Write these prompts on the board.
– A significant issue affecting us today is …
– A basic problem we have to solve is …
– … is one of the major factors to becoming a …
– … is a key quality to have if you want to …

👤 Learners choose a topic and write a sentence about it using one of the prompts.

👥/👥👥 Learners talk about their topic, including the sentence they wrote and get responses from other learners.

VOCABULARY Health problems and treatments

11 a *Vocabulary review.* Learners close their books. Learners tell you words from the unit referring to illnesses and treatments. Write them on the board.

Alternative

Learners brainstorm words in pairs and write them down.

b 👥/👥👥 *Focus on contexts.* Learners discuss who or what the pronouns refer to. Then discuss this together.

> 1 a wound or injury   2 a patient   3 a patient
> 4 a surgeon, a patient   5 a patient   6 an illness / disease
> 7 a doctor, a patient   8 a doctor, medicine

c *Focus on verbs.* Discuss the questions together.

> 1 heal (refers to a wound)
>   convalesce (= slowly recover from an illness), recover
>   cure (= make it better)
> 2 recover from (an illness), operate on (someone)
> 3 healing, convalescence, recovery, operation, cure,
>   treatment, prescription
>   ('undergo' has no noun form)
> 4 a The healing (or healing process) is taking a long time.
>   b She's still undergoing convalescence. (She's still a
>   convalescent)
>   c I'm sure he'll make a good recovery.
>   d I decided to give him an operation.
>   e It will be necessary to undergo heart surgery.
>   f Unfortunately there's no cure for it.
>   g I gave her treatment for shock.
>   h She wrote (or gave) me a prescription for
>   something called Antiflaxin.

12 a *Listening.* Play each conversation in turn from recording **2.26**. Learners listen and mark the words from **11** they hear. Then elicit other health and treatment words and write them on the board.

> 1 treat
>   Other words: attack, pain; painkillers, prescription
>   drugs
> 2 recovery
>   Other words: high temperature, symptoms, sore
>   throat, cough, ache, got ill; aspirin, paracetamol,
>   antibiotics, vitamins
> 3 convalescence, treatment
>   Other words: agony; stay in bed, stretching

b Play recording **2.26** again and pick up on any words that were missed before. Then discuss the questions.

> 1 migraine headache (lie down, nerves, darkened
>   room). She's OK at the moment.
> 2 'flu (temperature, cough, sore throat; but not worth
>   getting antibiotics). He's still ill.
> 3 slipped disc (vertebra) (agony, prostrate, no
>   treatment, posture, stretching). He's recovered.

Self-assessment

To help focus learners on the self-assessment, you could read it through, giving a few examples of the language they have leaned in each section (or asking learners to tell you). Then ask them to circle a number on each line.

Unit 7 Extra activities on the Teacher's DVD-ROM

Printable worksheets, activity instructions and answer keys are on your Teacher's DVD-ROM.

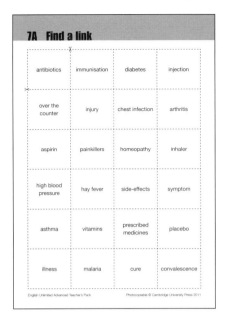

7A Find a link

Activity type: Speaking – Card game – Small groups

Aim: To make links between vocabulary items in the unit.

Language: Health problems and treatment – Coursebook p66 – Vocabulary

Preparation: Make one copy of the worksheet for each group. Cut into 20 individual cards.

Time: 15–20 minutes

7B Experiments in irrationality

Activity type: Speaking and reading – Prediction and jigsaw reading – Pairs

Aim: To describe and comment on experiments and their implications

Language: Describing processes and experiments – Coursebook p68 – Vocabulary

Preparation: Make one copy of worksheet A for each learner in half the class and one copy of worksheet B for each student in the other half.

Time: 30–40 minutes

7C Health issues

Activity type: Speaking – Discussion task – Groups of three

Aim: To discuss possible solutions to global health issues

Language: Discussing issues – Coursebook p70 – Target activity

Preparation: Make one copy of the worksheet for each group.

Time: 20–30 minutes

Unit 7 Self-study Pack

In the Workbook
Unit 7 of the *English Unlimited Advanced Self-study Pack Workbook* offers additional ways to practise the vocabulary and grammar taught in the Coursebook. There are also activities which build reading and writing skills, and a whole page of tasks to use with the DVD-ROM video, giving your learners the opportunity to hear and react to spoken English.

- **Vocabulary:** Health problems and treatment; Tests, processes and experiments; *consist, include*; All-purpose nouns
- **Grammar:** Passives and participles; Referencing and substitution
- **Explore writing:** Summarising information
- **DVD-ROM Extra:** Current affairs – *Raw foodists*

On the DVD-ROM
Unit 7 of the *English Unlimited Advanced Self-study Pack DVD-ROM* contains interactive games and activities for your learners to practise and improve their vocabulary, grammar and pronunciation, and also their speaking and listening. It also contains video material (with the possibility for learners to record themselves) to use with the *Workbook*.

- **Vocabulary and grammar:** Extra practice of the Coursebook language and Keywords
- **Explore listening:** An experiment
- **Explore speaking:** Opinions
- **Video:** Current affairs – *Raw foodists*

Unit 7 Health 83

8 Brand awareness

8.1

Goals: discuss brands
describe effects and influences
talk about the image and qualities of products

Core language:
LANGUAGE FOCUS   Effects and influences
LANGUAGE FOCUS   Image and qualities

Brands

LISTENING

1   a   Learners discuss the questions.

   b   Discuss the adverts together and focus on these points:

> 1 relaxed elegance, confidence, feeling at ease
> 2 elegance, power, dynamic woman in control

2   *Listening for main idea.* Read through the questions. Ask learners to predict what the speaker might say in answer to each question. Play recording **2.27**. Learners listen and answer the questions.

> 1 Very – she thinks brands are important.
> 2 Top designer labels: *they define you as belonging to a group.*
> Individuality and belonging: *you are an individual (because you choose the colour and cut) but you also belong to a family.*
> 3 He thinks brands pretend to make you different, but they don't really – so it's a lie.
> 4 (Possible answer) She probably wears fashionable clothes, is interested in fashion, takes care over her style and appearance, and is quite conventional (she doesn't question society or values).

LANGUAGE FOCUS Effects and influences

3   a   Learners complete the gaps, either from what they remember or from what they think could go in each gap.

   b   Go through the answers together. After discussing each sentence, play recording **2.28** to check.

> 1 make any difference
> 2 make people
> 3 be enhanced
> 4 define
> 5 has a positive effect
> 6 not influenced

   c   Learners read through the sentences and mark those they agree or disagree with.

   Discuss the sentences together and focus on these points:
   – how learners feel about wearing brands, and whether it is important to them to buy particular brands.
   – why people attach so much importance to brands and whether this is good or not.
   – the influence of adverts and the images they present.
   – whether the clothes you wear affect your attitude to life or personality, and if so, in what way.

Brand images

LANGUAGE FOCUS Image and qualities

1   a   Tell the class they will hear people talking about the images they associate with particular brands. Look at the word clouds and discuss the questions. Check the meaning of:
   – *retro* (adj.) = using an earlier style (e.g. from the 1960s or the 1920s).
   – *trendy* = fashionable, following the latest trends. The word is used about people, clothes and also places where trendy people (go e.g. *a trendy restaurant*).

   b   Play recording **2.29** which will give more clues as to what the brands might be.

> 1 Nike sportswear   2 Sony   3 The Mini (car)

   c   Learners decide which are adjectives and which are nouns.

   Discuss answers together and check learners know the noun forms of the adjectives and the adjective forms of the nouns (e.g. *reliable – reliability; success – successful*). Write any difficult pairs on the board.

> **Nouns:**
> A sport, ambition, comfort; (keeping fit)
> B success, innovation, reliability, perfection, sound quality
> C good design
> **Adjectives:**
> A trendy, fashionable
> B innovative
> C fast, dynamic, fun, speedy, retro, small

   d   *Listening.* Play recording **2.29** again, pausing after each speaker so that learners can note down other expressions.

   Go through the expressions together. Possible answers:

> 1 you look good, striving for something, getting to the top
> 2 easy to park, the perfect travelling companion, enjoy yourself
> 3 top quality, executive lifestyle, premier (= excellent, the best), perfect technology

   Ask which expressions refer to the product and which to lifestyle.

> **Optional discussion**
>
> Ask learners which of the qualities are actually true of the product or the people who buy it (e.g. *Do Sony products really have perfect technology? Are they bought mainly by executives? Does Nike sportswear make you look good? Does it help you get to the top?*).

2   a   Learners think of a brand and list words and expressions they associate with it.

   b   Learners read out their list without mentioning the brand. The others try to identify the brand.

 You could use photocopiable activity 8A on the Teacher's DVD-ROM at this point.

SPEAKING

3 a *Introduction.* Discuss what images soft drinks adverts usually present. Brainstorm a list of words and expressions and write them on the board.

b *Group discussion (1).* Divide the class into groups of three or six and give each group a letter: A, B or C. They look at their own adverts on page 132 and discuss questions 1–3.

Group discussion (2). Learners form new groups, so that each group has at least one A, one B and one C learner within it. They discuss questions 1–6 in relation to their own adverts.

Round-up. Ask a learner from each group to summarise what they said.

8.2

Goals: talk about advertising and marketing
describe an advert
Core language:
LANGUAGE FOCUS   Marketing words

Viral ads

READING

1 Learners cover the article or close their books. Ask if learners know what a viral ad is, or (if they don't) what they imagine it might be. If learners know about viral ads, ask them to give examples, but avoid talking about the ad which appears on p79.

2 a *Reading for main idea.* Learners read the article and find out why marketing companies are excited about viral ads.

Discuss the answer together. Point out that:
– it's an ideal way to market a product; people do the marketing for you by sending the clip to their friends.
– this enables companies to reach millions of customers without spending any money.

> **Optional check**
> If learners did not know before, check that they now understand what a viral ad is.

b *Focus on language.* Discuss question 1 together and establish that:
– these ads are 'viral' in the sense that they spread in the same way as a virus and people can 'catch' them from each other.
– diseases are infectious, but so are positive things (e.g. ideas, enthusiasm, sense of humour), so *infectious* also implies something that people can't resist.

For question 2, learners cover the article. Elicit adjectives and write them on the board, then let learners look at the article to find others.

> *short; compelling (= you have to watch it)*
> *edgy (= has a sharp edge, so it's interesting)*
> *surprising; original; emotional.*
> *These qualities all make people want to watch the ad*

For question 3, learners suggest an image that comes to mind for each word. Use this to focus on the precise meaning. Possible answers:

> a *like pulling apart wool or string (= pull apart)*
> b *like a new plant (= appeared unexpectedly)*
> c *like sowing seeds in different places (positioning them on different sites, e.g. YouTube)*
> d *like putting a pipe (or tap) into a spring to get water (= makes use of)*
> e *like launching a ship, a rocket (= a dramatic start)*
> f *like putting your arms round someone (= make it their own)*
> g *like a rocket going to the stars; very high (= 'stellar' is the adjective from 'star')*

c Discuss the question together.

> *The user decides whether to send it on to someone else or tell someone about it.*

LANGUAGE FOCUS Marketing words

3 *Focus on vocabulary.* Read through the questions and check that learners understand the highlighted items. Focus especially on:
– *sales pitch* = what a salesperson says to advertise their product to a buyer.
– *target audience* = the people their product is aimed at.
– *competitors* = the people going against them.

 Discussion. Learners discuss the questions.

Round-up. Talk about the questions together.

> You could use photocopiable activity 8B on the Teacher's DVD-ROM at this point.

A video clip

LISTENING

1 *Pre-listening.* Look at the video stills and discuss what they show. Ask further questions to prompt ideas, e.g. *What do you think is in the bottles? Why is it shooting into the air? How would you achieve this? Why are the men wearing lab coats?*

> **Note**
> Some learners may know about this video clip. If so, they should keep quiet during this phase.

2 a *Listening for main idea.* Play recording **2.30** and establish what it shows (an experiment in putting peppermint sweets into a bottle of cola). Discuss the questions.

> 1 50 million people watched it; people tried the experiment and made their own videos; people discussed it.
> 2 It was started for fun and general interest, not in order to sell the products. The Coca-Cola company had nothing to do with it.
> 3 It's edgy, surprising, original; not really emotional (though it's amusing). It taps into popular culture; the user is in control

b Ask how the speaker uses the words and check what they mean. Alternatively, learners could discuss these in pairs first. Possible answers:

> 1 The video wasn't *planned*
> 2 It *fizzes* up
> 3 It shoots out like a *geyser* (= a hot spring)
> 4 The second video was like a *firework display*
> 5 50 million people watched it *globally*
> 6 This included *user-generated* videos (= people made their own)
> 7 People contributed their own *eruption videos* (= videos showing coke shooting out of bottles)
> 8 There was a lot of *hype* (= publicity)
> 9 People discussed whether it was *lethal* to drink Diet Coke and Mentos (= it would kill you)
> 10 Coca-Cola and Mentos got a lot of *publicity*

c Play recording **2.30** again to check.

3 Learners practise telling each other about the video, using the words in **2b**.

Optional role-play

Give learners letters, A and B. B takes the role of someone who doesn't know about the video. A describes it and B asks questions.

---

4 Discuss the quote with the class. Consider these questions:
– *In what sense do we not understand the Internet?*
– *How are viral videos examples of this?*
– *In what ways is the Internet 'an experiment in anarchy'?*
– *Is this a good thing, or does it need to be controlled?*
– *Is it possible to control it?*

SPEAKING

5 *Preparation.* Learners choose an advert and prepare to talk about. They could make brief notes.

Learners tell each other about the advert they chose.

Round-up. Ask each group to choose their 'best' advert. One learner from the group describes it to the class.

Alternative: Preparation in pairs

Pairs choose an advert together and practise describing it. Then learners form groups, but with the members of each pair working in a different group. To do this, you could give learners letters, A or B – then some groups have only A learners and some have only Bs.

8.3 Target activity: Sell a product

Goals: talk about the image and qualities of products
talk about advertising and marketing
pass on detailed information

Core language:

8.1 LANGUAGE FOCUS	Image and qualities
8.2 LANGUAGE FOCUS	Marketing words
TASK LANGUAGE	Describing technology

TASK READING

1 Look at the photo and get ideas about how the car might work. You could also elicit a series of questions to ask about the AIRpod and write them on the board.

Talk about other alternatives to petrol-driven cars. Find out what learners know about them and why they might or might not be successful. These could include:
– cars using bio-fuels.
– electric vehicles and 'hybrids' (petrol-driven cars that can switch to electricity).
– gas-driven cars.
– cars using fuel cells or hydrogen.

2 a *Reading for main idea.* Learners read the article. When they have finished, discuss briefly what they found out about the AIRpod. If you wrote questions on the board, identify which of them are answered by the article.

b Ask what the advantages of air-powered cars are.

> – They produce fewer carbon emissions than a normal car.
> – They are cheaper to buy than electric cars.
> – They don't need expensive batteries.
> – They are quicker to recharge.

TASK LANGUAGE Describing technology

3 a Learners write the adjectives in three lists: positive, negative and neutral. When they have finished, they could compare answers with a partner.

Positive	Negative	Neutral
state-of-the-art	polluting	electric
efficient	expensive	conventional
superior	impractical	
	unproven	
	unreliable	

b Learners think of other adjectives to describe the AIRpod. Go through the answers together, building up adjectives on the board. Possible answers:

> *compact, fun, up-to-date, energy-saving, well-designed, uncomfortable, basic, slow, cramped, improbable, unrealistic, unsafe*

TASK

4 a *Reading and note-taking.* Tell learners they are going to prepare a marketing campaign for the AIRpod. Give each learner a letter, A or B. Learners read their own information about the AIRpod and note down features they think would be good selling points.

b *Discussion.* Learners work in A/B pairs. They tell each other the points they noted down and together prepare a marketing campaign, following the instructions in **4b**.

5   *Presentation.* In turn, pairs present their ideas to the class and deal with any questions or comments.

   Round-up. Discuss which of the ideas learners think are:
   – the most persuasive.
   – the most original.
   – the most visually appealing.
   – the most amusing.

8 Explore

Across cultures: Megabrands

Goal: to make learners aware of different attitudes to international brand names

Core language:
lifestyle, product, range

1 a *Books closed.* Write *Megabrand* on the board and ask the class what they think it might mean (= huge brands that operate internationally and produce different types of product). Ask learners to think of names of any companies they think fit this category. Discuss how companies might sell ideas as well as products. To focus on this, refer to the examples in lesson 8.1, e.g. ask what products Nike sells (clothing, sports shoes) and what lifestyle ideas it sells (fitness, sporting ability, success).

   b *Reading for main idea.* Read through the questions, then read the quotes.

   Discuss the questions together. Possible answers:

   > 1 Companies have moved from selling a product to selling a lifestyle idea.
   > 2 Coca-Cola: *youth lifestyle*
   >   Walt Disney: *the American dream*
   >   Nike: *athletic ability*
   > 3 Successful companies used to sell a single type of product, but now sell a whole range.

2 *Discussion.* Learners discuss the questions. To make this more focused, brainstorm the names of international brands that are sold in the learners' own country and write them on the board. Learners then refer to these brands in their discussion.

   Round-up. Ask different pairs or groups to tell you one thing they talked about.

3 a *Discussion.* Read through the opinion. Then learners mark their position on the line.

   b *Mingling activity.* Learners find someone who has a similar opinion, and discuss reasons for their opinion.

   c Learners find a new partner who doesn't agree with their point of view, and continue the discussion.

Keywords: *effect, affect*

Goal: to use *effect* and *affect* to describe influences

Core language:
effect, affect

1 *Focus on 'effect', 'affect'.* Read the examples and discuss the questions. Establish that:

   1 *affect* is a verb, *effect* (in the same sense) is a noun, so we can say:
      – It *affected* me.   – It *had an effect* on me.
   2 you say *the effect of* (something) and *have an effect on* (something).
   3 the adjective form is *effective*. You can also say *ineffective* (= not effective) and *ineffectual* (about people who are not good at getting results).

   > **Language note**
   > *Effect* also exists as a verb, but with a different meaning (= put into effect, bring about):
   > – *The government are trying to effect changes in the constitution.*
   > It is used in more formal (mainly written) styles.

2 a *Focus on verb collocations.* Learners complete the sentences.

   b Go through the answers together, then play recording **2.31** to check what the news reports are about.

   > 1 come into effect (combating street violence)
   > 2 take effect (the effect of subliminal advertising)
   > 3 produce a negative effect (relationship between lifestyle and health)
   > 4 reduce the effects (the effects of a medicine)

3 a *Focus on adjective / adverb collocations.* Ask which adjectives would change the meaning and how.

   > major, profound, great, important (similar meaning to 'significant')
   > positive (= good)
   > dramatic (= it changed it suddenly)
   > devastating (= it did a lot of harm)
   > lasting (= it continued for a long time)

   b Learners try saying the words as adverbs.

   > We could use: significantly, profoundly, dramatically, greatly.
   > The others are either impossible or unlikely.

4 a *Speaking.* Read through the questions and elicit ideas from the class. Focus on any difficult items.

   > 1 soft music, the sea, herbal tea (= makes you feel calm)
   > 2 pesticides in the soil, chemicals in your body (= slowly increasing, adding together)
   > 3 a new idea, an interesting conversation, a cup of coffee (= gives you new energy)
   > 4 alcohol, working too hard, eating junk food (= it's harmful)
   > 5 a good bus service, cycle tracks, a good local shop (= it improves it)
   > 6 electricity prices, diseases (= a greater effect than on richer people)
   > 7 pesticides, pollution, building motorways (= a negative effect)
   > 8 news of someone's death, a war (= it makes you very upset or causes great damage)
   > 9 a cup of coffee, a piece of news (= it happens instantly)
   > 10 an agreement about climate change, a world war (= it affects the world in many ways and for a long time)

Unit 8 Brand awareness   87

b 👥 Learners choose items in **4a** and say what things have these effects on them.

> **Alternative**
> Let learners work through the questions in pairs first (they may not be able to answer all of them). Then talk about them together and present any difficult items.

To introduce the items in question 2, tell the class about something that had a major effect on your life, someone who affected you positively, and something or someone you think is effective. Get learners to ask you further questions.

In turn, learners talk about the topics in question 2 in the same way.

5   Learners match the expressions with the images. Go through the items together and discuss how they would be used.

> A greenhouse effect (= carbon emissions in the atmosphere prevent heat from escaping, leading to global warming)
> B domino effect (one event triggers another, then another ...)
> C placebo effect (see Unit 7)
> D snowball effect (a process which develops in size or importance, like a snowball picking up snow)
> E butterfly effect (an insignificant event has an effect which leads eventually to a major change)
> F ripple effect (something happens and it gradually affects more and more people, like ripples spreading out on a lake)

Explore writing

Goal: use advertising language
Core language:
descriptive vocabulary

1   a   Look at photos A–C and ask learners what they can identify about the Tate Modern (e.g. it's an art gallery by the river in London; it's a converted power station; it's got great views of the city; it's got modern restaurants).

Reading for general idea. Learners read the introduction and the captions and match them with the photos.

> 1 B (mural).
> 2 A (glass walls, view of the skyline).
> 3 C (impressive, balconies).

b   Discuss which rooms would be suitable for each event. Expected answers:

> 1 the East Room (good views, natural light)
> 2 the Members' Room (balconies, good for outdoor evening receptions)
> 3 the restaurant (works of art, evening views; the East Room has an 'intimate setting', so is not so suitable for a large dinner)

2   a   👥 *Focus on style.* Learners work through the questions. Discuss the answers together. Possible answers (alternative words in brackets):

> 1 representing London (significant, well-known)
> 2 scenery at the back of a stage in the theatre (background)
> 3 a wonderful uninterrupted view (view)
> 4 proudly presenting (having, featuring)
> 5 smooth and vertical, like a cliff (straight, vertical)
> 6 surrounded by light as if by water (full of)
> 7 better than any other (wonderful)

Discuss why these words are used and focus on these points:
– they exaggerate the good qualities of the venues, emphasising their positive points.
– they give the impression the writer is very enthusiastic and loves the rooms, so it makes the writing more persuasive.

b   Learners find answers to the questions, then discuss them with a partner.

Discuss the questions together. Bring out these points:
1   there are more adjectives because the captions are static and descriptive (focusing on features and views, rather than events).
2   most of the verbs are passive, reinforcing the feeling of static description (focus on the place and atmosphere, not on what people do). The active verbs are similar in meaning and not very 'active': *offer*, *provide* (simply saying what there is).
3   *iconic*, *best-loved*, *unparalleled*, *dramatic*, *versatile*, *impressive*, *exclusive*, *uninterrupted*, *unique*: these make the description positive and persuasive.

c   Discuss the last question together. Establish that the writer portrays an evening at the venue as a wonderful, unforgettable experience.

3   *Group writing activity.* To introduce the writing activity, quickly summarise the features you looked at:
– descriptive, positive adjectives rather than verbs.
– passive rather than active verbs.
– verbs conveying what is available: *offer*, *provide*.
– words which have a dramatic effect (*iconic*, *sheer*, *unrivalled*).

👥 Learners choose a suitable venue and plan a description together.

They choose a 'secretary' to write the description, but they all contribute ideas. As they do this, go round checking and giving help. Make sure learners are choosing positive, persuasive language that presents their venue in the best possible light.

One person from each group goes to the next group and tries to 'sell' their venue.

Round-up. Ask each group if they decided to use the venue and why or why not.

8 Look again

GRAMMAR Measuring differences

1 a Read through the examples. Then elicit sentences using the expressions. Possible answers:

> *Air-powered cars take much less time to recharge.*
> *Electric cars take several hours longer to recharge.*
> *Electric cars take about 150 times as long to recharge.*

Alternative lead-in
Books closed. Write on the board:
  Recharging time
  Air-powered cars: 2 mins. Electric cars: 5 hrs.
Elicit sentences to express the difference. Prompt answers by writing expressions:
  a fraction   much less   several hours   150 times
Then open books and do **1b**.

b Learners continue the sentences to make a comparison between the two types of car. Focus on what word follows each expression.

> *Air-powered cars take much less time to recharge <u>than</u> electric cars.*
> *Electric cars take several hours longer to recharge <u>than</u> air-powered cars.*
> *Electric cars take about 150 times <u>as</u> long to recharge as air-powered cars.*
> *Air-powered cars cost a fraction <u>of</u> the price of electric cars.*
> *Air-powered cars take a fraction of the time to recharge <u>that</u> electric cars do.*

c Learners try making comparisons in different ways. They could also choose one sentence to write for each example. Possible answers:

> 1 *Vegetable oil is only a quarter of the price of extra virgin olive oil.*
> 2 *Our new flat is twice the size of the one we had before.*
> 3 *We live more than twice as far away from the university as we did before.*
> 4 *She looks at least 10 years younger than she actually is.*
> 5 *He managed to buy the painting for a tenth of its real value.*
> 6 *Only a fraction of the homes which were burgled last year had burglar alarms.*
> 7 *The average British school child spends 8 hours more every week watching TV than at school.*

GRAMMAR *whatever*

Optional lead-in
Books closed. Write *whatever* on the board. Learners suggest examples using the word. Ask what the word means in each case.
Then open books and look at the examples.

2 a Read through the examples and discuss what *whatever* means in each one. You could give other related examples of each one.

> 1 = it doesn't matter what your journey is.
> Other examples:
> *Whatever the time, he's happy to help.*
> *Whatever you want to buy, you can find it in Dubai.*
> 2 = and so on, or other things like that (a way of being vague)
> Other example:
> *Bring a coat or a jacket, or whatever (= something warm)*
> 3 = It doesn't matter what people tell you ..., In spite of what people tell you ...
> Other examples:
> *Whatever people think, ...*
> *Whatever you may say, ...*

b Learners match the expressions with their meanings.

> 1c   2a   3f   4e   5d   6b

c *Focus on intonation.* Play recording **2.32**, pausing after each remark to establish what feeling the speaker is expressing. Then learners practise saying them in the same way.

> 1 emphatic   2 emphatic   3 disbelief   4 lack of interest
> 5 agreeing unwillingly   6 lack of interest

3 a Books closed. Elicit the words (you could give prompts, e.g. *it doesn't matter when* → *whenever*) and write them on the board.

Learners suggest possible types of advert to go with each slogan, and say how it might continue. Possible answers:

> 1 shoes: *They will keep you dry, whatever the weather.*
> 2 a snack: *Whatever the time, it's time for a Lite Bite.*
> 3 perfume: *Wherever you go, Passion goes with you.*
> 4 chocolates: *The perfect gift, whatever the occasion.*
> 5 car: *Whoever you're with, they'll enjoy the new CX5.*
> 6 online bookshop: *Whatever you like to read, we've got it.*

b Learners choose a photo from A–D and write a caption to go with it.

c In turn, learners read out their caption. The others identify the photo.

VOCABULARY Multi-word expressions

4 a Look at the sentences and establish these points:
  – they function as adjectives (qualifying the nouns *backdrop* and *car*).
  – because the expressions are run together to make a single adjective, the individual words are linked by hyphens.

b Compare the highlighted examples and establish that:
  – *out of the blue* is an expression in its own right (functioning as an adverb), so the words are separate.
  – *out-of-the-blue* is a single adjective, so the words are joined with hyphens.

Unit 8 Brand awareness   89

c 👥 / 👥👥 Learners discuss what the expressions mean. Discuss the answers together.

> 1 = a unique opportunity (only comes once in your life)
> 2 do-it-yourself stores = shops that sell tools and materials to do home repairs, etc. yourself
> how-to classes = classes where you can learn how to do practical things, e.g. install your own central heating
> 3 = foods that you can eat immediately (without cooking), e.g. cheese, prepared salads
> 4 = a positive attitude (expressing 'I can do it')
> 5 = crucial, critical (he must succeed or his career will end)

5 a Learners match the expressions with the nouns.

b Go through the answers and play recording **2.33** to check. Ask what the expressions mean.

> no-win situation: *a situation where there is no good solution (you can't win whatever you do)*
> wake-up call: *literally, a phone call to wake you (e.g. in a hotel) / figuratively, an event that makes you realise how serious a situation is*
> peer-to-peer network: *a computer network connecting users directly without going through a server*
> hands-on experience: *direct, practical experience*

6 To demonstrate the activity, ask learners questions using one or two of the expressions from this section, e.g.
– Do you have any <u>ready-to-eat foods</u> in your fridge?
– If I offered you a <u>once-in-a-lifetime opportunity</u> to live in Antarctica for a month, what would you say?
Learners note down two or three questions.

👥 / 👥👥 Learners ask each other their questions.

Round-up. Learners tell you some of their questions and what reply they received.

VOCABULARY Influence and effect

7 a Look at the example sentence and discuss the questions. Establish that:
– the commonest expression with *influence* is *have an influence on*.
– we can also use other prepositions, e.g. *be under the influence of, be influenced by*.
– we can also use other verbs, e.g. *use your influence, exert an influence* (on), *gain / lose influence*.

b 👤 / 👥 Learners complete the sentences. Then go through the answers.

> 1 has had, has exerted
> 2 used
> 3 fall under
> 4 exert, have
> 5 lost

c Discuss how you could rephrase the sentences using the adjective *influential*.

> 2 ... was very influential in improving schools
> 3 We don't realise how influential advertising is.
> 4 'How to be influential and get what you want'.
> 5 ... is no longer as influential as it used to be.

8 👤 / 👥 Learners choose the best adjective.
Go through the answers and discuss the reasons for their choice.

> 1 Both.
> 'influential' = it was one of several factors that persuaded people
> 'effective' = it succeeded
> 2 Both.
> 'influential' = they had an influence on events
> 'effective' = they did their job successfully
> 3 'effective' (= does it work?)
> 4 'effective' (= it will work)

9 a Learners complete the sentences. Then discuss possible continuations together. Possible answers:

> 1 I was deeply affected by it.
> 2 His relatives were deeply affected by the news.
> 3 It has a significant influence on the way people decided to vote.
> 4 Even the neighbouring buildings were affected by the smoke.

b Learners write their sentences and then compare them in pairs.

 You could use photocopiable activity 8C on the Teacher's DVD-ROM at this point.

Self-assessment

To help focus learners on the self-assessment, you could read it through, giving a few examples of the language they have learned in each section (or asking learners to tell you). Then ask them to circle a number on each line.

Unit 8 Extra activities on the Teacher's DVD-ROM

Printable worksheets, activity instructions and answer keys are on your Teacher's DVD-ROM.

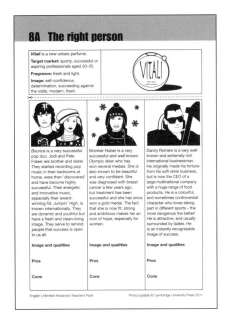  

8A The right person

Activity type: Speaking – Ranking and discussion – Groups of three or four

Aim: To discuss and agree on the best person for a product endorsement

Language: Image and qualities – Coursebook p77 – Vocabulary

Preparation: Make one copy of the worksheet for each learner. Cut it into two parts.

Time: 15–20 minutes

8B Make or break

Activity type: Speaking – Planning and presentation task – Groups / Whole class

Aim: To plan and present a marketing plan

Language: Marketing words – Coursebook p78 – Vocabulary

Preparation: Make one copy of the worksheet for each group.

Time: 40–60 minutes

8C Effects

Activity type: Speaking – Personalised guessing game – Pairs

Aim: To practise using vocabulary related to *effect* and *affect*

Language: *effect, affect* – Coursebook, p82 – Keywords

Preparation: Make one copy of the worksheet for each learner.

Time: 15–25 minutes

Unit 8 Self-study Pack

In the Workbook

Unit 8 of the *English Unlimited Advanced Self-study Pack Workbook* offers additional ways to practise the vocabulary and grammar taught in the Coursebook. There are also activities which build reading and writing skills, and two pages which give your learners the opportunity to develop their skills in extended reading.

- **Vocabulary:** Marketing words; Image and qualities; Effects and influences; Multi-word expressions
- **Grammar:** Measuring differences; *-ever*
- **Explore reading:** Blog entries and press releases

On the DVD-ROM

Unit 8 of the *English Unlimited Advanced Self-study Pack DVD-ROM* contains interactive games and activities for your learners to practise and improve their vocabulary, grammar and pronunciation, and also their speaking and listening.

- **Vocabulary and grammar:** Extra practice of the Coursebook language and Keywords
- **Explore listening:** Describing attitudes
- **Explore speaking:** Sounding persuasive

Icons

9.1

Goals: speculate about images and objects
interpret and respond to a story

Core language:
LANGUAGE FOCUS   Interpreting and defining

Apples

SPEAKING

1 a *Books closed.* Write the word *apple* on the board and ask learners to note down words or expressions they associate with it.

　　Learners compare their associations with a partner.

b Ask learners to picture an apple and write adjectives or expressions to describe it. Ask them to think about size, texture, colour, shape, taste, type.

In turn, a few learners describe their image of an apple to the class. Use this stage to explore vocabulary, e.g. *glossy, shrivelled, tart* (= slightly bitter), *crunchy, cooking / eating apple.*

2　　/　　*Pre-listening discussion.* Learners discuss the painting. They note down points they think are important.

Round-up. Ask different pairs or groups what ideas they had. Direct them to particular aspects of the painting (the apple, the people, the background, the colours) to focus on symbolic meaning in the painting.

LISTENING

3 a *Listening for general idea.* Play recording **3.1** once through. Then check what aspects of the painting the speakers talk about, but without going into details at this point.

> – They talk about: *the apple, the two men, the birds in the background*
> – They don't mention: *their clothes, the plaque, the colours in the painting*

b *Listening for main points.* Play recording **3.1** again. Learners listen and make brief notes on what the speakers say to complete sentences 1–4. Play it section by section, pausing to give learners time to make notes.

Discuss what the speakers say. Possible answers:

> 1 love, temptation, death, sin
> 2 brothers
> 3 the expression on their faces, the way he's holding the apple, the birds in the background
> 4 the contrast between youth / happiness and death

LANGUAGE FOCUS Interpreting and defining

4 a　　/　　Learners try to complete the sentences, either from memory or according to what they think could go in the gaps.

b Go through the answers together and play recording **3.2** to check.

> 1 was supposed   5 hard to tell
> 2 difficult to know   6 strikes me that
> 3 stands out for   7 are considered
> 4 appears that   8 seems to be saying

c Discuss what other expressions could be used in each sentence, or let learners discuss this in pairs first. Possible answers:

> 1 was thought; was believed
> 2 hard to guess; not very clear
> 3 strikes me; I find interesting
> 4 it appears that; they appear to; it looks as if
> 5 difficult to know; not clear
> 6 seems to me; occurs to me; I think
> 7 are considered to be; are regarded as; are often thought of as; are generally seen as
> 8 appears to be saying; The message of the painting seems to be

> **Optional discussion**
>
> Ask the class what they think of the painting:
> – Do they find it interesting? beautiful? disturbing? strange? Why?
> – Do they see it in a different way after hearing an interpretation from before?
> – What do they think of classical paintings of this kind? Do they have anything to say to people today?
> Ask learners what other old paintings (if any) they find worth looking at, and why.

SPEAKING

5　　Learners look at the images on p131. They consider each image in turn and discuss what connection it has with apples and what they think it shows or refers to. They make brief notes of their ideas. If they can't interpret an image, they leave it and move on to the next one.

Discuss the images together and get ideas from different groups. Explain any images that learners couldn't interpret. Possible answers:

> A Apple pie: US national dish and symbol of the American way of life ('as American as apple pie').
> B 'An apple for teacher': in Britain, children sometimes used to bring an apple to class for their teacher – implies being too good, or trying to gain favour with someone.
> C William (Wilhelm) Tell (Swiss legend – he was ordered to fire an arrow at an apple on his son's head).
> D Snow White (from the children's story 'Snow White and the Seven Dwarves') whose stepmother gave her a poisoned apple.
> E A Beatles LP record (recorded under the Apple label).
> F A man's larynx (called the 'Adam's apple' in English).
> G A painting by the French artist Matisse, showing an apple.
> H A caricature of Isaac Newton (who is said to have discovered gravity when an apple fell on his head).

Family story

READING

1 Look at the photo and establish that it shows New York, also called the Big Apple. Ask why it's called that (because it's the city of opportunity; everyone can have a 'bite').

2 a *Reading: interpreting meaning.* Learners read the story and think about the questions. When they have finished, they compare answers with a partner.

  b Discuss the questions and focus on these aspects of the story:
   – when we start a new phase in life we often have exaggerated hopes that have no connection with reality.
   – reality is often disappointing compared with our expectations.
   – New York appears to offer everything, but it may not be what it seems.
   – the children are looking back on their grandfather's experience as a new, naive immigrant. So for them, it's a key moment in their family history.

  c Read the next part of the anecdote. Then discuss what the speaker says in answer to the questions.

  > 1 Reality is always disappointing if it's different from your expectations.
  > 2 New York is the 'Big Apple'. America was seen by European immigrants as paradise (where Adam and Eve ate the apple).
  > 3 Because it seemed to symbolise what life is like, and because they found it funny.
  > 4 Because it symbolises expulsion from paradise and the contrast between expectation and reality.

  d *Reading: focus on style.* Learners look at both parts of the anecdote and discuss the questions.

  Discuss the answers together. Focus on these points in answer to the questions (1–4):

  > 1 She describes the events in the style of someone telling an anecdote (short sentences, a 'punch line', conversational style: 'the story goes that ...').
  > 2 To start the analysis in the second part, she goes back to the original 'scene' – she and her sisters enjoying the story ('My sisters and I loved ...', 'My sisters and I roared ...').
  > 3 'If you're thinking of getting an apple ...' involves the listener in the story (making you see it from the grandfather's point of view).
  > 4 Alliteration: 'chaos', 'colours' and 'crowds'. Combinations of adjectives: 'gorgeous', 'red', 'perfect'. Short dramatic 'turning point' expressing his disappointment: 'It was a tomato'. Choice of strongly descriptive words: 'flabbergasted' (= astonished), 'lusted after' (= wanted), 'splurged' (= spent a lot of money).

SPEAKING

3 a *Preparation.* Learners write down ten important words from the first part of the anecdote.

  b *Telling the story.* Learners take it in turns to tell the story. The others listen and notice how the stories are different.

  Round-up. Ask each group what differences they noticed between the stories and how that reflected different people's attitude to the story.

4 *Preparation.* To introduce this activity, tell a story about your own family. Start by writing key words on the board, then tell the story. Ask the class what significance they think the story has, or what it says about people in your family.

  Learners think of a true story on one of the topics. They make brief notes or write down key words, as they did in **3a**.

  Learners tell their story in turn. Their partner listens and comments on the story. Together they discuss what significance the story seems to have.

  Round-up. Ask a few learners to comment briefly on their two stories.

9.2

Goals: discuss icons
identify critical language in a text

Core language:
LANGUAGE FOCUS   Critical language

Iconic

SPEAKING and READING

1 a Discuss what the magazine cover shows and point out that:
   – the image is of Marilyn Monroe, illustrating the feature article on icons.
   – she was an 'icon' in that she was a world-famous actress and also represented the 1950s American ideal of beauty; also a tragic figure (she died very young).
   – the image of Marilyn Monroe is itself made up of smaller images of iconic figures.

  Check that learners understand the meaning of *icon* and *iconic* at this point.

  b Learners look at the cover and discuss what other iconic images they think appear.

2 a *Pre-reading.* Learners cover the article on 89. Look at photos A–F and check that learners recognise them all. Discuss what is 'iconic' about them. Possible answers:

  > A The US flag: known all over the world
  > B The Taj Mahal: possibly the world's most famous building, representing Indian civilisation
  > C The Mona Lisa: possibly the world's most famous painting
  > D Vespa: instantly recognisable design
  > E Mick Jagger: symbolises the 1960s
  > F Coca-Cola bottle: instantly recognisable shape, global brand

  b *Reading to check (scanning).* Learners quickly read through the article and check what it says about the icons in **2a**.

c *Reading for main ideas.* Learners compare the summary statements with the article.

Discuss the answers together.

> 1 Yes.
> 2 Yes.
> 3 Yes.
> 4 No. Artefacts must have certain characteristics to become iconic.
> 5 No. Usually, people only become iconic after their death, but there may be exceptions, e.g. Barack Obama.

d *Focus on expressions.* Discuss what the expressions mean.

> 1 words which are overused (so they 'invade' the language)
> 2 words misused by people with no sensitivity to language
> 3 people who deal with words (e.g. journalists) but who can't write well
> 4 the ready-made words (clichés) which they draw on in their job as writers ('props' = objects used in a play in the theatre)
> 5 its new, misused sense
> 6 stage sets (stage, lighting, etc.) used in rock concerts performed in stadiums

LANGUAGE FOCUS Critical language

3 a Learners read the first two paragraphs. Bring out these points about the writer's attitude:
   – he's very critical of the way language is misused.
   – he's contemptuous of popular journalism (whose job it is to smother page upon page with words).
   – he strongly dislikes the word 'iconic'.

b Learners list words with negative connotations.

Build up a list of words on the board. As you do this, discuss what connotations each word has and ask learners to suggest a more neutral equivalent. Possible words:

> jargon (words that are incomprehensible to most people) – language
> smother (cover so it can't breathe) – cover
> desperate (badly in need of help) – low quality
> trade (like a manual worker) – profession
> dismal (very sad, without hope) – dull
> tiresome (something that wears you out) – dull

c Learners find alternative words and discuss how they change the meaning.

> 1 mobbed (= they were out of control)
>   hemmed in (= he couldn't escape)
>   smothered (= he couldn't breathe)
> 2 irritating (= they annoy you)
>   inescapable (= you can't get away from them)
>   ubiquitous (= they seem to be everywhere)
>   invasive (= they intrude on your privacy)
> 3 brusque (= short and rude)
>   dismissive (= treating you as unimportant)
>   contemptuous (= without respect)
>   minimal (= as short as possible)
> 4 expensive:
>   a rip-off (= they cheated us)
>   overpriced (= too expensive, not good value)
>   crowded:
>   packed (= you could hardly move)
>   seething (= overcrowded, they were everywhere)
>   crawling (= they were like insects)
>   cloudy:
>   dismal (= miserable, without hope of change)
>   dreary (= dull and depressing)

d Discuss the choices together.

> **Alternative**
>
> Each group focuses on one of the sentences and finds suitable words. Then get feedback from each group and discuss the words together.

 You could use photocopiable activity 9A on the Teacher's DVD-ROM at this point.

SPEAKING

4 a Learners make a list of about five iconic people or things.

b Learners compare their ideas. Then they add one person or thing that is supposed to be iconic, but in fact won't survive as an icon.

Round-up. Ask each group to read out their list (write them on the board to avoid repetition) and explain why they chose them.

9.3 Target activity: Icons for today

Goals: discuss icons
talk about what something represents
present arguments and counter-arguments

Core language:

| 9.1 LANGUAGE FOCUS | Interpreting and defining |
| TASK LANGUAGE | Saying what things and people represent |

Icons for today

TASK LISTENING

1 a *Pre-listening.* Look at the poster and discuss the questions. Bring out these points:
   – it's a stylised image, in red, white and blue (colours of the US flag); it's not a photograph.
   – it glamorises Obama and makes him look heroic.
   – it looks a bit like revolutionary posters from the 1920s, stirring people to action.

b *Listening for main points.* Read through the questions and ask learners what they think the journalist might say. Then play recording **3.3** to check.

> 1 He has a vision, an ability to lead.
> 2 Lots of different people.
> 3 To make people curious about Obama.
> 4 He donated to the campaign.
> 5 He didn't mind. It shows how successful it was.

TASK LANGUAGE Saying what things and people represent

2 a Read the sentences and ask learners what verbs they think go in the gaps.

b If necessary, learners look at the script on p156 to check. Discuss other ways of expressing the same ideas.

> 1 portray (show, present, represent)
> 2 transcend (rise above, reach beyond, go beyond)
> 3 resonated (appealed to people, captured people's imagination, people have responded to the image)

3 a Learners look at the statements and identify the icons. Discuss the answers together. Possible answers:

> 1 Marilyn Monroe
> 2 The US flag
> 3 The Taj Mahal
> 4 The Mona Lisa
> 5 The Rolling Stones
> 6 The Taj Mahal
> 7 The Vespa

Focus on these words:
– *She epitomises* = she's a typical example of. We can also say *She's the epitome of ...* .
– *represent* and *stand for* mean the same.
– *They embody* = they represent, especially in their behaviour (we could also say *Gandhi embodied the spirit of non-violence*).
– *It encapsulates* = has all the qualities of, contains in itself (we could also say *Marilyn Monroe encapsulates the American ideal of beauty*).

b Learners choose three other icons and write a sentence about each.

Learners read out their sentences. The others identify who or what they refer to.

TASK

4 a *Introduction.* Explain the task: together learners are going to choose four iconic images that represent our time. They will discuss together which should be included and why.

Explain that first they will listen to people discussing whether to include the Barack Obama poster as one of the images.

Listening for main points. Play recording **3.4** and discuss the questions.

> 1 In favour:
>   – it captured people's imagination.
>   – he was an important figure, a great leader.
>   – he was the first African-American president of the US.
>   Against:
>   – it is not an enduring image.
>   – it is already out of date.
>   – politics is not 'worthy' enough.
> 2 They decide to include it.

b *Focus on language.* Elicit any expressions that learners remember (or can guess) and build them up on the board.

c Learners look at the script on p156 to find other expressions. Write them on the board.

> Pushing your own point of view:
> – I think we should go for it.
> – I think it's valid.
> Questioning / disagreeing:
> – I see your point but ...
> – I'm not really convinced.
> – I don't know.
> – I just don't see ...
> Agreeing:
> – I agree with ...
> – I'd be in favour of that.
> – As you say ...
> – That's right.
> – I'd be quite happy to go along with that.
> – Can you live with that?
> Suggesting an alternative:
> – I'd much rather ...
> – What about ...?

> **Language note**
> *go for it* = agree to it, do it
> *go along with* (an idea) = agree to it, accept it
> *Can you live with it?* = Can you accept it?
> *I'd rather* (+ infinitive without *to*) = I'd prefer to

5 *Preparatory discussion: choosing icons.* Give groups letters, A or B. They look at their own set of icons and decide which they think which are suitable. They should choose two or three and then add one of their own.

Groups discuss what arguments they would put forward for the icons they have chosen.

Then, they look at the other group's icons and discuss what arguments they will use against them.

Group debate: selecting four icons. Learners form new groups, so that each new group has people from both group A and group B. In turn, they propose the icons they chose and argue for and against them. Before they begin, remind them of the expressions on the board.

They should try to agree on four icons to represent our time.

Round-up. Ask each group which four icons they selected and why.

> **Note**
> The exact form this takes will depend on the size of your class.
> *Classes of 10 or fewer.* Form two groups, one A and one B. Then they could either form two new groups for the debate (with a mixture of As and Bs), or have a whole-class discussion.
> *Classes of more than 10.* Form four groups, two A and two B. Then form four new groups with a mixture of As and Bs for the debate.

> **Optional idea**
> Refer learners to the www.icons.org.uk website, where people are invited to suggest icons to represent modern Britain.

9 Explore

Across cultures: Loan words

Goal: to make learners aware of the mixing of words between languages

1 Ask learners what a *loan word* is (a word 'borrowed' from another language).

   Brainstorm English words that are used in the learners' language, focusing on words which have come into the language recently. Write these words on the board. Also, discuss whether the words mentioned really come from English or from some other language (e.g. *jeans* came from the USA, but is originally a French word; *burger* comes originally from the German word *Hamburger*).

2 Look at the photos and discuss the questions. Bring out these points:
   – in many languages, English words are seen as modern and 'trendy', so they are used in adverts to create this image.

3 a Focus learners on the words and discuss the questions together.

   b *Listening.* Play recording 3.5. Pause after each speaker and discuss the questions.

   > **Norman: Germany.** Language of marketing; computers.
   > cool, event, image, handy, email
   > **Olga: Russia.** Words that don't exist in Russian.
   > supermarket, training, marketing, manager She thinks it has gone too far, and there should be a balance.

   c Ask learners if they know of any English words in their language which are misused, or which have acquired a new meaning.

   d Discuss the questions with the class, or let them discuss in pairs first and then get feedback. To focus the discussion, you could ask further questions, e.g.
   – *Do people feel their language is 'threatened' by English or other languages? Do you think they are right?*
   – *Is it possible to keep a language 'pure'? Have people tried to do this with your own language? How successful has it been? Is it worth doing?*
   – *Some people think that a language becoming more 'international' is simply a natural process, and should be welcomed. Do you agree?*

Keywords: describing what things represent

Goal: to describe what things represent, depict or convey

Core language:
represent, depict, convey, portray, stand for, show, symbolise

1 a *Focus on verbs.* Learners close their books. Write on the board: *represent, depict, convey.* Ask what these verbs normally describe (many things, but especially images, photos, films, books …).

   b *Open books.* Learners choose the most appropriate verbs.

   > 1 convey
   > 2 portrayed
   > 3 shown
   > 4 depicted
   > 5 represents

   > **Language note**
   > *depict* and *portray* = represent something in a picture, film, story, etc. You can depict / portray a character, a place, or an event:
   > – *The film depicted / portrayed Elizabeth II.*
   > – *The film depicted / portrayed life in the 19th century.*
   > – *The film depicted / portrayed a small town in Russia.*
   > After *depict* and *portray* we can use *as*:
   > – *She was depicted as an evil character.*
   > You *convey* information, ideas, feelings etc. (= communicate):
   > – *The film conveys a powerful sense of optimism.*

   c Ask which verbs can be used in the sentence (*answer: portrays, depicts, shows*).

   d Use the question to establish that *stand for* has a very similar meaning to *represent* (so can be used in sentence 5).

2 a Learners complete the sentences. Discuss possible answers together.

   > 1 stand for, represent (= it's what they mean)
   > 2 shows (= it's clear from the logo)
   > 3 conveys (a message)
   > 4 represents, symbolises

   b *Focus on collocations.* Learners complete the sentences. Expected answers:

   > 1 depict his life
   > 2 conveys a more positive message
   > 3 depict the world / life
   > 4 depict scenes
   > 5 convey a sense of
   > 6 conveying information

3 *Speaking.* Learners choose a topic and make brief notes, using verbs from this section.

   Learners tell their partner about the topic and ask further questions.

   Round-up. Ask a few learners what their partner talked about and what significance it has for him / her.

    You could use photocopiable activity 9B on the Teacher's DVD-ROM at this point.

96   Unit 9 Icons

Explore speaking

Goal: give criticism
respond to criticism

Core language:
Ways of softening criticism
Ways of responding to criticism appropriately

1 a Look at the cover design and discuss what the article might be about (*answer:* financial crisis in the US, the dollar weakening against other currencies). Then ask how the cover illustrates this and attracts the reader's attention. Elicit these points:
  – it shows the dollar (symbolised by the image George Washington as he appears on the dollar bill) crashing, shot down as if in a war.
  – the style is of an action / war comic illustration (suggests US heroes).
  – it is an unexpected image to find on the cover of a serious magazine about economics, so it attracts attention.

You could ask the class what they think of the cover design: *Is it effective? Does it give a good idea of the article?*

b *Reading and listening.* Play recording **3.6**. Learners read the conversation as they listen. Discuss who the people are and what they are discussing.

> Two people on a design team. A has designed the cover for the next issue. B is a colleague or editor. They are going to discuss it in a meeting.

Alternative

Books closed. Play recording **3.6** and discuss the question. Then let learners read the conversation to check.

  c *Focus on language strategies.* Learners identify expressions. Ask for suggestions and bring out these points.
  – B criticises mainly by expressing an opinion:
    I think ..., I don't think ...
  – A responds by asking for clarification:
    What do you mean?
  – and by strongly disagreeing:
    I beg to differ.
  – A also responds by giving her opinion:
    I think ..., It seems to me ...

  d Ask how B softens the criticism:
  – starting with a positive remark:
    I like the basic idea, but ...
  – using 'hedging' and 'softening' expressions:
    I don't know, I'm not sure; quite, a bit
  – leaving the conclusion open:
    Let's see what the others think.

2 a *Criticising.* Learners put the remarks in order, from least to most critical.

b Learners compare answers and discuss which remarks are too harsh.

Discuss the order together and ask how the critical remarks could be softened. Possible order:

> 1 g (emphasises what's positive)
> 2 d (gently suggests a different direction, using conditionals to sound tentative)
> 3 f (a negative comment, but softened with 'quite' and 'really')
> 4 a (more direct, but softened with 'actually')
> 5 e (critical, softer version: 'I was actually expecting something a bit different')
> 6 c (harshly critical, sounds like a command, softer version: 'It isn't really what we want. Maybe you should re-think it.')
> 7 b (harshly critical, ridicules the other person, softer version: "So this is your idea for the design, is it? I'm not sure it's quite what we want.')

Summarise the main ways of softening criticism:
  – hedging expressions: *I don't know; I'm not sure*
  – softening adverbs: *really, a bit, quite, actually*
  – conditionals: *It would be better to...; You could ...*
  – not + a positive adjective: *It's wrong → It isn't quite right.*

3 a *Responding to criticism.* Learners put the remarks in order.

b Learners compare answers and discuss which remarks are too aggressive.

Discuss the remarks together. Possible order:

> 1 a (agrees to change it too readily)
> 2 d (accepts the criticism and gives an explanation)
> 3 g (agrees to think about it)
> 4 c (asks for clarification, neither agreeing nor disagreeing)
> 5 e (asks for an explanation, sounding defensive)
> 6 b (responds with a criticism, sounding aggressive)
> 7 f (responds with a challenge, sounding very aggressive)

Establish that the best ways of deflecting criticism are probably g, c and e.

4 *Introduction.* Look at the topics together and choose one of them.

Discussion: developing ideas. Learners work in groups: A, B and C. In their group, they discuss ideas and find solutions together. They should make brief notes.

Discussion: presenting ideas and commenting. Learners form new groups, so that each group has one A, one B and one C. In turn, they present their ideas. The others listen and criticise, using the strategies they have studied. If possible, they should agree on the best ideas.

Round-up. Ask each group to summarise their ideas. Then ask how they felt about each other's criticisms.

 You could use photocopiable activity 9C on the Teacher's DVD-ROM at this point.

9 Look again

GRAMMAR *It's no ...*

> **Optional presentation**
>
> *Books closed*. Write sentence beginnings on the board:
> – *It's no coincidence ...*
> – *It's no use ...*
> Learners suggest possible continuations.
> Use this to focus on the structure of expressions with *It's* followed by *that* or verb *+-ing*.
> Open books and read the examples.

1 a Look at the examples and focus on the structure of expressions with *It's*.

  b 👤/👥 Learners complete the sentences. Go through the exercise together and elicit a range of possible answers. Discuss what the context might be.

> 1 it's no wonder / surprise, it's no coincidence
>   (about the stock market)
> 2 it's no good, it's no use
>   (someone's girlfriend has left him, or a relative has died)
> 3 It's no secret, It's no coincidence
>   (report on tobacco advertising)
> 4 it's no different
>   (about being born disabled, or about people's skin colour)
> 5 it's no use, it's no good
>   (marketing advice)
> 6 it's no trouble / big deal / problem
>   (an offer in a conversation – e.g. someone needs an electrician)

  c Discuss the questions together and establish these points:
  – *It's no good / use* are followed by *-ing*.
  – *It's no coincidence / secret / wonder / surprise* are followed by *that*.
  – *It's no trouble / problem / big deal* are followed by *to* + infinitive (or by *-ing*).
  – *it's no good* and *it's no use* both mean 'there's no purpose / point'.
  – *it's no wonder / surprise* mean the same.
  – *it's no problem / trouble / big deal* mean the same (*It's no big deal* is more conversational).
  – *It's no different* is followed by *from*.

  d Discuss the example together (*answer: simply, absolutely*).

GRAMMAR Modifying a sentence

2 Look at the sentences and discuss where the modifying expressions should go.

Point out that most of the expressions can go in several different places in the sentence. Common positions are:
– at the beginning or end to modify the whole sentence:
  Really, all is forgiven ...
  In that sense I'm very happy ...
  ... the way I see them, hopefully.
– before a main verb:
  So I actually made something ...
  ... was maybe going to transcend
– before a particular phrase that they modify:
  in a way well-suited
Discuss question 2.

> '*really*' adds emphasis.
> The others soften the sentence and make a comment on it.

3 a 👤/👥 Learners add expressions to the sentences.

Go through the answers and get a range of possible suggestions. Possible answers (many variations are possible):

> 1 That was a really terrible mistake!
>   In a way, that was a terrible mistake!
> 2 Maybe it would be better to do something different.
>   It would actually be better to do something different.
> 3 I don't think that was the right decision, actually.
>   I really don't think that was the right decision.
> 4 She'll be earning next year, hopefully, so she'll be more independent.
>   She'll be earning next year, so for better or worse she'll be more independent.

  b 👥 Learners choose a sentence and develop it into a dialogue. Then they practise saying it.

In turn, pairs act out their conversation. The others listen and guess the situation.

VOCABULARY Uses of *suppose*

4 a *Meaning and form*. Read the examples and ask what *suppose* means in each case.

> 1 think, assume
> 2 people thought / believed that
> 3 what does it mean? (expressing irritation or confusion)
> 4 people say she is

Discuss the form of the verbs and establish that:
– you use *I suppose* as a set expression (1).
– you often use the passive form *is supposed to* + infinitive (2, 3, 4), meaning 'people say or think ...'.

  b, c 👥/👥👥 Learners find synonyms for *suppose* and match the sentences with the meanings. Possible answers:

> 1 If ..., imagine that ... (e)
> 2 is said to ... (f)
> 3 I think so, I guess so (b)
> 4 should be (d)
> 5 Presumably, Possibly (a)
> 6 guess, assume (c)

  d *Negatives*. Discuss how to make *suppose* negative.

> 1 Supposing it isn't ...
> 2 ... isn't supposed to be
> 3 I don't suppose so. / I suppose not.
> 4 isn't supposed to be here
> 5 I don't suppose you would be able ...?
> 6 –

Point out that:
– there are two possible negative forms of *I suppose so*: *I suppose not* and *I don't suppose so*.
– *I don't suppose you could (possibly) ..., could you?* is a common way of making a careful request.

e Introduce the adverb *supposedly* and focus on its pronunciation /sə'pəʊzɪdli/. Learners try using it in the sentences. Possible sentences:

> 2 Supposedly, a little salt is good for you.
> 3 Supposedly, yeah.
> 4 The plane should be here by now, supposedly.
> 5 Supposedly they made a mistake.

5 a Look at each photo in turn. Learners suggest a conversation that each might illustrate (e.g. people in a restaurant ordering octopus, people discussing how to cook octopus). Then learners suggest sentences with *suppose* that might appear in the conversation, e.g. for A:
– Grilled octopus is supposed to taste very good.
– I don't suppose you know how to cook octopus, do you?
– A Is that octopus for sale?
  B I suppose so.

b Learners choose one sentence and develop it into a conversation that might relate to one of the photos.

Ask a few pairs to read out their conversations.

c Play recording **3.7**, pausing after each conversation to check the situation and ask what they said using *suppose*.

> 1 Two friends discussing how to prepare octopus: "I think you're supposed to bash them to make them tender."
> 2 Two people photographing an elephant: "Come on, supposing it suddenly charges at you?"
> 3 Two people queuing to get into an art gallery: "It is supposed to be a really good exhibition."
> 4 Mother asking son to take the rubbish out: "I suppose you couldn't take the rubbish out, could you?"
> 5 Woman met by man at airport (just arrived from Brazil): "If you leave it on the wish comes true, supposedly."

6 a Learners write sentences about their country.

b Learners read out their sentences. After each one, ask if he / she thinks it is true and ask other people if they agree.

Self-assessment

To help focus learners on the self-assessment, you could read it through, giving a few examples of the language they have learned in each section (or asking learners to tell you). Then ask them to circle a number on each line.

Unit 9 Extra activities on the Teacher's DVD-ROM

Printable worksheets, activity instructions and answer keys are on your Teacher's DVD-ROM.

9A Word grab

Activity type: Speaking – Game – Groups of three or five

Aim: To practise using negative connotations

Language: Critical language – Coursebook p88 – Vocabulary

Preparation: Make one copy of the worksheet for each group. Cut the words up into separate cards.

Time: 20–30 minutes

9B Find a picture which …

Activity type: Speaking – Activity creation – Pairs / Small groups

Aim: To improve oral and written use of verbs related to representation

Language: Talking about what something represents – Coursebook p92 – Keywords

Preparation: Make one copy of the worksheet for each learner. Cut each worksheet into two parts.

Time: 20–30 minutes

9C Critical conversations

Activity type: Speaking – Role play – Pairs

Aim: To practise criticising appropriately and deflecting criticism

Language: Giving and responding to criticism – Coursebook, p93 – Explore speaking

Preparation: Make one copy of the worksheet for each pair. Cut the worksheet into two.

Time: 15–20 minutes

Unit 9 Self-study Pack

In the Workbook

Unit 9 of the *English Unlimited Advanced Self-study Pack Workbook* offers additional ways to practise the vocabulary and grammar taught in the Coursebook. There are also activities which build reading and writing skills, and a whole page of tasks to use with the DVD-ROM video, giving your learners the opportunity to hear and react to spoken English.

- **Vocabulary:** Interpreting and defining; Saying what things and people represent; Critical language
- **Grammar:** *It's no …*; Modifying a sentence;
- **Explore writing:** Tribute texts
- **DVD-ROM Extra:** News clip – *The death of icons*

On the DVD-ROM

Unit 9 of the *English Unlimited Advanced Self-study Pack DVD-ROM* contains interactive games and activities for your learners to practise and improve their vocabulary, grammar and pronunciation, and also their speaking and listening. It also contains video material (with the possibility for learners to record themselves) to use with the *Workbook*.

- **Vocabulary and grammar:** Extra practice of the Coursebook language and Keywords
- **Explore listening:** An interview
- **Explore speaking:** Softening criticism
- **Video:** News clip – *The death of icons*

10 A sense of belonging

10.1

Goals: describe groups and membership
describe feelings about belonging

Core language:
LANGUAGE FOCUS Belonging to a group
LANGUAGE FOCUS Talk about membership

Groups

SPEAKING

1   / *Discussion.* Learners discuss the questions. Then talk about questions 1 and 2 together. Possible answers:

> A Demonstration or concert in support of giving aid to poor people in Africa (Make Poverty History campaign). They're listening to speeches or music. The people are mostly in their 20s, they all believe in fighting poverty, and they like similar music.
> B Outdoor festival or party (Carnival in Recife, Brazil). They're chatting, dancing to music, having a good time. They are mostly people from the same place, and they want to celebrate together.
> C Fans at a football match. They're supporting their team.
> D A procession of Buddhist monks (novices). They could be taking part in a ceremony. They have the same religion and occupation, and are dressed in the same way.

Discuss question 3. Bring out these ideas:

> – they all show groups or crowds of people who have something in common.
> – all the people have an identity or sense of belonging (because of political views, religion, social group, interests).
> – some are there to have a good time (A, B, C), some are there out of duty (D), some are there to give their support (A, C).

2 a *Discussion: groups that learners belong to.* Together, brainstorm different words for groups that people belong to. These might include general groups (e.g. sports clubs, football fans, a language class) and also specific organisations (e.g. the army, a political party).

b Learners list groups that they belong to. To introduce this, tell the class about some of the groups that you belong to and write them on the board.
  / Learners show each other their lists and ask further questions.

Feedback. Ask students which is the most important group on their and their partner's list.

LISTENING

3 *Pre-listening.* Look at the photo of Grover and read through the questions. Ask learners to guess what group Grover will talk about and what he might say.
Listening for main points. Play recording **3.8**. Learners listen and answer the questions.

> 1 The US army
> 2 Pride in and loyalty to the army unit
> 3 Because he's naturally an open, honest, loyal person; other people had to learn to share things
> 4 He became a stronger person; made lifelong friends; learned to like himself.
> 5 Yes. Life is easier, you don't have to think for yourself.

LANGUAGE FOCUS Belonging to a group

4 a Learners complete the sentences, either from memory or according what they think might go in the gaps.

b *Listening to check.* Discuss the answers together, then play recording **3.9** to check.

> 1 part of a larger group
> 2 a sense of loyalty
> 3 belonging to
> 4 get territorial
> 5 bonded with

Focus on these expressions:
– *be / get territorial about* = want to have your own territory (space that belongs to you, e.g. an animal fights for its own territory).
– *bond with* = develop close ties with someone (like a family).
– *loyalty*: the noun from *loyal*.

Joining a group

LANGUAGE FOCUS Talk about membership

1 a   / Learners match the expressions and discuss the questions. Talk about the expressions together. Expected answers:

> 1b, d   2f, (b)   3a, c   4a, (c)   5d, e   6d, e, (b)   7b   8a, c

Establish these points:
– *join* and *become a member of* mean the same: you join an organisation, e.g. a political party or club.
– *sign up for* and *enrol in* mean the same = join a course or a class, where you register your name.
– *team up with* and *collaborate with* mean the same = work with someone else on a project.
– *get involved in* = become interested or feel part of something.

> **Language note**
> *Collaborate with* can have a negative connotation:
> *They collaborated with the enemy* (they were collaborators).
> It can also be used with a neutral or positive meaning:
> *We collaborated* (= worked together) *on the project.*
> *It was an excellent collaboration.*

b *Listening to check.* Play recording **3.10** and establish what each person is talking about.

> 1 got involved in politics; joined the Scottish National Party (about when she was a university student)
> 2 teamed up with a few colleagues (about setting up an unsuccessful software company)
> 3 signed up for one of their training courses (about a management or secretarial training course)
> 4 enrolled in a drawing class, got to know a lot of new people (someone saying how he met his partner or a friend)

 You could use photocopiable activity 10A on the Teacher's DVD-ROM at this point.

LISTENING and SPEAKING

2 *Listening for general idea.* Play recording **3.11**. Learners listen and answer questions 1 and 2.

> 1 a team of carers for old people ('the organisation', 'an elderly couple', 'other carers')
> 2 she enjoys it, she likes helping people, it gives her something to do

Focus on language. Ask learners what expressions they noticed. Then play recording **3.11** again. Learners listen and note down expressions from **1a**.

> <u>became a member of</u> this group recently
> <u>got involved with</u> the organisation
> when somebody new <u>joins</u>
> I <u>teamed up with</u> some other carers
> can meet up and <u>get to know</u> new people

> **Language note**
> We can say *get involved in* or *get involved with*, with almost no difference in meaning.

3 *Preparation.* To introduce the activity, think of a group you belong to and tell the class about it, but without mentioning what the group is. They listen and guess which group you are talking about.

Learners choose a group and make a few notes.

Speaking activity. In turn, learners tell their partner about their group. Their partner guesses what the group is.

Round-up. Ask a few learners to tell you about their partner's group and whether they guessed it correctly.

> **Optional extension**
> Learners form new pairs and repeat the activity.

10.2

Goals: give opinions emphatically
explore strategies for analysing authentic texts

Core language:
LANGUAGE FOCUS   Being emphatic

Football

READING

1 a *Pre-reading.* Cover the extracts and look at photos 1–4. Ask what each photo seems to show and how it might be connected with the idea of 'belonging'. Possible answers:

> 1 The Homeless World Cup – a football championship organised by and for homeless people; people belonging to a team.
> 2 Iranian women playing football. They share a common interest.
> 3 Children playing football in the street. Children identify with football teams (some are wearing football strips) – it's a game that friends play together.
> 4 A crowd of football spectators from the 1950s. Football supporters identify with their home team.

b Ask learners what they think each extract might say.

2 a *Reading for main idea.* Learners read extracts A–D quickly (you could set a time limit). When they have finished, they could discuss the answers with a partner.

Discuss the answers together. Bring out these points about each extract:

> A A novel or autobiography: it has a condensed, literary style, it's a reminiscence about the past. The author used to be a fan (he went to football matches at weekends). He's telling the modern-day reader about the atmosphere of football matches in the 1950s.
> B Could be a speech, or a message on a website, by a famous footballer who sponsors the Homeless World Cup: it has a rhetorical style used in speeches. He's saying that he has been through difficult times and now wants to help other people.
> C Could be a feature article in a magazine, written by an academic or journalist about the international nature of football: written in an abstract, academic style.
> D Interview in a newspaper with someone who made a film about football, which included female supporters; it contains direct quotes from the interview. Written by a film critic or a journalist, probably for people who are interested in films.

b Discuss the questions together.

> 1 B (about homeless people as outside society);
>   D (about women and football)
> 2 A
> 3 A (brought people together, gave them an escape from routine)
> 4 A (they were members of a community)
> 5 D (a film)
> 6 C (it can be played everywhere)

c *Focus on style.* Learners identify the techniques. Then discuss these together.

> Questions: C (Is there any cultural practice ...?)
> Nouns: A
> Inversion: A (not only had you ...)
> Exclamations: B
> Rhetorical questions: C (McDonalds? MTV?)
> Descriptive language: A
> Use of direct quotations: D

d Ask learners to imagine they are in a bookshop and have come across these extracts. Ask: *Which one would you want to carry on reading?* You could give learners a few moments to think and make a choice, then find out which extract most people chose and why.

LANGUAGE FOCUS Being emphatic

3 a *Focus on sentence stress.* Learners read the sentences in turn round the class, or they could try reading them in pairs first. Focus on these points:
   – words and expressions like *not only, no single, not merely, exactly, yes* emphasise particular points in the sentence, so they are stressed.
   – *not only* and *not merely* are used to make a contrast between two ideas (*not only ... but; not merely consumed ... embraced*)

   b *Listening to check.* Play recording **3.12** to check. You could pause after each sentence and ask learners to copy the stress pattern.

   c Discuss questions 1–3 together.

   > 1 After 'not only', the subject and verb change places (you had → had you)
   > 2 no: *not a, not one*
   >   merely: *only, just*
   >   exactly: *precisely, at the very moment when*
   >   yes: *certainly, of course, absolutely*
   > 3 The emphasising in sentences 1–4 is more common in writing or a formal spoken style (e.g. a speech); in sentence 5, 'yes' is more likely to be used in speaking (it appears here as part of a quotation).

   Learners try saying the sentences in a less emphatic way. Possible answers:

   > 1 You hadn't only escaped ...
   > 2 World religions can't match ... / There aren't any world religions that can ...
   > 3 Football has been consumed by the world's societies, and it has also ...
   > 4 When chaos ...
   > 5 (omit 'yes')

   Language note
   Adverbial expressions followed by inversion are focused on in **Look again**, p104.

   > You could use photocopiable activity 10B on the Teacher's DVD-ROM at this point.

SPEAKING

4 a   *Preparation.* Learners read through the statements and decide which they agree and disagree with.

   b   Learners practise changing the sentences to reflect their opinion. They could do this alone or try out sentences with a partner. To show what to do, you could give more examples with sentence 1, e.g.
   – (You agree) *No single sport in my country is anywhere near as popular as football.*
   – (You agree) *As far as popularity is concerned, yes, football is definitely the most popular sport.*
   – (You disagree) *Not only is it not very popular, most people don't even watch it on TV.*

   c Taking each topic in turn, a few learners express opinions about it and find out if other people agree.

10.3 Target activity: Prepare a campaign

Goal: persuade others to take action
Core language:
10.1 LANGUAGE FOCUS Talk about membership
10.2 LANGUAGE FOCUS Being emphatic

TASK PREPARATION

1 a Look at photos A–B in turn. Discuss what they might show and how they might be connected with the subject of homelessness.

   b Learners read the summaries on p133 to check.

   > 1 B Gives homeless people a chance to change their lives.
   > 2 A People camp on the street to make the public aware of homelessness.

   Discuss which campaign is likely to be most effective and why.

   Discuss the other questions together and explore some of these points:
   – how visible homelessness is; where do homeless people go and where do you see them (if at all).
   – whether homeless people can change their situation, and if so how.
   – what attitudes most people have to people sleeping rough or begging (sympathetic? unsympathetic?).
   – what attitude the learners have (e.g. how do they react if they see a homeless person on the street?).

   Alternative
   Books closed. Begin by discussing the questions in **1b**. Then open books and look at the photos.

2 a *Pre-reading.* Learners cover the campaign message. Tell the class they will read a campaign message from the Homeless World Cup website. Discuss how people might support or help the organisation and write ideas on the board (e.g. giving money, buying something from them, helping to organise events).

   b *Reading to check.* Learners read the campaign message. Then discuss which kinds of support learners did and didn't think of.

   Focus on key words and establish that:
   – a *partner* = someone who becomes part of the organisation (probably paid).
   – a *volunteer* = someone who works for no money (voluntarily).
   – a *fan* is someone who supports them at football matches.
   – a *donation* is money you give to an organisation.

Unit 10 A sense of belonging

3   a, b   *Focus on language.* Learners find examples of each item in the text. Possible examples:

> imperatives: *Become ... , Help ...*
> present progressive: *We are looking ...*
> exaggeration: *change the world*
> compliments: *Bring your spirit of co-operation, your skills and talents*
> positive adjectives: *powerful positive message, unforgettable event*
> slogans: *spread the word, a ball can change the world*
> pledges and claims: *to reach one million players*
> expressions from p97: *sign up for, join*
> alliteration: *engage employees; help the homeless*

Point out that these features are typical of campaign messages. You could discuss why a campaign message is likely to use this kind of language, and bring out these points:
– it presents the campaign in a very positive light.
– it conveys a feeling of optimism and enthusiasm.
– it persuades people to respond and support the campaign.

TASK

4   a   *Preparation: group planning.* Learners choose a campaign – this could be real or invented. You could also give ideas if learners find it hard to think of anything suitable.

Together, each group plans a campaign message and one person in the group writes it down, including ideas for visuals and layout.

b   Groups pass their campaign message to the next group to read.

c   *Presentation.* One person from each group moves to the next group. They present their campaign and answer any questions. Their aim is to persuade the group to contribute to the campaign.

Repeat the procedure, until the group representatives have visited all the other groups.

d   *Evaluation.* Groups discuss which of the campaigns they will support and how. They could decide to support only one campaign or more than one.

Round-up. Ask each group to report what they decided and why.

> **Optional game**
>
> To introduce a game element, you could give each group a certain sum of money (e.g. $5,000) and a certain number of free hours (e.g. two weeks) which they can either devote to one campaign, or spread over more than one. They could of course decide not to spend time or money on any of them.

10 Explore

Across cultures: Football rivalries

Goal: to make learners more aware of different attitudes to sports teams

Core language:

squad, match, season, strip, clubs, fans, supporters, stadium, pitch, player

1   Learners match the shields to the cities. Discuss the answers.

> 1 B (Milan) AC Milan, Internazionale
> 2 A (Istanbul) Galatasaray, Fenerbahçe
> 3 C (Buenos Aires) River Plate, Boca Juniors

> **Note**
>
> If only a few people in the class know much about football, make sure that each group contains one 'football fan', who can help their group answer the questions.

2   *Listening for main ideas.* Read through the questions, then play recording **3.13**. Discuss the questions together.

> 1 Boca Juniors: *working-class team*
>   River Plate: *more upper-class support base*
>   Inter Milan: *supported by the bourgeoisie*
>   AC Milan: *working class support*
>   Galatasaray: *'upper crust' (= middle class), European side of Istanbul*
>   Fenerbahçe: *working class, Asian side*
> 2 Surrounded by money and media coverage
> 3 There's a social class difference between the teams.

3   *Focus on language.* Learners find football words in the script. Elicit words and build them up on the board.

> Football: *footballing calendar, squad (= team)*
> Football / other sports:
> *match, season, strip, clubs, fans, supporters, stadium, pitch, player*

4   a   *Discussion.* Learners discuss the questions.

Feedback. Ask each group to tell you one thing they discussed and what they said about it.

b   Learners write a suitable caption for the photo. Then they turn to a partner to compare.

Feedback. Learners read out their captions. You could tell them the original caption: *Rivals on the pitch, but friends for life.*

104   Unit 10   A sense of belonging

Keyword: *together*

Goal: to use *together* to describe time, relationships, positions and states

Core language:
together, put together, get together, work together, go together

> **Optional lead-in**
>
> Books closed. Write *together* on the board. Ask learners to write a sentence using the word.
> Then open books and read the examples.

1 *Focus on 'together'.* Read the examples. For each one, discuss a possible context and the meaning of *together*. Answers (possible contexts in brackets):

> 1 at the same time (complaining about trains or buses)
> 2 in a relationship (talking about a couple)
> 3 round each other (telling someone how to tie up e.g. a boat or a parcel)
> 4 against each other (= clap your hands) (introducing a guest on a chat show)
> 5 as a whole (commenting on two paintings, or gossip about a millionaire and his wealthy wife)
> 6 side by side (a speech about fighting a disease or terrorism)

2 a *Focus on collocations.* Point out that the missing verbs all commonly collocate with *together*. Learners complete the sentences.

 b Go through the answers and ask learners to suggest single verbs that would have a similar meaning.

> 1 got together (met)
> 2 work together, pull together (co-operate)
> 3 put together, get together (pack, collect)
> 4 go together (match, suit each other)
> 5 put together, get together (write, design, work out)

3 a Read the examples and ask learners to suggest synonyms.

> 1 wrote, made, devised
> 2 made, produced
> 3 written
> 4 employ, take on

 b *Focus on idioms.* Learners decide what the expressions mean. Then discuss this together. Possible answers:

> 1 ... than over the whole of the last four years (= the total of the last four years was less than this year)
> 2 an informal party (where people decide to get together (= meet))
> 3 stable, in control, self-aware (conversational English)
> 4 I worked out the situation (as if doing a simple calculation)
> 5 organise it, organise myself to do it (conversational English)

4 a *Speaking activity.* Learners complete the questions. Then check the answers.

> 1 been together
> 2 put together
> 3 get together, put together
> 4 work together, pull together
> 5 go together

 b Learners ask and answer the questions and ask follow-up questions to find out more.
 Round-up. Ask each pair or group to tell you the most interesting thing they talked about or found out from their partner.

> **Alternative: Mingling activity**
>
> Give each learner one of the questions to ask. Learners move freely round the class, asking their question to three or four learners.
> *Round-up.* Ask learners to tell you the most interesting answer they received.

Explore writing

Goals: describe an organisation
present something in the best possible light

Core language:
Positive language

1 a Books closed. Write the word *Shelter* on the board. Ask what a shelter is (= a simple building that protects you from the weather or from bombs). Tell the class that this is the name of a charity in the UK, and ask what they think its purpose might be (*answer:* it campaigns to provide homes for homeless people).

 Open books. Cover the webpage and look at the poster. Discuss what message the poster conveys and how it achieves it. Bring out these points:
 – it's about people losing their homes (*repossessed* = the mortgage company takes the home away from the owners because they can't pay).
 – the house of cards = owning your home is very insecure; it could collapse at any moment.

 b *Pre-reading.* Discuss what else Shelter possibly fights for. Try to get a few different ideas (e.g. the rights of home owners, the rights of homeless people, providing cheap accommodation).

2 a *Reading to check.* Learners read the webpage. Possible answers:

> They help homeless people, make their lives better (alleviate distress)
> They help people in bad housing
> They give information
> They fight for people's legal rights (advocacy)
> They lobby (try to persuade) the government to improve housing
> They pass information to the media

 b, c Learners choose headings, then choose an overall heading. Discuss the answers together. Expected answers (1–4):

> 1 About us
> 2 Help and advice
> 3 Informing professionals
> 4 Fighting for change

3 a *Focus on language.* Discuss how the ideas in the sentences are expressed on the webpage and use this to focus on features of style:
 1 Shelter *alleviates* (= makes less severe) the *distress* caused by homelessness.
 This sounds more serious and more caring.

2 *We can give* confidential help to people with *all kinds of* housing problems.
Active verb forms sound more personal / positive; *can* implies they are ready, available; they can give help to a wide range of people.

3 Shelter *tackles* the *root causes* of bad housing.
Sounds more thorough – they go to the root of the problem.

4 *Our influential campaigns bring … to the attention.*
Making *our campaigns* the subject suggests they play an active role, they take the initiative.

5 We *develop* practical solutions to *address …*
Again, this makes them sound active and successful.

b Discuss other ways in which the webpage casts the organisation in a good light. Focus on:
– the use of positive adjectives and phrases: *lasting change, for good, influential campaigns, a leading expert, practical solutions, proud, creative ways.*
– the use of *we*, which conveys directness and action.
– the division into short sections with headings, which makes the message clear and convincing.

c Focus on the verbs used:

> Helping and solving problems: *alleviate, give help, tackles, lobbying, address, improve, develop*
> Fighting: *campaigning, join forces, fight for*

d Discuss why these verbs are used.

> They give an impression they are effective and they solve problems.
> They give the impression that homelessness is a battle that they need to win.

4 Learners form the same groups as for the activity on p100. Together, they write a description of their own campaign in the style of the Shelter webpage.

> **Alternative: Individual writing**
> Working alone, learners write material for a webpage. Then they form the same groups as for the activity on p100 and compare what they have written.

10 Look again

GRAMMAR Inversion

1 a Read through the example and discuss the questions. Point out that:
– because there is an adverbial expression at the start, the subject and verb change places (so the word order is the same as for questions). We call this 'inversion'.
– this makes the sentence more emphatic, because *not only* is given special prominence (and is stressed).

b Learners suggest other possible expressions. Build them up on the board. As you do this, you could give simple examples.

> not until (Not until I left home did he start speaking to me again)
> not once (Not once did they phone me)
> very / only rarely (Very rarely do I get a chance to relax)
> at no time (At no time should you turn the electricity off)
> in no way (In no way do I regret what I said)
> only once (Only once did I have a problem with my employees)
> only recently (Only recently did I read in the paper …)

2 a Learners complete the gaps.

b Discuss which sentences seem formal or informal.

c Try saying the sentences and decide where to put the stress.

d Play recording **3.14** to check and quickly practise saying each sentence with the class. Answers (alternative possibilities in brackets):

> 1 not once, (at no time)
> 2 In no way
> 3 at no time, (not once, only rarely)
> 4 Only rarely
> 5 Only recently, (Only now)

3 Learners re-write the sentences. Possible answers:

> 1 Only recently did we start making a profit.
> 2 At no time did he pick up the phone to see how I was.
> 3 Very rarely does it rain here in July.
> 4 Not until we were leaving the bar did I realise my bag was gone.
> 5 Not only is it pouring with rain, (but) it's also freezing!

4 a Books closed. To introduce this stage, write on the board *No way …* . Ask learners what might come next and build up a sentence word by word, getting learners to predict what will come next:
No way am I going to let him use the car.
Ask what it means (*answer:* I'm certainly not going to). Open books. Discuss the examples.

> 1 United certainly won't win the league (about a football team)
> 2 He certainly didn't write it (about a student's essay or assignment)
> 3 I certainly wouldn't want to (about a holiday resort)

b Play recording **3.15**. Learners mark the main stress (*answer:* see script).

> **Alternative**
> Learners say where they think the main stress should be in each sentence. Then play recording **3.15** to check.

5 a Learners write true sentences, using one of the expressions from this section.

b In turn, learners read out their sentence. Other learners ask further questions.

6 a Learners write captions for the pictures.

b Learners compare their captions.

Feedback. Ask each pair or group to read out the caption for each photo they think is best.

VOCABULARY Collective nouns for people

7 a Books closed. Write *group* on the board. Ask learners what other synonyms for *group* they remember from the unit, and any other synonyms they can think of.

b Learners look at the sentences and discuss the questions.

Discuss the answers together. Possible answers:

a *A film star, pop singer, sports celebrity.* = a large group, negative (other words: crowds, masses)
b *Report on a trial.* = a large, uncontrolled group, negative (other words: crowd, rabble)
c *Parent talking to a teenager who has been out late.* = a small, select group, negative or neutral (other words: group of friends, crowd)
d *A cinema listing.* = a small group of professionals, neutral (other words: team)
e *Someone talking about children at a new school.* = a very small exclusive group, negative (other words: gang, group)
f *Report on a band or pop group.* = a large group, neutral (other words: audience, listeners, fans)
g *Football news item.* = a small group playing together, neutral (other words: side, squad)

8 a *Focus on collocations.* Learners suggest collocations. Write the most likely ones on the board and check the meaning.

hordes of tourists	flight crew (on a plane)
crowds of tourists	crowd capacity (of a stadium)
mob violence	capacity crowds (= full)
gang violence	fans of the team
team member	hordes of children
gang member	crowds of children
mob rule	gang leader
	team leader

b Learners replace *group* with a more precise word.

1 crowd	4 crowds, hordes
2 team	5 crew
3 gang	6 gang, mob

9 *Writing.* Together, each pair writes a sentence with one of the words from this section. They pass it to the next pair.

They continue the story they received, then pass the paper to another pair. Continue in the same way with four or five sentences.

In turn, learners read out their story.

Alternative
To make this more challenging, ask learners to try to include a 'group' noun in each sentence they add. If necessary, they may need to add more than one sentence to include their noun.

VOCABULARY Collective adjectives

10 a Discuss what *the rich* and *the elderly* mean (= rich people and elderly people). Point out that:
– you use these expressions to talk about people in general, as a general class.
– they always function as plural nouns, so we say e.g.:
The elderly <u>need</u> to feel their life has a purpose.

Learners complete the sentences.

1 the disabled
2 the homeless
3 the rich and the poor
4 the elderly
5 the needy (= those in need)

b Ask how learners would express the same ideas in their language and whether they have a similar system of collective adjectives. The aim of this is to give them insight into differences between English and their own language.

c Learners look at each category in turn and discuss how attitudes have changed.

Round-up. Taking each category in turn, ask the class what conclusions they came to. Ask follow-up questions, e.g.
– *Do you think the elderly are better cared for now?*
– *Do you think they should be cared for in homes or in the family?*
– *Is the gap between the rich and poor bigger or smaller than 50 years ago? Why do you think that has happened? Do you think this will change?*
– *How have attitudes changed towards the disabled? If so, how?*
– *What facilities does your society provide for the disabled?*

Alternative: Group interview activity
Give each group a different category (*the elderly*, *the rich*, etc.) to think about. Together, they write a few questions they could ask to find out people's opinion (e.g. *Do you think the rich should pay more tax?*).
One person from each group goes to the next group and asks the questions. Then they move to the next group and repeat the procedure, and so on until they have asked all the other groups.
Learners return to their original group and report back on what the 'interviewees' said.

 You could use photocopiable activity 10C on the Teacher's DVD-ROM at this point.

Self-assessment

To help focus learners on the self-assessment, you could read it through, giving a few examples of the language they have learned in each section (or asking learners to tell you). Then ask them to circle a number on each line.

Unit 10 A sense of belonging 107

Unit 10 Extra activities on the Teacher's DVD-ROM

Printable worksheets, activity instructions and answer keys are on your Teacher's DVD-ROM.

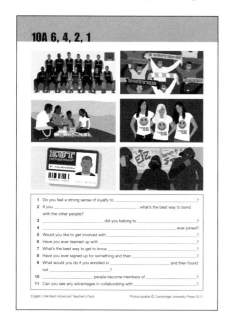
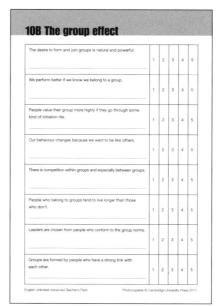

10A 6, 4, 2, 1

Activity type: Speaking – Personalised discussion – Whole class

Aim: To discuss ways of learning English

Language: Talking about membership – use at any point after Language focus, p97

Preparation: Make one copy of the worksheet for each learner.

Time: 25–35 minutes

10B The group effect

Activity type: Speaking and reading – Discussion – Pairs

Aim: To practise language used to add emphasis

Language: Being emphatic – use at any point after Language focus, p99

Preparation: Make one copy of the worksheet for each learner.

Time: 25–35 minutes

10C Manifesto

Activity type: Speaking – Role-play discussion task – Groups of three

Aim: To develop oral fluency in decision-making tasks

Language: Collective adjectives – Coursebook, p105 – Vocabulary

Preparation: Make one copy of the worksheets for each group. Cut along the dotted line.

Time: 40–60 minutes, depending on group size

Unit 10 Self-study Pack

In the Workbook

Unit 10 of the *English Unlimited Advanced Self-study Pack Workbook* offers additional ways to practise the vocabulary and grammar taught in the Coursebook. There are also activities which build reading and writing skills, and two pages which give your learners the opportunity to develop their skills in extended reading.

- **Vocabulary:** Collective nouns for people; Groups and membership; *together*
- **Grammar:** Being emphatic; Inversion

On the DVD-ROM

Unit 10 of the *English Unlimited Advanced Self-study Pack DVD-ROM* contains interactive games and activities for your learners to practise and improve their vocabulary, grammar and pronunciation, and also their speaking and listening

- **Vocabulary and grammar:** Extra practice of the Coursebook language and Keywords
- **Explore listening:** A football tournament
- **Explore speaking:** Emphasising opinions

11 Climate

11.1

Goals: talk about climate change
describe inventions and how they work
discuss proposals

Core language:
LANGUAGE FOCUS   Climate change
LANGUAGE FOCUS   Active and passive infinitives

Radical ways to save the planet

LISTENING

1 a Ask if learners have heard of Richard Branson and if so, what they know about him. If they don't know, tell them a few things about him, e.g.:
– he's a British billionaire entrepreneur.
– he founded the record label Virgin Records and the airline Virgin Atlantic.

> **Alternative: Homework preparation**
> Before the lesson, learners find out about Richard Branson on the Internet. Start the lesson by asking what they found out.

Discuss why the photo was taken. Learners will probably guess that it had something to do with saving the planet.

b *Listening for general idea.* Play recording **3.16**. Learners listen and answer the questions.

> 1 $25 million to anyone who could find a way to reduce greenhouse gases.
> 2 Because he wants to reverse global warming. Probably also for publicity.

Ask whether learners think his offer is a good idea and why or why not, but don't get involved in lengthy discussion about global warming at this point.

LANGUAGE FOCUS Climate change

2 a Ask which words are connected with climate change and explain any that learners don't know.

> atmosphere
> carbon dioxide (= CO_2)
> global warming
> climate change
> greenhouse gases
> temperatures

👤/👥 Learners write sentences to show the connections between the words in the word cloud. Possible answers:

> *Billionaire Richard Branson offered a prize of $25 million.*
> *Greenhouse gases such as carbon dioxide are causing global warming.*
> *The United Nations has said that climate change is 90% likely to be caused by humans.*
> *Temperatures will rise by six degrees by the end of the century.*

Learners say what the report said, using the words and phrases from the word cloud. You could do this round the class, with each learner adding a new piece of information.

b *Listening to check.* Play recording **3.16** again and focus on any words or expressions that are different from what learners said.

READING and SPEAKING

3 a *Pre-reading.* Learners look at images A–E without reading the article and say what they think each one shows.

b *Reading to check.* Learners read the article, then check the answers. If necessary, present the meaning of *plankton* (= tiny plants and animals that live in the sea), *sulphur* (chemical symbol S) and *yacht* (= sailing boat).

> A giant sunshade
> B cloud yacht
> D sulphur rocket
> E plankton farms

Discuss that the ideas involve:

> – Reducing CO_2 levels: plankton farms
> – Absorbing the sun's heat: sulphur rockets
> – Deflecting the sun's rays: sunshade; pumping water

Artificial trees

LANGUAGE FOCUS Active and passive infinitives

1 *Reading for main idea.* Look at the 'artificial tree' in picture C and ask how it might work. Learners read the article and find answers to the questions. When they have finished, they discuss answers with a partner.

> 1 Like a tree: *they have the equivalent of a trunk, branches and leaves; the 'leaves' collect CO_2 from the air.*
> Unlike a tree: *the 'leaves' are packed more tightly, so it's more efficient.*
> 2 By a chemical reaction as the wind passes through it.
> 3 It's turned into concentrated CO_2 which can be buried.

2 a *Focus on passive infinitives.* Read the examples and write the passive sentence on the board: *Carbon dioxide would be extracted.* Check that learners can form the passive infinitive (*be* + past participle).

b Learners note down examples of infinitives from the article.

Check the answers, and for each one discuss alternative forms and how this would affect the meaning.

Unit 11 Climate   109

Active	Passive
could solve	could be removed
would have	could be stored
would hold	could be packed
would stand	could be planted
would look like	would be coated
could extract	would be extracted
would work	could be buried
would extract	
would collect	

Focus on these points:
- the passive gives distance and objectivity to the article; it is typical of scientific writing of this kind.
- using active forms instead of passives (*you could pack*) would sound more informal.
- an alternative active form *It would be possible to pack* ... would be clumsy and long-winded.
- generally, active forms are used in the article only where the agent (subject) is important, e.g. *each tree would collect* ... or where the verb is intransitive: *the apparatus would work* ... .

3 a Learners cover the article and continue the sentences.

  b Check the answers together, or let learners check in the article to see if the verbs were the same. Possible answers:

  > 1 be reduced
  > 2 be released; form a thin cloud-like layer
  > 3 increase the thickness of the clouds; be reflected
  > 4 be fed huge quantities of fertiliser; absorb CO_2 from the air

  > You could use photocopiable activity 11A on the Teacher's DVD-ROM at this point.

SPEAKING

4 *Introduction.* Explain the point of the discussion: each group should make a case for one of the inventions.

  Group preparation. Divide the class into five groups and give each group one of the proposals. They discuss together how they think it would work, and what arguments they will present in favour of it. They should consider:
  - how it would affect the climate, and how effective it would be.
  - what risks might be involved and how they would prevent them.
  - how much it would cost and how much energy it would use.

  Discussion. One person from each group presents their proposal to the class and responds to any questions or comments.

  Learners vote for the proposal they think is best.

  > **Alternative: Group discussion**
  >
  > For the discussion, learners form new groups, so that the groups contain one person from each original group. In turn, they present their idea to the group. They vote in their group for the best proposal.

11.2

Goals: describe an ongoing process
understand imagery in a poem

Core language:
LANGUAGE FOCUS   Processes

Glaciers

READING

1 Discuss photos A and B. Focus on these points:
  - the glaciers have receded dramatically (the first photo is the Upsala glacier, Argentina, in 1928; the second is the same glacier in 2004).
  - this was caused by global warming / climate change; less snow fell in the winter to replace the lost ice.
  - most scientists believe this was caused by increased greenhouse gases in the atmosphere.

2 a *Reading to predict.* Learners read the beginning of the article (you could ask them to cover the main part of the article).

  Establish what it is about (*answer:* icebergs breaking off a glacier in Greenland), and discuss the expressions.

  > calving season: *in summer, icebergs break off the glacier and float away; this is called 'calving', like a cow giving birth to a calf*
  > a flotilla of icebergs: *they are like a group of sailing ships (drifting slowly and magnificently)*
  > eerily beautiful: *beautiful but also strange*

  b Discuss why the writer uses the expressions. Either draw attention to these points now, or return to them after learners have read the main article:

  > - 'a chilling view' = a view of ice and snow ('chilling' = makes you cold), but also a view that makes you scared for the future, because it's a sign of climate change ('chilling' = makes you afraid).
  > - it's 'utterly terrifying' because icebergs are huge and dangerous; but what is happening (= the retreat of glaciers) is also terrifying because of what it means for the world.

3 a *Reading for general idea.* Learners read the article quickly (you could give them a time limit).

  Establish the main point of the article.

  > Glaciers are losing ice faster than they can replace it; the ice sheet is melting.
  > Scientists understand what is happening but not why it is happening so fast.

  b *Reading for detail.* Learners read and make brief notes. When they have finished, they could compare their notes with a partner, but don't discuss them together yet.

LANGUAGE FOCUS Processes

4 a Learners answer the questions using verbs from the box.

  b Check the answers together or let learners check in the article. Possible answers:

110   Unit 11 Climate

> 1 The ice is melting, is disappearing, is vanishing.
> The ice isn't being replenished, it's shedding ice.
> This could trigger a new effect.
> The glacier is marching forwards, has accelerated, is flowing at a greater pace.
> It's transmitting ice from the ice sheet to the ocean.
> The level of the ocean could rise.
> 2 The ice sheets maintained an equilibrium.
> Ice was replenished every winter.

Focus on these words:
– *shedding ice* = losing it (e.g. a snake *sheds* its skin)
– *trigger* an effect = it suddenly happens (like pressing the *trigger* on a gun)
– *replenish* = replace, fill up again (e.g. you *replenish* stocks of food)

c Discuss the topics in **3b** together. Possible points:

> 1 It's vanishing / disappearing faster than expected.
> 2 He's a glaciologist. He discovered the glacier had accelerated, was flowing faster.
> 3 They have risen (now five degrees above normal).
> 4 The melting ice triggers new effects which can't be predicted, so it is not a steady process.

d Discuss other 'dynamic effects', e.g.
– permafrost melting, triggering the release of trapped methane into the atmosphere.
– climate change leading to drying out of the rainforest, causing fires.
– CO_2 causing increased acidity in the oceans, leading to coral reefs dying.

2084

READING

1 a *Reading.* Learners read about Phaethon. Quickly check the information about him, and discuss what the story might represent (*possible answer:* the irresponsibility of humans, they have taken over the world, but they don't know what they are doing and will destroy it).

b Discuss the significance of 1984. If necessary, explain that it is the title of a novel by George Orwell (written in 1948): a vision of a totalitarian society in the future where everyone is kept under constant surveillance by 'Big Brother'. So this poem will also be about a future society where people are controlled.

2 a Play recording **3.17** and let learners follow the poem, or let them read the first part of the poem in their own time, then play the recording afterwards.

Optional discussion

Discuss what the poem seems to be about in general, and bring out these ideas:
– it's a vision of society in 2084.
– it seems to be a farming community (ponds, fields) and religious (scripture-safe).
– they seem to be very ecological (they have windmills, they've abolished runways).

Focus on expressions that refer to climate change and discuss what they might mean:

> ice-bar (floating ice or the edge of an ice-sheet, or perhaps a bar to keep ice away)
> that flood, in motion inches from the cross-roads (the sea level has risen)
> the world will sail over the carbon peak (they have reduced carbon emissions, so the world will become safe again)

b Learners find expressions, then discuss them together.

> bicycles: *paired wheels*
> solar heating: *PV (= photovoltaic) panels*
> computers: *one screen only, daily rationing of downloads*
> a group of houses / flats: *each estate (= housing estate)*

3 Learners read the second part of the poem. Play recording **3.18** at the same time. Discuss the questions.

> 1 borrowed chariot, thunder of gold tyres, infelix Phaethon, drove, children
> 2 burn, brand (= piece of burning wood), spark (= start a fire), blazing (can refer to bright light or a brightly burning fire), fires
> 3 humans (they destroyed everything)

LISTENING and SPEAKING

4 a Play recording **3.19** and establish what the speaker says the main message is (*answer:* that humans will survive, but our children will blame us for what we did to the world).

b ♟ / ♟♟ Learners identify parts of the poem that refer to each point.

> Lifestyle: *lines 1–6: ponds, hives, fields, windmills*
> Society: *scripture-safe (religious); one screen, rationing of downloads, the government says so (totalitarian, controlled)*
> Children: *2nd part, lines 1–7 (they want to burn things, drive fast cars)*
> Parents: *last part of the poem (they drove the chariot earth to destruction)*

5 a Play recording **3.20** of the complete poem. Discuss what connection there is with the article (*possible answer:* the article warns of climate change, the poem imagines life after it has happened).

b Ask learners if they know of other visions of the future. Discuss whether they are positive or negative. You could refer to films such as *The Matrix*, *The Road*, *Bladerunner*, among other science fiction novels and films.

11.3 Target activity: The Doomsday debate

Goals: talk about climate change
describe an ongoing process
say if actions are justified
conduct a debate

Core language:
11.1 LANGUAGE FOCUS   Climate change
11.2 LANGUAGE FOCUS   Processes
TASK LANGUAGE   Saying if actions are justified

TASK LISTENING

1 a *Pre-listening.* Discuss the questions and bring out these points:

1 *Gaia* is the Greek word for Mother Earth.
2 clearly pessimistic, he thinks the world is being destroyed.

b *Listening for main idea.* Read through the opinions, then play recording **3.21**.

Discuss the answers together.

> 1 • Yes.
>   • No. Lovelock thinks they are responsible.
>   • Yes (like someone playing with a gun).
>   • No. But Lovelock thinks it is very unlikely.
> 2 Because it seems a very irresponsible idea.

TASK LANGUAGE Saying if actions are justified

2 a Learners choose sentences that match (*answer:* 1, 2, 3, 5).

b Discuss the highlighted adjectives.

> a pointless
> b feasible
> c isn't really justified
> d crucial
> e inevitable
> f worthwhile

c Learners express the sentences using words from the box. Possible answers:

> 3 There's no point in using low-energy light bulbs.
>   Using low-energy light bulbs makes no sense.
>   Using low-energy light bulbs makes no difference.
> 5 There's no real justification for the amount of money we invest in wind power.
> 6 It's certainly worth holding conferences on climate change.
>   Conferences on climate change will achieve a lot.

TASK PREPARATION

3 a *Introduction.* Read out each opinion and find out who agrees with it.

b Divide the class into two or four groups according to their opinion. Each group reads their text and answers the questions. Go from group to group, checking and discussing the answers.

> **Note**
> If nearly all learners have the same point of view, simply divide them into random groups. In the task, they argue for the point of view they have read about.

TASK

4 a *Preparation.* Groups discuss what arguments they will present. They could make brief notes of what they might say.

b *Debate.* Groups choose one person to be their 'speaker'. In turn, the speakers present their case. If there are two speakers for each side, the second speaker should add further arguments not already covered by the first speaker.

After the speakers have each presented their case, the debate is 'thrown open to the floor'. Other people in the class can add further points or ask questions of any of the speakers.

> **Alternative: Group discussion**
> For the discussion phase, learners form new groups, each containing both A and B learners. They discuss the issue together, taking it in turns to make their case.
> *Round-up.* Ask each group what points they agreed and disagreed about.

11 Explore

Across cultures: Living 'off-grid'

Goal: to make learners aware of different attitudes towards an environmentally friendly lifestyle

Core language:
off-grid, self-sufficiency, energy consumption, fossil fuels

1 *Pre-reading.* Look at the photo and discuss the meaning of *off-grid* (= providing your own power, so you don't depend on the national grid; the photo shows a cottage with solar power).

2 a *Reading to check.* Learners read the first two paragraphs. Establish these points:
– living 'off-grid' applies to electricity, gas, water supplies and sewage. So if you are 'off-grid', you supply all these independently.
– people do it because it gives them independence and security, and they feel less guilty (because they know their power comes from renewable energy).

b Cover the article. Learners suggest collocations. Then they check in the article.

> He doesn't pay electricity bills.
> He has his own electricity company.
> He generates electricity.
> He sources his own water.
> He manages his own waste disposal.

3 *Vocabulary focus.* Learners find nouns and adjectives in the article.

Elicit words and write them on the board in two lists, positive and negative. Possible answers:

(+)	(-)
glee	maverick
guilt-free	hippie
unconnected	survivalist
security	pipe dream
peace of mind	
good life	
pioneer	
self-sufficiency	

Focus on any new or difficult words, e.g. *maverick* (= someone who acts independently and isn't always taken seriously), *survivalist* (= someone who believes civilisation is going to end, so sets up an alternative lifestyle to survive), *pipe dream* (= an impossible plan).

4 *Discussion.* Learners discuss the questions.

Feedback. Look at each question in turn and ask different pairs or groups what they thought about it.

Keywords: describing similarities and differences

Goal: to say how things are similar or different

Core language:

like, unlike, equivalent to, identical to, just as, in the same way as, tantamount to, as opposed to, in contrast to

1 *Focus on key words.* Read the examples, then ask learners to rephrase the sentences using the expressions in the box. Possible answers:

> 1 Just like a real tree, …
> Just as a real tree has, …
> An artificial tree is similar to a real tree in having …
> 2 Unlike in a real tree …
> Rather than the leaves being spread out, as with a real tree, the leaves …

> **Language note**
>
> *like / unlike* are followed by a noun or noun phrase, so we can say:
> – *like / unlike a real tree …*
>
> You cannot say *as a real tree*. You have to say *as with a real tree* (= *as is the case with*), or use a complete sentence:
> – *(just) as a real tree does …*
>
> After *whereas* we need a complete sentence:
> – *Whereas a real tree has leaves …*
>
> After *rather than*, you can use an *-ing* form:
> – *Rather than the leaves being spread out …*
> – *Rather than having spread-out leaves …*

2 a *Focus on 'like', 'unlike'.* Learners complete the sentences.

Go through the answers by discussing what words in each sentence give a clue to the answer.

> 1 Unlike (rugged – wide / sandy = a contrast)
> 2 unlike (without disciplinary problems – stormy = a contrast)
> 3 Like (all forms of art: popular music is a form of art)
> 4 unlike (prohibitively expensive: notebook computers are obviously cheaper to ship)
> 5 like (lime juice, sour: we know lime juice has a sour taste)
> 6 like (pram, box on wheels: they are similar)

b Learners think of possible additions.

Discuss the sentences together and elicit a range of ideas. Possible answers:

> 1 unlike his predecessor
> 2 unlike other colas / like all our drinks
> 3 like many people of my age / unlike you
> 4 unlike bears
> 5 like tennis players / unlike golfers

3 a *Other expressions.* Learners think of possible continuations.

Discuss the answers together. Focus on the word following each highlighted expression and write the complete collocations on the board. Check that learners understand what each expression means. Answers (possible continuations in brackets):

> 1 the equivalent of (branches and leaves)
> = has the same function or purpose
> 2 identical to (those of the suspect)
> = exactly the same as
> 3 equivalent to (one pound)
> = the same value
> 4 just as (their grandparents did)
> = in the same way as
> 5 in the same way as (state-owned companies)
> in the same way that (the government is)
> 6 tantamount to (admitting she was guilty)
> = almost the same as
> 7 as opposed to (taking the car)
> = rather than
> 8 in contrast to (most Latin American countries)
> = unlike, different from

b Play recording **3.22** to check and compare answers.

4 a *Speaking.* Learners write sentences about images A–D.

Learners read out one of their sentences. Other people identify which image it is about.

b Learners write four or five sentences about where they live, using words and expressions from this section.

Learners read out what they have written. See if other people in the class agree, or (if learners come from a different place) whether the same is also true for where they live.

Explore speaking

Goals: report a point of view
react to a point of view

Core language:

Ways of reporting what someone says
Ways of agreeing and disagreeing with what someone says

1 a Quickly ask learners what they remember about James Lovelock and his views about climate change.

Listening for main point. Play recording **3.23**. Pause after each speaker and establish if they agree or disagree and what their opinion is.

> Pilar: *Disagrees. She thinks things aren't as bad as he says.*
> Uri: *Partly agrees, but thinks it's worth trying to combat climate change.*
> Patrick: *He agrees that politicians don't say how bad things really are.*
> Jane: *She agrees. She thinks we'd have to invent new technology to combat climate change.*

b *Agreeing and disagreeing.* Learners suggest possible ways to complete the gaps, either from memory or according to what they think the speakers could say.

c Play the recording again, pausing to check the answers. Write the expressions on the board in two lists: agreeing and disagreeing.

> Agreeing:
> *I partly agree.*
> *I think he's got a point.*
> *I think that's a valid point.*
> *What he says is spot on.*
> *I think he's absolutely right.*
> Disagreeing:
> *I don't really agree with him.*
> *I think he's exaggerating.*
> *I don't really see that.*

2 a *Reporting a point of view.* Look at the expressions and discuss how they change the meaning. Establish that:
– the expressions in B give added emphasis to what follows.
– the present progressive (*is saying*, *is making*) conveys the meaning 'at this point in his argument', so also gives the statement more focus.

   b Play recording **3.24** and ask which words are emphasised (*answer: really, point*). Learners practise saying the sentences with the correct emphasis.

   c Learners identify similar expressions in the script.

> *That's exactly what he's saying.*
> *Lovelock makes the point that …*
> *When he says it's too late …*

   Ask where the stress should be and practise saying the sentences.

3 a *Listening.* Play recording **3.25**. Pause after each speaker and ask what they are talking about.

> Jane   B travelling by plane – she thinks it's necessary.
> Tina   D battery chicken farms – she thinks they are terrible.
> Pilar C downloading music – he thinks it doesn't do any harm, everyone does it.
> Uri   A war – he thinks it doesn't achieve anything and you can't control it.

   b Play recording **3.26** to check. Pause after each speaker and ask learners to briefly say if they agree or not. Don't ask them to give reasons at this point.

   c *Preparation.* Learners choose one opinion and prepare to comment on it. They note down a few expressions they could use.

   d *Discussion.* In turn, learners report the opinion and comment on it. Their partner (or others in the group) say if they agree.

   Round-up. Ask pairs or groups what their opinions were and whether they agreed or not.

> **Alternative: Mingling activity**
> Learners move freely round the class, reporting and commenting on their opinion to three or four different people. Each time, they find out if the other person agrees with them.
> *Round-up.* Ask learners to tell you their opinion about the topic they chose and whether most people they spoke to agreed or not.

 You could use photocopiable activity 11B on the Teacher's DVD-ROM at this point.

11 Look again

GRAMMAR Present progressive active and passive

> **Optional lead-in**
> Books closed. Ask the class when we use the present progressive and ask for some examples. Then ask them how we form the passive.

1 a Look at the examples. Ask which use each one shows and which uses the passive.

> 1a (passive)   2b   3b   4b   5a

   b Learners find other examples in the article.

> Use a:
> *It is melting*
> *The ice is vanishing*
> *Arctic temperatures are warming*
> *The Greenland ice sheet is now shedding …*
> *… it is accumulating*
> *We can't explain why they are happening*
> Use b:
> *Straneo's research is looking at …*

2 a Learners continue the sentences. Discuss the answers together. Possible answers:

> 1 are disappearing
> 2 is being eroded
> 3 are being introduced
> 4 is declining / increasing
> 5 is increasing

   b Discuss which adverbs you could add to each sentence. Most likely adverbs:

> gradually (1, 2, 3, 4, 5)
> rapidly (1, 2, 3, 4, 5)
> noticeably (1, 2, 3, 4, 5)
> steadily (1, 2, 3, 4, 5)
> dramatically (2, 4, 5)
> alarmingly (2, 4, 5)
> imperceptibly (= you don't notice it) (2)
> experimentally (3)

   Make these points about the position of the adverbs:
   – adverbs that indicate the speed or pace of change most naturally come before the main verb:
   The fish are gradually disappearing.
   The coast is being steadily eroded.
   – adverbs which have an additional meaning are likely to come after the main verb:
   The crops are being introduced experimentally.
   The number of sea turtles is declining alarmingly.

3 Learners write four or five sentences, using adverbs if possible.

   In turn, learners tell each other their sentences and ask and answer further questions.

   Round-up. Ask a few pairs to tell you their most interesting sentences.

GRAMMAR Cleft sentences

> **Optional presentation**
>
> Books closed. Write on the board:
> – *I'd really like to live in Vancouver.*
> – *I'd like a good, strong cup of coffee.*
> Ask how you could emphasise *Vancouver* and *coffee* more strongly. If necessary, prompt them by writing sentence beginnings:
> – *The place …*
> – *What …*
> Point out that we call these 'cleft' sentences (because they are split into two parts).
> You could also ask learners whether there is an equivalent way to give emphasis in their own language (this may be done in a different way, e.g. by changing the word order).

4 a Read the examples and show how they emphasise the idea more strongly than a normal sentence (*I'd really like to live in Vancouver*).

b Discuss how to emphasise the underlined items in the examples, using cleft sentences. Possible answers:

> 1 *The colour that really works well for a bedroom is light green.* (or *What really works well …*)
> 2 *I think what she's really trying to do is get attention.*
> 3 *The people I really hate are rude shop assistants.*
>   *What I really hate is rude shop assistants.*
> 4 *What I remember most clearly is our first holiday together.*
> 5 *The main reason I like living here is that it's close to the sea.*
>   *What I really like about living here is that it's close to the sea.*

c Play recording **3.27** to check and compare answers. Identify additional words:

> 1 one colour
> 2 really trying
> 3 more than anyone else in the whole world
> 4 most clearly of all
> 5 most of all

Ask which words were stressed (*answer:* the words that give emphasis: *really, most, all*). You could ask learners to practise saying the sentences, paying attention to the stress pattern.

5 a Discuss the examples together, or let learners discuss them in pairs and then talk about them together. Possible answers:

> A 1 *People leaving rubbish instead of putting it in bins.*
>   2 *People who don't put things in bins have no responsibility.*
> B 1 *Talking about someone who has just died.*
>   2 *Erika always had time for you, which was a rare gift.*
> C 1 *Talking about dogs (or some other pet, e.g. cats)*
>   2 *No other animal can give you such special company as dogs.*
> D 1 *Someone explaining why they moved out of a flat.*
>   2 *I could hear everything and I couldn't stand the noise any more, so I left.*

b To introduce this, tell the class about something that irritates or pleases you, using a cleft sentence structure.

Learners write a sentence about themselves. As they do this, go round and check that they include an appropriate cleft sentence structure.

In turn, learners say what irritates / pleases them, using their sentence and expanding on it. The others could ask follow-up questions.

VOCABULARY Adverb / adjective collocations

> **Optional lead-in**
>
> Books closed. Ask learners if they remember what adjective was used to describe the icebergs in the article (*answer: beautiful*), and what adverb was used with *beautiful* (*answer: eerily*).
> Open books. Read the example.

6 a Look at the adverb / adjective collocations and ask how they would affect the meaning. As you discuss this, focus on any unfamiliar adverbs.

> – *strangely beautiful* = beautiful and strange
> – *breathtakingly beautiful* = so beautiful it takes your breath away, it's almost too much
> – *exquisitely beautiful* = with beautiful details (usually used of small things)
> – *astonishingly beautiful* = it astonishes you
> – *stunningly beautiful* = extremely beautiful (it's so beautiful you almost lose consciousness – it stuns you)
> – *heart-rendingly beautiful* = so beautiful it makes you want to cry (it tears at your heart)

b Learners discuss suitable expressions for each item.

Point out that some of the items can be used as adjectives with the meaning 'very beautiful':
– *She looks stunning.*
– *It's an exquisite piece of jewellery.*
– *The view was breathtaking.*

7 Learners choose suitable adverbs. Point out that all the adverbs in the box have the meaning 'very'. Discuss what additional meaning they give.

> 1 *stiflingly hot* (= you can hardly breathe)
> 2 *a bitterly cold wind* (= extremely cold, very unpleasant)
> 3 *hideously ugly* (= you don't want to look at them)
> 4 *highly intelligent* (= he / she has a very high IQ)
> 5 *notoriously dangerous* (= it's known to be dangerous, there have been lots of accidents)
> 6 *blissfully happy* (= their life is perfect, they have no problems)
> 7 *wildly successful* (= its success had no limits)

> **Language note**
>
> These are commonly used adverb / adjective collocations. You could also try out other less likely collocations and discuss what connotation they would have, e.g.
> – *a notoriously cold wind*
> – *a stiflingly intelligent person*
> – *blissfully hot weather*
> – *a hideously happy couple*

8 Learners find a pair of adverbs for each gap. Go through the answers and focus on differences in meaning:

> 1 critically (= dangerously)
>   terminally (= he won't recover)
> 2 resolutely (= she made up her mind)
>   irrepressibly (= nothing could prevent her)
> 3 obstinately (= he refused to speak)
>   tactfully (= he didn't want to embarrass anyone by saying something)
> 4 dangerously (= it was dangerous)
>   terrifyingly (= I was very scared)
> 5 reassuringly (= it made me feel less worried)
>   strangely (= I recognised them, but I couldn't think who they were)
> 6 deceptively (= you think it's easy but it isn't – it deceives you)
>   relatively (= easier than many rivers)
> 7 impossibly (= I couldn't do it)
>   frustratingly (= it annoyed me, I gave up)
> 8 eerily (= a strange atmosphere, something was wrong)
>   pleasantly (= it was nice, you could relax)

9 a Learners write a sentence for each photo, A–C, using an expression from this section.

   Learners compare what they have written.

 b For each photo, ask a few learners what they wrote, then play recording **3.28** to compare.

10 a Learners choose three expressions and write them in sentences about themselves or someone they know.

 b In turn, learners tell their partner a sentence and elaborate on it. They ask and answer questions to find out more.

> **Alternative: class game**
>
> In turn, learners read out one of their sentences. The others guess what the sentence is about. Then the person who read out the sentence explains.

> You could use photocopiable activity 11C on the Teacher's DVD-ROM at this point.

Self-assessment

To help focus learners on the self-assessment, you could read it through, giving a few examples of the language they have learned in each section (or asking learners to tell you). Then ask them to circle a number on each line.

Unit 11 Extra activities on the Teacher's DVD-ROM

Printable worksheets, activity instructions and answer keys are on your Teacher's DVD-ROM.

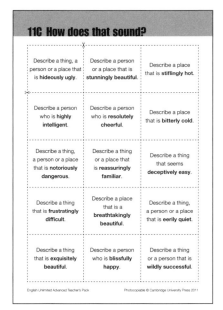

11A Survival!

Activity type: Speaking – Game – Groups of four

Aim: To practise making suggestions

Language: Active and passive infinitives – Coursebook p107 – Grammar

Preparation: Make one copy of the worksheet for each group. Cut into 16 cards.

Time: 30–40 minutes

11B It's not my fault!

Activity type: Speaking – discussion – Groups of four

Aim: To develop oral fluency on the subject of lifestyle changes

Language: Reacting to a point of view – Coursebook p113 – Explore speaking

Preparation: Make one copy of the worksheet for each group. Cut it into four role cards.

Time: 20–30 minutes

11C How does that sound?

Activity type: Speaking – Game – Pairs

Aim: To practise describing people, places and things

Language: Adverb / Adjective collocations – Coursebook p115 – Vocabulary

Preparation: Make one copy of the worksheet for each pair. Cut into 15 cards.

Time: 15–20 minutes

Unit 11 Self-study Pack

In the Workbook

Unit 11 of the *English Unlimited Advanced Self-study Pack Workbook* offers additional ways to practise the vocabulary and grammar taught in the Coursebook. There are also activities which build reading and writing skills, and a whole page of tasks to use with the DVD-ROM video, giving your learners the opportunity to hear and react to spoken English.

- **Vocabulary:** Climate change; Processes; Saying if things are justified; Adverb / adjective collocations; Describing similarities and differences
- **Grammar:** Present progressive active and passive; Cleft sentences
- **Explore writing:** Essays
- **DVD-ROM Extra:** Film excerpt – *Off-grid living*

On the DVD-ROM

Unit 11 of the *English Unlimited Advanced Self-study Pack DVD-ROM* contains interactive games and activities for your learners to practise and improve their vocabulary, grammar and pronunciation, and also their speaking and listening. It also contains video material (with the possibility for learners to record themselves) to use with the *Workbook*.

- **Vocabulary and grammar:** Extra practice of the Coursebook language and Keywords
- **Explore listening:** A discussion
- **Explore speaking:** Expressing agreement
- **Video:** Film excerpt – *Off-grid living*

12 Technology

12.1
Goals: talk about knowledge and technology
discuss how to access information

Core language:
LANGUAGE FOCUS: talking about information and knowledge

The end of general knowledge?

SPEAKING

1 *Discussion.* Learners discuss the questions. Encourage them to consider:
   - the advantages and disadvantages of different ways of finding out the information.
   - whether they would choose not to use the Internet for any of them and if so, why not.
   - if they would use the Internet, what sites they would look on and why.

   Ask what most learners would do and tell them what you would do yourself. An idea should emerge from this of how much the learners rely on computer technology (e.g. the Internet, navigation systems) to access information.

READING

2 a *Reading to make predictions.* Learners cover the main article and read just the first part.

   Discuss the questions and get learners to predict what the article might go on to say.

   b *Reading for general idea.* Learners read the article.

   Discuss in general what the main point of the article is and how it relates to the story at the beginning. Establish that:
   - it is about our reliance on technology, and whether this has led to a loss of general knowledge
   - the story is an example of people relying on technology (here, Sat-Nav) instead of their own knowledge or common sense.

3 a Discuss the connection between the image and the article. Ask learners for ideas, and establish that:
   - it shows a quiz show with 'Google' in a chair instead of a contestant.
   - this symbolises the way information from the Internet has replaced our own general knowledge (it gives the answers instead of us).

   b Learners discuss the questions. Possible answers:

   > 1 Increasingly, people look up information rather than committing it to memory. The more quickly you can access information, the less need there is to know it yourself.
   > 2 Knowledge about the world, facts, where places are, etc.

   > 3 In the story, writing was a new invention, like the Internet today. Writing, like the Internet, makes it less necessary to learn things by heart. The king believed writing would destroy learning and knowledge, as people do now about the Internet.
   > 4 Jones sees the Internet as a useful tool, like writing, and not a threat to knowledge. Swift thinks it might make people not bother to learn information themselves, but he also thinks it will increase people's knowledge by making it more available.

   c Discuss what the writer will go on to say.
   d Learners read the paragraph on p134 to check.

LANGUAGE FOCUS Talking about information and knowledge

4 a Learners cover the article and answer the questions.

   b Discuss the answer to question 1. Learners could check answers in the article. Write the collocations in two lists on the board:

Information / facts	Knowledge
look up	value
find out	acquire
commit to memory	pick up
know	
absorb	

   Focus on these expressions:
   - *acquire knowledge* = get, gain
   - *absorb information* = we take it in without being aware of it (like a sponge)
   - *commit something to memory* = consciously memorise it (you might do this with someone's name or a PIN)
   - *look something up* = find it in a book or on the Internet

   Discuss the other questions. Possible answers:

   > 2 look up, find out (both ways to get information)
   > acquire, pick up (both mean 'get new knowledge')
   > 3 absorb, value, pick up
   > 4 You key words into a search engine.
   > The man handed over responsibility to a machine.
   > You click on a search engine.
   > He outsourced the job of knowing the information to a computer.
   > The Internet gives people an opportunity to boost their general knowledge.

    You could use photocopiable activity 12A on the Teacher's DVD-ROM at this point.

LISTENING and SPEAKING

5 a *Listening for general idea.* Play recording **3.29**. Pause after each speaker and discuss the questions.

   b Answer the questions. If necessary, play the recording again, pausing to focus on the relevant parts of what the people say.

   c Ask learners which opinions they agree with.

118 Unit 12 Technology

6   *Preparation.* Learners think about the questions and make a few notes.

   Speaking activity. Learners exchange experiences, using their notes to help.

   Round-up. Ask a few learners to tell you some of their experiences and what they think about obtaining information online.

12.2

Goals: describe technological advances
talk about how things develop

Core language:
LANGUAGE FOCUS   Developments and advances

The Hole in the Wall

LISTENING

1 a *Prediction task.* Discuss what the photos show. Try to draw attention to these points:
   – It's in India, it seems to be a poor area of a city.
   – There are screens or windows built into the wall and keyboards.
   – The low cover suggests it's for use by children; the boys seem to be using it for something.

   b Learners read the extract, then ask what it indicates about the project (*answer:* it seems to be to observe children using computers for the first time).

   c Learners check their ideas on p139.

2 a *Listening for main idea.* Read through the questions, then play recording **3.30**. Discuss the questions together. Possible answers:

   > 1 They could teach themselves.
   > 2 By experimenting and watching each other.
   > 3 Educational software, word-processing software, educational games
   > 4 Believing in children can improve their lives. The Internet can give them access to the world.

   b Point out that the report was on TV, so it was accompanied by video images. Discuss what the images might have been at each point. Possible answers:

   > 1 children gathering round the Hole in the Wall
   > 2 one of the children using the computer
   > 3 an image from the film
   > 4 young adults working with computers

READING

3 a *Pre-reading.* Learners cover the interview. Discuss the questions and try to get a range of ideas.

   b Learners read the interview to check and compare answers.

   > 1 news, travel
   > 2 not specifically mentioned, but probably clicking around the Internet and improving their skills
   > 3 It makes their aspirations more realistic, makes them more tolerant; they have improved their computer skills

   c Learners write a question for each answer. Discuss the questions together or let them check on p135.

   d Learners think of arguments for and against the project and make brief notes. Discuss the arguments together. You could build up brief notes on the board in two lists.

   Possible arguments might be:
   In favour:
   – it gives insight into how children learn.
   – it gives poor children access to computers and the Internet, and so improves their lives.
   – it has educational value: it encourages children to experiment and acquire new skills.
   – it increases children's curiosity about the world and increases their self-confidence.
   Against:
   – it turns children into 'guinea pigs': they are being used for an educational experiment.
   – it seems to favour boys over girls, and probably more assertive children over shy ones.
   – it's not clear what the children really get from clicking around the Internet: the learning could be made more focused.

LANGUAGE FOCUS Developments and advances

4 a Learners write the verbs in three lists.

become popular	improve	increase
catch on	enhance	boost
spread	raise	soar
thrive	advance	expand
gain ground		

   Focus on these verbs and expressions:
   – *it caught on* = people heard about it, started applying it themselves.
   – *spread like wildfire* = very quickly.
   – *gain ground* = become more popular or accepted (e.g. a new idea, a product, a political party).
   – *his self-confidence soared* = like a bird flying up in the air.

   b Learners write a sentence using one of the verbs.

   c In turn, learners read out their sentence without mentioning the topic. The others listen and guess what it is about.

    You could use photocopiable activity 12B on the Teacher's DVD-ROM at this point.

SPEAKING

5 *Discussion.* Learners discuss the questions.
   Feedback. Taking each question in turn, ask each group what conclusion they came to.

12.3 Target activity: Deliver a confident message

Goals: explain an idea
deliver a positive message

Core language:
12.1 LANGUAGE FOCUS   Talking about information and knowledge
12.2 LANGUAGE FOCUS   Developments and advances

TASK PREPARATION

1 a   Ask learners to suggest questions that people might ask. To give this more focus, ask learners to note down two or three questions that they would want to ask.

b   *Reading to check.* Learners read the article on p137 and answer the questions. When they have finished, they compare their answers with a partner.

Discuss the questions together and ask what information in the article helped them decide. Possible answers:

> 1 a false. He's freelance (Demand Media is his 'employer for the day').
> b true. ('thousands of filmmakers', 'an army')
> c false. No, they work as quickly as possible (the videos are 'slapdash').
> d true. They mine search data, keywords, etc.
> e false. It's done automatically by an algorithm ('automatic, random and endless').
> f true. The algorithm can 'determine what people want to know'.
> 2 He thinks the quality is poor: 'good enough', 'loose standards', 'slapdash'.
> He thinks the company is very ambitious: 'enormous', 'surreal', 'aggressively', 'single-mindedly'.
> 3 He starts with a 'snapshot' of a typical photographer's work.
> He gives extreme examples of the content (e.g. 'How to draw a Greek helmet').
> He describes the excess of current Internet content as 'logorrhoea' (like 'diarrhoea').
> He thinks people's interests are quite random (e.g. the final sentence).

c   Discuss which part of the article is most surprising. Focus especially on:
– the way in which the topics are selected and the fact that this is possible.
– the way people are used (or exploited) to provide low-quality content quickly.

2   *Listening for main points.* Play recording **3.31**. Learners listen and answer the questions. As the listening is short but quite difficult to follow, you could play it a second time. Possible answers:

> 1 He gives an idea of the business model: to find a new way of providing media content.
> 2 Instead of creating content first, they find out what people want first and then create the content to match.
> 3 Instead of guessing what people want, they track search data to find out what information people are searching for (so the basis is scientific).
> 4 enthusiastic, optimistic, self-assured.

3 a, b   *Focus on language.* Look at the statements and discuss question 1. Bring out these points:
– he uses adjectives and adverbs that express certainty and which reinforce what he says: *whole, definitely, with surety* (= certainly), *successful*.

– he uses verbs which express confidence and determination: *set out, create, rethink, going to be*.

Get learners to say the statements aloud and discuss which words are emphasised.

c   After trying out each one, play recording **3.32** to check.

d   Learners try using the expressions in the sentences.

Discuss the answers together and focus on the meaning of any new items. Possible answers:

> We set out to create <u>cutting-edge</u> content. (= at the forefront of knowledge, most developed)
> <u>There's no question</u> that it's going to be successful.
> We set out to create a <u>totally unique</u> form of content. (= nothing else is like it)
> We set out to create an <u>innovative</u> form of content. (= it uses new ideas)
> We can know with surety that it's going <u>to flourish</u>. (= grow successfully)
> <u>Without any doubt</u>, it's causing people to rethink their business models.
> I'm <u>absolutely certain</u> that it's going to be successful.
> We set out to create a <u>ground-breaking</u> form of content. (= it breaks new ground, it does something no one has done before)
> We can know with surety that it's going to <u>catch on</u>. (= become popular)

TASK

4 a   *Preparation.* To show what to do, you could think of an idea yourself (for example, an improvement to the school where you are teaching). Explain your idea to the class, making it sound as convincing as possible.

Learners think of an idea and make brief notes to help them prepare. They should think how to include expressions like those in **3**.

b   *Explaining the idea.* In turn, learners 'interview' each other. They explain their idea to their partner and answer any questions. They could then form new pairs and repeat the interviews.

Round-up. Ask a few learners to tell you their partner's idea and whether they found it convincing.

Alternative: Preparation in pairs

Learners prepare their idea together with a partner. Then they form new pairs or groups for the interview stage.

12 Explore

Across cultures: Technology

Goal: to make learners aware of different attitudes towards technology

Core language:
gadget, fancy, status (symbol), innovate, innovation

1 a   Learners cover the texts. Look at the photos together and discuss the questions. Try and get ideas from the class:
– about what's going on in the first photo (*Why are there so many computers in one place? What are the people doing? Does it look like an office? a market?*

120   Unit 12 Technology

a stock exchange? something different? What do the people look like?)
– about what the second photo shows (*What can you tell about the people? What do they seem to be doing, and why? What part of the world is it?*)

b Learners read the captions. Then discuss the questions again and establish these answers:

> 1 A a computer programmers' conference
>   B a rubbish dump for computers
> 2 A Norway
>   B Ghana
> 3 They show a contrast: people who own and programme computers; people who make money from computer waste.
>   They also show a connection: the computers people used in the West will end up on a rubbish tip in Ghana.
> 4 They say something about:
>   – the gap between rich and poor
>   – 'throw-away' consumer society and waste
>   – exploitation of children.

Ask learners whether they think this is an accurate picture of the modern world.

2 a Play recording **3.33** and discuss the questions. Establish that:
– he seems to be saying that there isn't a growing gap in technology between rich and poor countries.
– mobile phones are probably an example of this.

b Play recording, **3.34**. Learners listen and note down answers to the questions.

👥 Learners compare answers.

Discuss the answers together.

> 1 the USA (she compares the USA with other countries)
> 2 in the USA, people want new and expensive gadgets. In developing countries, people want more uses from simple, cheap technology.
> 3 poorer countries are finding new ways of using basic technology.
> 4 India: text messages for job hunters
>   Kenya: personal finance (sending money)
>   Moldova: political protest
> 5 that you can do a lot with simple technology.
> 6 that the USA may get left behind in innovation, because it's concerned with producing expensive technology.

3 👥 / 👥👥 Learners discuss the questions.

Round-up. Ask each pair or group to tell you one conclusion they came to.

Keywords: *sure, certain*

Goal: to use *sure* and *certain* to describe a situation, or what you think will happen

Core language:
sure, surely, certain, certainly

Optional lead-in
Books closed. Write *sure* and *surely* on the board. Ask learners to suggest sentences using each word. Then open books and read the examples.

1 a *Focus on 'sure' and 'certain'.* Read the examples and discuss how the meaning changes if you substitute *certain* or *certainly*. Establish these points:

1 *sure* and *certain* mean the same (*Be sure / certain to write ...* = you should certainly do this). Other examples:
   – *They're sure / certain to phone soon.* (= they certainly will)
   – *I'm sure / certain this is his coat.*
   – A *They live at number 18.*
     B *Are you sure / certain?*

2 In British English *surely* is slightly different in meaning from *certainly*:
   – *Schools are certainly right to ...* is a neutral statement (= I'm sure / certain they are right).
   – *Schools are surely right to ...* implies a question or an argument (= I think they are right – don't you agree?).
   This difference doesn't apply in US English.

b 👥 / 👥👥 Learners discuss how to use the words in the box in the example sentences. Focus on these points.
– *make sure*, *be sure* and *ensure* can all be used in example 1, with roughly the same meaning. *Ensure* is more formal.
– *unquestionably* = there's no question about it. We could also say *There's no question that ...*
– *doubt* can be used in various ways:
  Without (any) doubt, it's ...
  There's no doubt that it's ...
  I have no doubt that it's ...

2 a 👤 / 👥👥 *Collocations with 'sure'.* Learners continue the sentences. Discuss the answers together. Try to get a few different answers for each sentence and discuss what they are about. Possible answers:

> 1 ... started crying a lot.
>   (two-year-old daughter's behaviour)
> 2 ... better value for money.
>   (a music CD or DVD)
> 3 ... competition from mainland China.
>   (the economy of China)
> 4 ... would be to shake hands.
>   (a cross-cultural misunderstanding)
> 5 ... he lost his concentration in the third set.
>   (a tennis match)

b Play recording **3.35** to check.

3 a, b *Use and position of 'surely'.* Remind learners of the way *surely* is often used to question or argue a point of view (refer back to the examples in **1a**). Then discuss where *surely* might go in each sentence and how it would affect the meaning. Ask which examples might be replies. Possible answers:

> 1 Surely they wouldn't have forgotten ...
>   They surely wouldn't have forgotten ...
>   (= I can't believe it)
> 2 ... must surely be viewed as a success
>   (= I strongly believe this)
> 3 You're joking with me, surely!
>   Surely you're joking with me!
>   (= You're joking, aren't you? replying to someone saying e.g. 'I'm over 70.')
> 4 Surely it's never happened before, though.
>   It's never happened before, though, surely.
>   (= questioning whether that really is true, replying to someone saying e.g. 'She's failed her exams again.')
> 5 But surely that's not the point.
>   But that's not the point, surely.
>   (= I don't believe it, replying to a point in an argument)

Point out that *surely* can come:
- in the normal adverb position (before the main verb).
- at the beginning or end of a sentence. In this position it is more emphatic and so suggests doubt or disbelief.

c Look at the examples and establish that *sure* and *surely* are typically used in conversational English or informal written style.

4 a *Focus on expressing certainty.* Learners try expressing the sentences using words from the box. Possible answers:

> 1 It's bound to be successful.
> It's sure to be successful.
> There's no shadow of a doubt it's going to be successful.
> 2 The Democrats will undoubtedly win again.
> The Democrats are going to win again – it's a foregone conclusion.
> The Democrats are certain to win again.

Focus on these points:
- *is bound to*, *is certain to*, *is sure to* are used for making predictions. They all mean roughly the same.
- *it's a foregone conclusion* = everyone already knows it will happen.
- *there's no shadow of a doubt* = it's completely certain.
- *undoubtedly* is a formal equivalent of *There's no doubt that ...*
- *chances are ...* is informal / conversational.

b Learners write sentences about photos A–D, using expressions from this section.

c Learners read out their sentences. Ask other people if they agree.

Explore writing

Goals: give written advice
write steps in a process
describe how to do something

Core language:
Giving advice in a text

1 a Books closed. Choose one of the 'How to ...' articles mentioned in the article in 12.2 (e.g. How to stop snoring) and discuss what kind of information it might contain and what form it might take. Bring out these ideas:
- it would probably have a series of short practical 'tips'.
- it might be in the form of a simple list with bullet points.
- it would probably include illustrations or diagrams to support the text.

Open books. Look at the two articles and establish that these are giving advice to people who want to write an informational article for a website.

Reading and gap-filling task. Learners read the articles and add imperative verbs in the gaps. Possible answers:

A	B
1 Choose / Select	1 be
2 bear	2 add
3 bore / annoy	3 try
4 get	4 remember
5 learn	5 write

b, c Discuss the two articles and bring out these points:
- A seems to be from a more specialised website (finance, business), pitched at a higher level, including expert advice.
- B seems to be from a general-interest website (hobbies, interests) and the writers themselves are not so qualified (they need reminding about spelling).
- both articles are in the form of quick tips and hints.
- other advice might be: don't spend too long researching the topic, as it's not worth it; keep language direct and simple; divide the content up into separate 'tips' to make it easier to read.

2 *Focus on language.* Learners give examples of typical language from the articles. Focus on expressions that are generally useful for giving advice. You could build useful words and expressions up on the board under two headings:

Imperatives and modals	Linking words
Try to ...	if ... then ...
Be sure to ...	so that ...
Remember to ...	or ...
Remember, ...	because ...
Don't ...	as long as ...
Simply ...	
Think about ...	
You should ...	
You need to ...	
You don't have to ...	
You'll want to ...	
... should be (written)	

3 a Discuss what expressions could go in the gaps. Possible answers:

> 1 Before, After
> 2 shopping
> 3 takes, needs, requires
> 4 key, trick
> 5 no one
> 6 When, As soon as

b Discuss possible article titles for each extract.

4 *Group writing.* Learners in each group choose a topic and plan an article. After brainstorming ideas, they could either write the article together (with one learner as 'secretary'), or they could split up and write different parts each, then put them together afterwards.

5 *Round-up.* In turn, one person from each group reads out their article. At the end, learners could vote on the best advice article (or the most unusual one, most useful one, most amusing one, etc.).

Alternative: Individual writing
1 Learners choose a topic and write a 'How to' article.
2 Learners read out their article in turn. Then they decide on the best one.
3 Each group reads out the article they chose to the rest of the class.

12 Look again

GRAMMAR Participle clauses

1 a Learners underline the participles. If necessary, point out that:
   - present participles are formed verb + -ing (*play* → *playing*, *choose* → *choosing*).
   - past participles are formed verb + -ed (*play* → *played*), or irregular forms (*choose* → *chosen*).

   | 1 coming   2 starting   3 asked |

   b Learners suggest other ways to say each sentence.

   | 1 When you come up with … / When you want to come up with …
   2 … information which is shared …
   3 Try to use words that people will search for on the Internet. This should start with the title.
   4 If they are asked a factual question, … |

   Point out that:
   - participles often replace a complete clause (*When you…, If they are …, which is …*).
   - past participles often replace a passive form (*is shared, are asked*).
   - participles are more likely to be used in written styles, because they give a 'tighter' structure to the sentence.

   Optional presentation
   To introduce present and past participle clauses, write two example sentences on the board, e.g.:
   – *When you choose a topic, follow your own interests.*
   – *When you have chosen a topic, make a few notes.*
   Ask how you express the same ideas with participles and elicit these examples:
   – *When choosing a topic, follow your own interests.*
   – *(After) Having chosen a topic, make a few notes.*

2 Learners change the sentences using a participle clause if possible. Go through the answers by discussing why a participle clause isn't possible in some cases.

   | 1 Not possible, because the subject changes ('I put …', 'she referred')
   2 The subject changes ('you have keyed …', 'it takes …'), so only a passive clause is possible: 'The words having been keyed in, an Internet search …'.
   3 'playing with …' (present participle)
   4 The subject changes ('she told …', 'he delivered …'), so only a passive clause is possible: 'In spite of having been told 'Stamford Bridge' … the driver delivered them.'
   5 'When shopping for clothes, …' (present participle) |

   Point out that:
   - participle clauses can only be used when the subject stays the same (so we can't say *Putting that to Moira Jones, she referred me …*, although this is a common mistake made by English speakers!).
   - in order to keep the same subject, you can use a passive participle clause, as in sentences 2 and 4. However, this makes the sentence sound formal and rather awkward.

3 a Learners think of possible contexts. Discuss the expressions together. Example answers:

   | – He carried on playing, despite being injured.
   – After resigning from his job, he went abroad for a year.
   – She walked out without saying goodbye.
   – Before opening the door, he listened carefully.
   – Far from apologising, he kept insisting that it was my fault.
   – They managed to get onto the plane without being searched.
   – On arriving at the airport, we joined the queue for check-in.
   – She was delighted on hearing the news of our engagement. |

   b Each pair chooses an expression and writes sentences based on it on a piece of paper. They pass their paper to the next pair.

   They add one or two more sentences, either before or after the ones they received. They should include one more expression from **3a**.

   You could continue for one more round, with pairs adding a third expression from **3a**.

   Pairs read out their story in turn.

4 a Learners write a paragraph using participle clauses.

   b Learners check on p138 to compare with what they wrote.

5 a To introduce the activity, read out one or two of the sentences, adding information about yourself or your opinions, e.g.:
   – *Having lived here for 25 years, I feel this is my home.*
   – *When asked why I'm a vegetarian, I usually ask people why they eat meat.*
   – *Looking to the future, I hope to travel a lot more while I have the chance.*

   Learners choose one sentence and continue it so that it is true for them.

   b In turn, learners stand up and read out their sentence, as if they are giving a speech. Other learners can ask questions to find out more information.

VOCABULARY Computer icons and collocations

6 a Learners look at the icons and see how many they recognise. Discuss the answers together. Possible answers:

   | A – Address book
   B – Burn CD
   C – Settings
   D – Recycling bin
   E – Chat
   F – Web-cam |

   b Learners brainstorm possible collocations. Elicit answers from the class. Possible answers:

   | 1 the net   2 a file   3 the cursor   4 a program
   5 an image / a file   6 a system / a program |

c Discuss the questions together and focus on any unfamiliar items, e.g.:
– you *browse* through books (in a bookshop)
– *bug* = a small insect
– *cookie* = a biscuit
– *spam* = a type of cheap tinned meat

> You could use photocopiable activity 12C on the Teacher's DVD-ROM at this point.

VOCABULARY *knowledge* and *information*

7 a Elicit collocations from the class.

> new information
> further / additional information (or knowledge)
> background information (or knowledge)
> relevant / useful information (or knowledge)
> common knowledge
> confidential information
> general information (or knowledge)

Focus on these common collocations:
– *background information / knowledge* (= other things you need to know to help you understand a problem or an issue).
– *it's common knowledge* = everyone knows this.
– *confidential information* = secret, you shouldn't tell other people.
– *general knowledge* = basic facts about the world, famous people, etc.

b Learners complete the gaps. Possible answers:

> 1 background knowledge
> 2 common knowledge
> 3 general knowledge
> 4 further information / additional information
> 5 new information
> 6 confidential information
> 7 accurate information
> 8 relevant information

c To introduce the activity, tell the class your own answers to the questions, e.g. *I read the paper, so I get a lot of information from that about the news and current affairs; in my work, I get information from the Internet; I receive emails*, etc.

Learners think about the questions and make a few notes. To make this more focused, elicit categories and write them on the board, e.g. books, other people, the Internet, newspapers, notices. Then ask learners to think where most of their information comes from in a typical day.

Ask different learners to tell you what ideas they had

Self-assessment

To help focus learners on the self-assessment, you could read it through, giving a few examples of the language they have learned in each section (or asking learners to tell you). Then ask them to circle a number on each line.

Unit 12 Extra activities on the Teacher's DVD-ROM

Printable worksheets, activity instructions and answer keys are on your Teacher's DVD-ROM.

12A Half a joke

Activity type: Speaking – Collaborative task – Groups of four

Aim: To practise language related to technology

Language: Talking about information and knowledge – Coursebook p117 – Vocabulary

Preparation: Make one copy of the worksheet for each group. Cut the worksheet into two.

Time: 25–30 minutes

12B Something survey

Activity type: Speaking – Personalised survey – Pairs / Whole class

Aim: To increase confidence in talking about developments and advances

Language: Developments and advances – Coursebook p119 – Vocabulary

Preparation: Make one copy of the worksheet for each learner.

Time: 25–30 minutes

12C How can I explain?

Activity type: Speaking – Word game – Pairs / Small groups

Aim: To practise paraphrasing vocabulary related to technology

Language: Computer icons and collocations – Coursebook p125 – Vocabulary

Preparation: Make one copy of the worksheet for every four learners. Cut it into four.

Time: 25–30 minutes

Unit 12 Self-study Pack

In the Workbook

Unit 12 of the *English Unlimited Advanced Self-study Pack Workbook* offers additional ways to practise the vocabulary and grammar taught in the Coursebook. There are also activities which build reading and writing skills, and two pages which give your learners the opportunity to develop their skills in extended reading.

- **Vocabulary:** Knowledge and information; Developments and advances; *sure, certain*; Sounding confident
- **Grammar:** Participle clauses
- **Explore reading:** Register and formality in business emails

On the DVD-ROM

Unit 12 of the *English Unlimited Advanced Self-study Pack DVD-ROM* contains interactive games and activities for your learners to practise and improve their vocabulary, grammar and pronunciation, and also their speaking and listening.

- **Vocabulary and grammar:** Extra practice of the Coursebook language and Keywords
- **Explore listening:** A report
- **Explore speaking:** Giving an explanation

Unit 12 Technology 125

Acknowledgements

Adrian Doff would like to thank Karen Momber and Keith Sands at Cambridge University Press for overseeing the project and for their invaluable help and support throughout the development of this course. He would also like to thank his editor, Andrew Reid, for his commitment and hard work and help in bringing the book into its final form.

He would also like to thank Gabriella Zaharias for consistently supporting and encouraging him during the writing of this book.

Johanna Stirling would like to thank her colleagues and students for all their help and inspiration. She also acknowledges the contribution of those in her online social network who often rallied to the cry of help. Thanks to Andrew Reid for simplifying the over-complicated. Above all, she would like to thank Daryl for his unfailing support and for doing more than his fair share of the washing-up.

Sarah Ackroyd would like to thank all the editors who have provided invaluable support throughout.

The authors and publishers are grateful to:
Text design and page make-up: Stephanie White at Kamae Design
Video content: all the team at Phaebus Media Group

Illustrations by Kate Charlesworth, Nick Kobyluch, Nigel Sanderson, Sean Simms, Vicky Woodgate

The authors and publishers acknowledge the following sources of copyright material and are grateful for the permissions granted. While every effort has been made, it has not always been possible to identify the sources of all the material used, or to trace all copyright holders. If any omissions are brought to our notice, we will be happy to include the appropriate acknowledgements on reprinting.

For the tables on the DVD-ROM and the text on pages 4 and 22 of the Teacher's book © *Common European Framework of Reference for Languages: Learning, teaching, assessment* (2001) Council of Europe Modern Languages Division, Strasbourg, Cambridge University Press